We

MW01678484

Webs of Meaning

WRITING IN THE ELEMENTARY SCHOOL

Weaving *Webs of Meaning*

WRITING IN THE ELEMENTARY SCHOOL

MARILYN L. CHAPMAN

University of British Columbia

TREVOR J. GAMBELL

Consulting Editor

University of Saskatchewan

I(T)P Nelson

an International Thomson Publishing company

Toronto • Albany • Bonn • Boston • Cincinnati • Detroit • London • Madrid • Melbourne
Mexico City • New York • Pacific Grove • Paris • San Francisco • Singapore • Tokyo • Washington

I(T)P® International Thomson Publishing
The ITP logo is a trademark under licence

Published in 1997 by
I(T)P® Nelson
A division of Thomson Canada Limited
1120 Birchmount Road
Scarborough, Ontario M1K 5G4

Visit our Web site at **http://www.nelson.com/nelson.html**

All rights reserved. No part of this work covered by the copyrights hereon may be reproduced or used in any form or by any means—graphic, electronic, or mechanical, including photocopying, recording, taping, or information storage and retrieval systems—without prior written permission of the publisher.

To show your appreciation for the time and effort that the authors and publisher have invested in this book, please choose **not** to photocopy it. Choose instead to add it to your own personal library. The investment will be well worth it.

Every effort has been made to trace ownership of all copyrighted material and to secure permission from copyright holders. In the event of any question arising as to the use of any material, we will be pleased to make the necessary corrections in future printings.

Canadian Cataloguing in Publication Data

Chapman, Marilyn L. (Marilyn Lesley), 1946–
Weaving webs of meaning : writing in the elementary school

Includes bibliographical references and index.
ISBN 0-17-605644-0

1. English language – Composition and exercises – Study and teaching (Elementary). I. Gambell, Trevor J. II. Title.

LB1576.C419 1997 372.62'3 C97-930380-X

Publisher and Team Leader	Michael Young
Executive Editor	Charlotte Forbes
Senior Production Editor	Bob Kohlmeier
Project Editor	Claudia Kutchukian
Production Coordinator	Brad Horning
Art Director	Angela Cluer
Cover Art	Eric Colquhoun
Technical Art	Deborah Crowle
Series Design (cover and interior)	Kevin Connolly
Senior Composition Analyst	Alicja Jamorski

Printed and bound in Canada

1 2 3 4 (BG) 00 99 98 97

Dedication

To my parents, with love and gratitude:

James Alexander Mitchell
Sylvia Myra Mitchell (née Jepson)

Contents

A Note to the Reader

BY TREVOR J. GAMBELL
COLLEGE OF EDUCATION, UNIVERSITY OF SASKATCHEWAN
CONSULTING EDITOR

Language is at the heart of education—language is the essential learning that links the subject areas in primary through secondary school, and beyond into postsecondary and tertiary education. This book is bound both by a holistic understanding of the language arts and by a belief in language as the core of teaching and learning across the curriculum.

We have produced this book specifically for two groups of educators. One group consists of pre-service teachers who are studying teacher education in colleges or faculties of education, especially students in their senior years who have been student teachers, possibly for lengthy internships (likely entire terms). Pre-service teachers will be able to reflect on their own experiences, as well as on those of their cooperating or supervising teachers and students. The other group consists of practising teachers at all levels of education, with varying responsibilities, including classroom teaching, resource room teaching, curriculum development, supervision, instructional development, and evaluation of curriculum, program, and students.

The following premises underlie this text:

- ***Language learning takes place not only in language arts and English programs but in all subject areas.*** Language is the primary mode of teaching, learning, and assessing in all areas of curriculum. Furthermore, no aspect of the language arts—listening, speaking, reading, writing—stands independent of the others in teaching and learning. Thus, this book addresses the language arts and, at the same time, reflects language learning and development across the curriculum.
- ***Teachers are professionals who make decisions about curriculum and instruction in their classrooms.*** They develop and select their own instructional resources from a number of sources in various media. Teachers are more than mere technicians who implement curriculum and "teach the textbook."

- ***Teachers learn from one another and through their own reflective practice.*** Thus, this book addresses the importance of reflection and of teachers-as-researchers in their own classrooms. It demonstrates these aspects through classroom vignettes, and through scenarios that depict real teaching situations.
- ***Pre-service and in-service teachers are more likely to develop a philosophy of language education and to change their practice when they can successfully meld theory with practice.*** Thus, this book provides a theoretical base and shows how theory is applied in the classroom. Examples of students' work, teaching and learning techniques that address both teachers and students, and suggested resources help to translate theory into practice.
- ***Cooperative and collaborative learning environments are most effective in developing language skills and are consistent with holistic instruction.*** This book promotes all social aspects of language learning, including peer, small group, large group, mixed age, mixed ability, multilingual, and multicultural learning environments.
- ***Teachers realize their professional and personal potential when they are empowered to take initiatives in their own classrooms and schools.*** These initiatives address curriculum, instruction, and student and program evaluation, as well as resource development and selection. This book provides guidance for how teachers may be empowered in these ways.

Features of the Book

- ***Chapter objectives*** appear at the beginning of each chapter and serve as the basis for organizing each chapter.
- ***Reflection boxes*** invite you to think back on your own knowledge and experiences and to compare and contrast them with the information and perspectives offered.
- ***Scenarios*** offer vignettes and case studies of students, teachers, classrooms, situations, and teaching methods.
- ***Samples of student language*** include writing samples, drawings, and extracts from students' oral discussions.

- ***Photographs*** illustrate some of the learning situations described in the book.
- ***Activity boxes*** provide details of writing/learning activities.
- ***Kindergarten Corners*** suggest ideas for addressing the needs of kindergarten children and beginning writers, including ESL students.
- ***Charts and other visuals*** relate to key issues in writing instruction and are specially designed for classroom use.
- ***References and further readings*** describe resources that you might want to look up and are listed at the end of each chapter.

◆ ◆ ◆

In *Weaving Webs of Meaning: Writing in the Elementary School,* Marilyn Chapman uses weaving as a metaphor for meaning-making through writing. The author draws on more than thirty years of teaching in both elementary schools and universities to reflect on the process of teaching writing. She invites readers to reflect on their own writing practices, personal and professional: thoughtful questions at the end of each chapter provide opportunities to ponder, discuss, and debate the points made in the chapter. The questions provide an interactive, socioconstructivist summary of the philosophy of writing and the teaching of writing advanced in this book.

In the first chapter, Marilyn Chapman establishes ten principles that form a foundation for learning and teaching writing, and for the book. She returns to them in the instructional strategies chapters and in the final chapter on assessment and evaluation. Chapter 2 is somewhat of an autobiographical reflection, a personal retrospective of the evolution of writing instruction during the author's thirty years of teaching writing; readers will be able to empathize with stages in her development as a teacher of writing.

In the chapters on classroom practices, we visit the classrooms of two teachers, one primary and one junior and, with the author, we peer over the shoulders of teacher and children, listening to what they say (in written script) and seeing what they write.

The author describes her carefully developed version of process writing, one that fosters fluency in writing while addressing the place of skills, including syntax and usage. She also shows how teaching different writing genres can be successfully interwoven with a process approach to teaching writing. The five major genres examined in Chapter 7 are description, narration, poetry, argument, and exposition, along with various forms of these major genres.

Finally, the book deals with how teachers can assess and evaluate students' writing in a way that is consistent with a process approach. Using authentic assessment strategies, the author weaves together the strands of writing/learning, assessment, and evaluation, based on an action research model.

You are an important part of this book in two ways. First, you are encouraged to write, prompted by personal experience and professional practice. Second, you may want to implement some of the ideas you will find in this book. There is a wealth of sound practices and innovative suggestions along with examples and materials to put them to work in your own classroom.

Acknowledgments

I am indebted to many people for their ideas and support, without which writing this book would have been next to impossible. I would like to thank Trevor Gambell, the Education Series editor, first, for honouring me by inviting me to write this book and, second, for his insights and ideas as it took shape and for his thoughtful responses to the first drafts. I would also like to thank Mary Clare Courtland, of Lakehead University, who reviewed the manuscript and made invaluable suggestions for making the book more useful for its intended audience. Thanks also to Claudia Kutchukian, Project Editor, for helping me refine and fine-tune words and ideas.

Although I began to write this book a year or so ago, the ideas in it have developed over a long period of time. I would like to thank Dr. Marv Klein, my graduate supervisor at Western Washington University, for introducing me to the work of Vygotsky, thus changing forever my thinking about language, learning, and writing. I would also like to thank my professors at the University of Victoria, especially Dr. Norma Mickelson and Dr. Terry Johnson, for the numerous ways in which they extended my thinking and learning. Thank-you also to my colleagues in the Department of Language Education at the University of British Columbia, especially Dr. Marion Crowhurst, from whom I learned much about the writing process in workshops in the early 1980s. I have been delighted to join her as a colleague at UBC, where I continue to learn from her and to receive encouragement and inspiration.

I have learned so much from the many teachers I have worked with over the years. Where possible, I have acknowledged them individually in the text. I particularly want to thank Brian Bennest and Julie Corday, with whom I worked in implementing a process approach to teaching writing in Delta School District; teachers in Richmond School District involved in the Young Writers Project, especially Linda Kaser and Faye Brownlie; and the teacher–friends who willingly allowed me to do research in their classrooms, particularly Margaret Reinhard in Victoria and Colleen Politano in Sooke, British Columbia. I extend special thanks to Colleen and Leon Politano and the children in their classrooms for the photographs that appear in this book.

Finally, I would like to express my deep appreciation to my family and friends, who provided me with invaluable support and encouragement and did not complain when I spent hours researching and writing rather than spending time with them. Thank-you, each and every one, especially my husband, Roland Chapman.

Marilyn L. Chapman

Prologue

This book explores the learning and teaching of writing. It is a *texere,* or "a woven thing," in that ideas are introduced and then picked up like thematic threads and elaborated in other parts of the text. This reflects the integrated nature and connectedness of knowledge about writing and learning and also my process of writing, which was very much a back-and-forth, recursive approach. You will notice that I have interwoven my personal reflections and recollections throughout. I have been a teacher for more than thirty years, mostly at the elementary level, and much of what I know and believe about writing has been constructed through my experiences of teaching in the elementary school. I continue to be actively involved with writing through teaching and research as an Associate Professor in the Department of Language Education at the University of British Columbia in Vancouver. I apply the principles and practices I describe in this book in my courses with pre-service and practising teachers; for example, I integrate process and genre approaches (discussed in Chapters 6 and 7) when I teach lesson and unit planning. I am also actively involved in writing research and spend a considerable amount of time in classrooms observing children and teachers engaged in writing/learning activities, talking to them about writing and learning, and collecting samples of children's writing. I am a writer, a teacher, and a teacher of writing, so I often use the term "we" when I talk about writers and teachers. Since I believe that making connections and generating questions are integral to learning, at various points in a discussion and at the end of each chapter I also invite you to think about key ideas—to reflect on your own experiences, to formulate questions and develop hypotheses about learning and writing.

While this is not a "recipe book" for teaching writing, I try to integrate theory and practice in a variety of ways. For example, I include teaching ideas for writing activities interspersed with discussions by way of Activity boxes. To address the needs of diverse learners, I include specific suggestions for teaching kindergarten and primary children, students in the junior grades, and ESL (English as a Second Language) and ESD (English as a second Dialect) students. (Throughout the book I use *primary* to refer to kindergarten through Grade 3, and *junior* for Grades 4 to 7. I use the term *elementary school* to refer to kindergarten through Grade 7.) Since many of my student teachers ask me about how I would address a particular writing issue or adapt a learning-writing activity for kindergarten children, I thought that readers of this book might have similar concerns, so I created Kindergarten Corners. These incorporate suggestions and ideas addressed particularly to teachers of kindergarten children. Teachers of Grade 1 classes may also be interested in some of the ideas in Kindergarten Corners, especially early in the school year or to meet the needs of some of their children. As well, some of the Kindergarten Corner ideas may be useful for teachers who have in their classes learners for whom English is a second language or a second dialect.

Throughout the book I weave together many different strands related to learning, teaching, and writing. In Chapter 1, I explore the multiple meanings of the word "writing" and develop a set of principles that form a framework, like warp strands on a loom, for the rest of the book. In Chapter 2, I weave in what we know about teaching and learning writing—the research and theory strands. Chapters 3 through 5 focus on the decision-making processes of creating, planning, and organizing classrooms that foster writing. Chapter 3, delves into the creation of the classroom learning/writing community, and Chapter 4, explores planning and organizing classroom learning experiences and activities for writing. To help you visualize what these ideas might look like, Chapter 5. illustrates how teachers can weave writing through the day with two vignettes: a day in a primary classroom and a day with a junior class. Chapter 6 takes an integrated and holistic approach to teaching the craft of writing, including strategies for teaching composing processes, from prewriting to presenting; and how to integrate the teaching of writing "skills," such as spelling, punctuation, syntax (grammar), and usage. In Chapter 7, I discuss ways of integrating process and genre approaches to expand children's writing repertoires within the language arts and across the curriculum. Finally, in Chapter 8, I examine how assessment and evaluation can be woven into the writing program.

CHAPTER 1

Understanding Writing: A Web of Meanings

CHAPTER OBJECTIVES

To provide a conceptual framework for understanding the nature and purposes of writing

To establish a set of principles that form a foundation for learning and teaching writing

To introduce specific vocabulary related to writing

PERSONAL REFLECTION

I remember many times when I taught primary children and they would ask, "Can't I please *print* my story instead of *writing* it?" I also remember trying to explain the different ways we use the word "writing"—that it can mean "writing a story" and also "cursive handwriting." However, it was not until many years later that I began to appreciate the multiple meanings of the word *write* and how these different meanings influence the way we think about learning and teaching writing.

What are the different meanings that come to your mind when you think of the word *write*?

We use the word *writing* in many different ways. As the above anecdote illustrates, this can be confusing for children when we talk about writing. More importantly, the way teachers think about writing has a strong impact on the way they approach teaching it. In this chapter, I explore key ideas about writing that are important for all teachers in the elementary school to consider. From this perspective, I establish a set of guiding principles that provide a foundation for the discussion of learning and teaching writing throughout this book. Understanding the key issues and guiding principles are particularly important in the elementary school, since it is the setting in which most children are formally introduced to writing. Children learn about what writing is by what teachers do and say about writing.

Writing Is Written Language

When we write, we are engaging in a means of **discourse**, communicating thoughts in words. First and foremost, writing is a means of *communication* and, as such, it is related to other types of communication such as speaking and reading. Some people consider writing to be secondary to and derived from oral language which they view as the "primary," "real," or "natural" form of language. Related to this idea is the notion that writing is "talk written down." Others conceive of speaking and writing as separate but equal modes of communication that are distinct not only in structure but also in function or use. However, the work of Deborah Tannen (1985) and others reveals that oral and written language overlap in function and form and that each affects the other. We can find "written" uses of language in conversation, and features of oral language in written texts; for example, a sermon is written language presented orally, and notes are often verbatim transcriptions of something spoken.

Writing is **written language**, the linguistic expression of meanings in written form. In language, words are used as symbols for something else; for example, an object or a concept. Likewise, writing is symbolic in nature—it refers to something else, a word or an idea. When we speak and when we write, we orchestrate these symbols in complex ways according to various subsystems, which include

- **pragmatics**—relationship between language and the context in which it is used; how writing **functions** in a particular **context**, the roles it plays, and the purposes it serves.
- **semantics**—relationship between words and their meanings; sometimes referred to as *meaning vocabulary*.
- **syntax**—relationship between words; the ways words are organized and sequenced, and structural patterns of word order, including sentence, paragraph, and discourse-level structures; sometimes referred to as **grammar**.

Understanding writing as written language, its relationship to speech, its symbolic nature, and the complexity of the symbolic system leads us to the following principles:

Principle 1. *Writing is written language, a complex system of linguistic expression related to other forms of language, such as speaking and reading.*

Principle 2. *Communication and meaning-making are central to writing and should always be the primary focus.*

Writing Is a Notational System

One of the things that makes writing distinct from oral language is that it is also a **notational system** based on visual or graphic marks that function according to certain rules. Twenty-six letters can be used in various combinations to represent all the **phonemes**, or speech sounds, that make up spoken English. But even though written English is considered to be alphabetic (that is, the letters of the alphabet can represent sounds and words), it has many nonalphabetic features that convey information; for example, word segmentation marked by spaces (speech is more like a running stream of words), use of upper and lower case, and punctuation marks. In addition to conveying ideas, writers must also manipulate the notational system to express their meanings in written form. This adds yet another subsystem to those listed in the previous section:

- **Graphophonics**—relationship between speech and writing, involving all of the elements of the written code, e.g., layout and directionality of print (front-to-back in a book, top-to-bottom of a page, left-to-right on a line), segmentation into words, letter–sound relationships, spelling and punctuation; sometimes referred to as **conventions of print.**

Understanding the role of the notational or graphophonics subsystem leads to another principle:

Principle 3. *Conventions of print are a part of writing, not ends unto themselves.*

Figure 1.1 Dimensions of Written Language

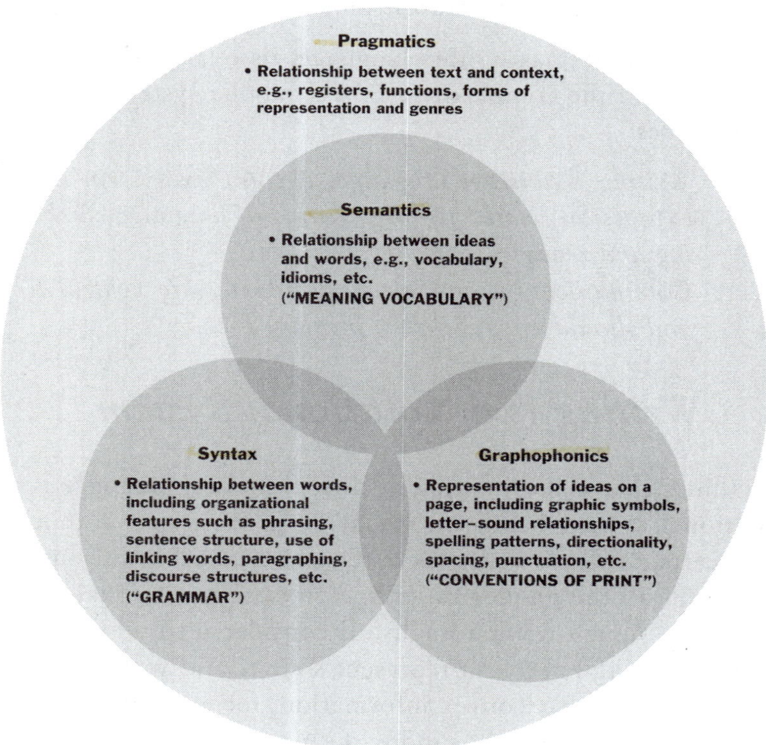

Writing Is a Multifaceted Process

Writing is a complex process that involves coordinating and integrating both linguistic and notational systems. We often use **composing** to refer to the processes of construction of meaning and **encoding** to refer to the recording or representation of ideas on the page in written symbols. Composing and encoding can also occur separately from each other. For example, we can compose through talk, movement, music, or drawing as well as in writing. Similarly, we can encode when we transcribe a spoken message or when we record someone else's ideas that are dictated to us. Other disciplines, such as mathematics and music, have their own notational systems.

In this book, "writing" always refers to the integration of composing and encoding, and thus the interaction of the subsystems of pragmatics, semantics, syntax, and graphophonics. It is important to remember that while we often talk about these subprocesses as though they are separate, in reality they occur simultaneously, in concert with one another. While some take the view that writing has only two basic components, ideation and spelling, it is my view that writing is multifaceted, a complex coordination of many types of knowledge. The various sources of knowledge we use when we write are the same ones that we use when we read; this is one of the ways in which writing and reading are interrelated. However, while writing and reading are similar in many ways, they are not identical processes—writing is not the inverse of reading.

Another way of looking at writing focuses on the cognitive processes involved, often referred to as the composing process or the writing process. This includes strategies for *planning* or generating ideas, *translating* or putting ideas into words, and *reviewing* or revising. Each term is something of a misnomer in that there is no single process for writing—different writers

Something to think about

The meanings of *literacy* and *writing* have changed over time. For example, the early monks who copied the Bible laboriously by hand could do beautiful lettering but usually could not read what they had copied. Are you aware of any changes in the meanings of *literacy* and of *writing* in your own lifetime?

have different ways of composing, and we approach writing differently depending on many factors; for example, our purpose for writing and the context or situation in which we are writing. Furthermore, planning, translating, and reviewing do not occur in a linear manner, but throughout the composing process in a recursive fashion (Flower & Hayes, 1980).

Principle 4. *Writers compose meanings and encode them in writing in an integrated, simultaneous fashion.*

Principle 5. *Writing involves many cognitive processes such as planning, generating and organizing ideas, putting ideas into words, and reviewing for meaning and form.*

Writing Is a Purposeful Human Activity

> Literacy is an activity, a way of thinking—not a set of skills. And it is a purposeful activity—people read, write, talk, and think about real ideas and information in order to ponder and extend what they know, to communicate with others, to present their points of view, and to understand and be understood. (Langer, 1987, p. 4)

As Michael Halliday (1973) has said, "All language is doing something." Writing is a human *activity,* and like all human activities, it is goal-directed, driven by meaning and purpose, and must be understood in terms both of the individual and of the context in which it occurs (Rogoff, 1990). In order to explore the idea of writing as a human activity, I will discuss purposes for writing, individual and social dimensions of writing, and the various layers of context.

Something to think about

What are all the ways you use writing in your own life?

Purposes for Writing

The origins of writing appear to have been based on the storage function of writing as record-keeping for transactions. The earliest forms were found in

Sumeria as clay tokens shaped like the objects they represented and placed inside clay "envelopes." These were used like bills of lading. By 4000 B.C., envelopes bore markings corresponding to the shapes of the tokens inside; by 3500 B.C., markings similar to the ones on envelopes were found on clay tablets. The use of clay envelopes died out at about the time that cuneiform writing began—what had been written on the outside of envelopes was now written on clay tablets with a stylus. With the advent of this "technology," there was no need for tokens and envelopes. Instead, records were kept on tablets, primarily for economic and legal record-keeping purposes (Goody, 1986).

Writing is used for many purposes or **functions.** These can be classified into two broad categories: **writing for communication,** which is primarily other-oriented, and **writing to facilitate thinking and learning,** which is primarily self-oriented. It is the storage or recording function of writing that contributes to its uniqueness as a tool for thinking and learning, what Wells and Chang-Wells (1992) refer to as the **epistemic mode.** Because writing can be recorded, it is easier to "revisit" ideas and thus rework and revise them. Since thinking and learning are what schools are all about, the epistemic function of writing is particularly important.

An overview of major functions of writing are shown in Figure 1.2. (This chart is general in nature. In Chapter 3, I discuss writing in the classroom from a functional perspective and provide examples of the different functions of writing in various classroom contexts.) As you examine this chart, keep in mind that the function categories are overlapping rather than discrete and that writing can (and usually does) serve many functions simultaneously. My own research on young children's writing shows that from the very beginning, children can use writing in many ways (Chapman, 1995a; 1995b; 1996). In fact, examples of all of the functions of writing shown on this chart were found in the writing of the Grade 1 children I studied.

Principle 6. *Writing is a purposeful activity, and people use writing for a wide array of functions. Two major categories of writing functions are to communicate and to facilitate thinking and learning.*

Figure 1.2 Functions of Writing

Instrumental/self-maintaining	To satisfy needs and wants, protect self and interests *Tasks:* Request; persuade; argue (present a case); defend oneself, ideas, feelings, or opinions; indicate ownership; justify behaviour
Regulatory/directing	To monitor own actions and direct/control actions of others *Tasks:* Establish and follow rules, procedures, contracts; make plans; make reminders; keep track; give directions; negotiate; collaborate, cooperate
Personal/expressive	To discover oneself; express individuality, feelings, and opinions *Tasks:* Express emotions; state opinions; reflect on meaning of personal experience; respond emotionally; extend knowledge of self; empathize with others; project into experiences, feelings, reactions of others or to situations never experienced
Interactive/interpersonal	To establish, define, and maintain social relationships *Tasks:* Show friendship; extend invitations; show gratitude (thank yous); share ideas; engage in a variety of social exchanges such as contests, ceremonies, rituals, celebrations
Imaginative/creative	To create images, moods, imaginary worlds; engage in pretend or make-believe *Tasks:* Create imaginative places, characters, events, or situations in stories, drama, poems; engage in dramatic play, role-play; write in role
Representational/informative	To communicate information, report facts or conclusions from facts; report on experience *Tasks:* Provide information; label, identify, or describe something; recall, tell, or retell what you know; report facts, conclusions; report on experience; explain a process; summarize; elaborate; give instructions or directions

Figure 1.2 Functions of Writing (cont.)

Divertive/entertaining	To enjoy, amuse oneself and others *Tasks:* Play with words; make jokes, riddles, puns; create or re-create amusing people, places, events, situations
Perpetuating/recording	To store or record events, ideas, feelings *Tasks:* Aid memory; store information or ideas; recall, examine, and savour ideas; re-create events or situations, remind oneself
Heuristic/epistemic	To explore, investigate, acquire knowledge and understanding; make personal meaning or sense of something
• inquiring	*Tasks:* Ask questions; collect, record ideas and information; pose problems and alternative solutions; generate ideas
• predicting	*Tasks:* Anticipate events, problems, and possible solutions or consequences; wonder; speculate; predict; hypothesize
• reviewing	*Tasks:* Recall; remember; access prior knowledge; synthesize; reflect on what was learned; reflect on learning process (how one learned)
• reasoning	*Tasks:* Explore, expand, clarify, develop, analyze, elaborate, revise, refine, apply, interpret, evaluate ideas and information; make connections; make inferences; compare, contrast; clarify issues; identify themes or main ideas; recognize cause and effect, problems and solutions; draw conclusions, justify judgments; reflect on ideas

Sources: Based on Goffman, 1974; Gundlach, 1981; Halliday, 1973; Perera, 1984; Smith, 1977; Stubbs, 1980; Tough, 1976.

Writing is a purposeful human activity.

Individual and Social Dimensions of Writing

Current interest in writing began in the 1970s with research that focused on individual writers and psychological aspects of writing. These studies, influenced to a great extent by the work of Jean Piaget (1983), contributed much to our understanding of cognitive processes for writing, stages of development, and individual differences. For example, we now appreciate both that there are both common patterns in the development of writing and that people differ in terms of their individual styles, interests, rates of development, and experiences. In the 1980s there was a shift toward an interest in the social dimensions of writing; this was influenced significantly by Lev Vygotsky (1978). The two perspectives, both of which view writing as a constructive process, are compared in the box on page 11:

Rather than view these two perspectives as alternative or competing explanations, it is perhaps more appropriate to see the contributions of each in help-

Cognitive Constructivist	Social Constructivist
• The focus is on the individual writer; context is not a factor.	• The focus is on people writing in specific contexts.
• Cognitive processes of writing are emphasized.	• There is a focus on the social dimension of writing.
• Interactions with the social world are not significant.	• Writers' interactions within their social worlds are emphasized.
• Thinking is considered to be primary; language is a reflection or manifestation of thought.	• Language and thinking are seen as interactive, with each influencing and enhancing the other.
• Literacy is thought of as a unified construct, with writing and reading seen as similar processes.	• Literacy is thought of as a differentiated construct, with writing and reading seen as processes that are alike or related in some ways, yet different in other ways.

ing us to understand writing—to see them as complementary, each providing insights into different dimensions of writing. Clearly, writing is both a personal and a social activity. While it is determined to a great extent by the experiences and intentions of the individual writer, rather than being a biological, adaptive reaction to the environment, writing is better thought of as a purposive and culturally meaningful activity, a social practice that varies with context of use (Farr, 1986).

Language grows out of and is embedded in every aspect of people's lives. Each sphere of human activity has its own variety of language or **register**; for example, lawyers use the register of law in their professional work, the register of sport (such as weight training) in their athletic pursuits, the register of parenting in interactions with their children at home, the academic register when they take courses at the university, and so on. Each register has related vocabulary and syntax, and various forms of oral and written discourse.

Mikhail Bakhtin (1979/1986) has provided important insights that can help us understand the interplay between the individual and the social dimensions of writing. He suggests that all language is *dialogue* because our understandings of words and how to use them are shaped by and developed in and through interactions with others. Even when we write to and for ourselves, we use words in ways in ways that we have learned from our communities and cultures. An important contribution of Bakhtin's work is his discussion of **genres**, which, he explains, are structures that are embedded in and develop out of the various spheres of human activity. Genres are flexible models, not merely generic forms that writers slot ideas into—they reflect an integration of content (what we want to express), form (ways of organizing our words and ideas), function (purposes for writing), and context of situation. "Each sphere of activity contains an entire repertoire of ... genres [oral and written] that differentiate and grow as the particular sphere develops and becomes more complex" (p. 60). These socially constructed genres provide a set of signals that enable a speaker/writer and listener/reader to interpret the particulars of a specific communicative interaction. Yet genres are sufficiently open-ended to allow for individual choice, creativity, and **voice**—writers make choices about what they write about and how they write it, and they express the uniqueness of their own personalities in their writing—so writing is very much an individual creative process as well as a social one.

Principle 7. *Writing is both an individual and a social activity.*

Principle 8. *Each sphere of activity has a language register, which includes vocabulary, syntax, and forms of discourse. Writers express their ideas in various forms of representation and genres, which are ways of using language to suit particular contexts and functions.*

The Nature and Importance of Context

We often speak of writing as occurring in a context—literally, "that which surrounds a text"—but context is multidimensional and fluid. Writing occurs in and is influenced by all layers of context:

- **Sociocultural context**—the global setting encompasses such things as socioeconomic class, language, ethnicity, power relations, and gender; the sociocultural context includes a variety of communities in which people live and interact.
- **Community context**—a person is a member of several communities; for example, a professional community, an academic community, a religious community, a recreational community, a neighbourhood community, and so on; while a teacher and students may share the same classroom community, other communities to which they belong may overlap or be quite different.
- **Sphere of activity**—each community encompasses several spheres of activity, recurring contexts that give rise to particular functions and varieties of language (registers), forms of representation, and genres.

The classroom writing context is multilayered and is both social and personal.

- **Immediate context**—the particular writing situation is comprised of a specific set of circumstances, including the people (in this case, teachers and students), the environment (physical, intellectual, and emotional dimensions), and the task (e.g., purpose of the task, how the task is structured); it occurs at a particular moment in time and is bound by events immediately preceding and following.
- **Personal context**—as well as being viewed from a social perspective, context can also be considered in relation to the life of the individual writer(s); it is part of a personal historical timeline, influenced by what has gone on before in a person's life and in turn affecting what will follow.

Individuals and groups represented in all layers of context bring with them their particular knowledge, experiences, and skills; their attitudes, beliefs, and values in relation to language, writing, teaching, and learning; their ways of using literacy and their literacy tools and resources. We often refer to a group of people who share ways of using language as a **discourse community.**

Layers of context, as with all social relationships, are not neutral, but rather reveal issues of values, ethics, and power. And all of these layers are dynamic—constantly changing. For example, in many places in Canada we are undergoing rapid changes in the ethnic compositions of our communities; this affects the makeup of our classrooms, local communities, and Canadian society and culture. In fact, the whole idea of "Canadian culture" is undergoing a redefinition. (It is beyond the scope of this book to explore this issue completely. For a more in-depth discussion, see Chapman & Anderson, 1995, and Chapman & Froese, 1994.) Rather than being homogeneous, Canada is pluralistic in nature, multicultural, and multilingual. And this cultural and linguistic diversity creates a wide array of functions and forms of writing.

Something to think about

How would you describe your own sociocultural and community contexts and spheres of activity that affect the ways you use writing?

Principle 9. *Writing occurs in and is influenced by context, which is multidimensional. The immediate writing context is both social—embedded in a sphere of activity, community, and sociocultural context—and personal, part of an individual writer's life.*

Writing as a Product

When we think about the "products" of writing, something that is produced and can be reproduced, something visible, we think of written texts. (Reader response theorists and curriculum researchers studying narratives have a different perspective on the word "text." Their use of the term includes personal narratives that are not necessarily written.) The word "text" comes from the past participle of the Latin *texere*, to weave. So a text is "something that is woven." This provides a wonderful metaphor for thinking about written products—fabrics or tapestries of meaning woven from words. When we look

REFLECTION

In most Canadian societies, we value writing. We expect that everyone will learn to write, and we teach children about writing from an early age. Not being able to write is seen as a handicap. Other cultures in other countries do not share the same values. For instance, in Guatemala, being able to weave cloth is highly valued. It is expected that everyone will learn how to weave, and the children are taught to weave from a very early age. On the other hand, far fewer Guatemalan children learn to read and write than to weave, and the levels of literacy they achieve are far lower than what we expect of Canadian children. This contrast between Guatemala and Canada shows us that values are culturally situated and constructed.

Since most Canadians learn to write rather than to weave cloth, would most of us be considered handicapped in Guatemala? What might our communities be like without writing?

at them from a functional perspective, we can see that some are practical, the fabrics of our daily lives; others are like tapestries, forms of art. When we look at them from afar we see them as wholes; when we focus on particular aspects, we can identify their patterns and textures. When we examine them closely we can see the various threads and appreciate how they are interlaced. And an informed eye can identify both the craftsmanship and the creativity of the individual writer/weaver.

As well as communicating ideas, a piece of writing reveals information about its author. It documents, for example, a writer's knowledge of discourse structures, word meanings and syntax, and control of conventions of print such as spelling and punctuation. It may also provide evidence of planning and revision. As will be discussed in Chapter 8, written products provide powerful evidence about a child's knowledge and abilities. When we look at texts through an anthropologist's eye, we see them not only as an individual's products, but as cultural artifacts. Writing reveals much about the layers of context in which the writing was produced and the cultural tools, such as genres and notational systems, used by the social group to which the writer belongs.

Writing is an artifact in another sense too. A notational system is a cultural artifact that has evolved over time and continues to evolve. Because our alphabetic writing system is so much a part of our everyday lives, we fail to appreciate that it is a cultural tool for expressing our ideas. In fact, it is often not until we look at writing systems from other cultures that we understand the nature and significance of written English.

Principle 10. *Writing is a product in many senses: a text containing a message, a document that reveals information about its writer, and a cultural artifact.*

Warp and Weft

As I have written about the various dimensions of writing and how we use the word "writing" to mean many things—language that is written, a notational system, a process, an activity, and a product—I have woven into the text two conceptual strands. One set of strands, the principles of writing, are like the lengthwise warp threads of a weaving, and they will form the foundation of the rest of this book. Our explorations of the various dimensions of teaching and learning writing will be interwoven with these principles. The second strand I have introduced is vocabulary that we will use to talk about writing.

Principles of Writing

Here is a list of the principles stated in the chapter:

1. Writing is written language, a complex system of linguistic expression related to other forms of language, such as speaking and reading.
2. Communication and meaning-making are central to writing and should always be the primary focus.
3. Conventions of print are a part of writing, not ends unto themselves.
4. Writers compose meanings and encode them in writing in an integrated, simultaneous fashion.
5. Writing involves many cognitive processes such as planning, generating and organizing ideas, putting ideas into words, and reviewing for meaning and form.
6. Writing is a purposeful activity, and people use writing for a wide array of functions. Two major categories of writing functions are to communicate and to facilitate thinking and learning.
7. Writing is both an individual and a social activity.
8. Each sphere of activity has a language register, which includes vocabulary, syntax, and forms of discourse. Writers express their ideas in various forms of representation and genres, which are ways of using language to suit particular contexts and functions.
9. Writing occurs in and is influenced by context, which is multidimensional. The immediate writing context is both social—embedded in a sphere of activity, community, and sociocultural context—and personal, part of an individual writer's life.
10. Writing is a product in many senses: a text containing a message, a document that reveals information about its writer, and a cultural artifact.

Metalanguage

You may have noticed that some words in the text appear in boldface type. Sometimes I have used bold print to emphasize particularly important ideas. Some of these words or phrases are the "technical" vocabulary that we use when we talk about writing. (I have included many of these key words and phrases in the Glossary at the end of the book as a reference as well.) I introduce these words not because I particularly like "jargon," but because when we talk about language we use words in particular ways, just as scientists, doctors, and other professionals talk about their areas of study. Words about language are referred to as **metalanguage**. Metalanguage is part of the vocabulary of all literate people, but particularly of teachers. I think that while it is important to be straightforward and clear when we speak and write, we should not shy away from precise terms as long as we introduce them and use them in context. I believe this is so not only for teachers, but also for the children we teach. It is through using metalanguage purposefully, in developmentally and contextually appropriate ways, that we can help children develop **metalinguistic awareness**, so that they too can become aware of the many dimensions of language, including writing.

Reflections on the Chapter

Think about/talk about/write about:

Your Understanding of Writing

- What significance does writing have/has it had to you as a person? How and why do you think this has happened?
- Do you know any notational systems other than written English? How are they the same? How are they different?
- Consider some of the ways that you may have been ethnocentric about writing. What things have you taken for granted or considered "neutral?"
- How and why has your thinking about writing changed?

Your Own Uses of Writing

- In what ways do you use writing? In what contexts?
- To what discourse communities do you belong?
- In what ways do your various discourse communities use writing? How has this affected your own writing?
- What genres do you use most frequently (or would like to)?
- Consider some of the ways that writing is/has been politically powerful or not for you personally.

REFERENCES AND FURTHER READING

Bakhtin, M.M. (1986). *Speech genres and other late essays.* (V.W. McGee, Trans., C. Emerson & M. Holquist, Eds.). Austin, TX: University of Texas Press. (Original work published 1979.)

Chapman, M.L. (1995a). The sociocognitive construction of written genres in first grade. *Research in the Teaching of English, 29*(2), 164–92.

———. (1995b). Living, loving, and learning: Writing in first grade. *Canadian Children, 20*(2), 8–13, 50.

———. (1996). Why write? A functional analysis of "writers' workshop" compositions in first grade. *The Canadian Journal of Research in Early Childhood Education, 5*(2), 75–99.

Chapman, M.L., and Anderson, J. (Eds.). (1995). *Thinking globally about language education.* Vancouver: Research and Development in Global Studies, Centre for the Study of Curriculum and Instruction, University of British Columbia.

Chapman, M.L., and Froese, V. (1994). Literacy research, curriculum and instruction. In T. Gambell & M.C. Courtland (Eds.), *Curriculum planning in the language arts K–12: An holistic perspective* (pp. 350–78). North York, ON: Captus Press Inc.

Farr, M. (1986). Language, culture and writing: Sociolinguistic foundations of research on writing. *Review of Research in Education, 13*, 195–223.

Flower, L., and Hayes, J. (1980). The dynamics of composing: Making plans and juggling constraints. In L. Gregg and E. Steinberg (Eds.), *Cognitive processes in writing* (pp. 3–30). Hillsdale, NJ: Lawrence Erlbaum Associates.

Goffman, E. (1974). *Frame analysis.* Cambridge, MA: Harvard University Press.

Goody, J. (1986). *The logic of writing and the organization of society.* New York: Cambridge University Press.

Gundlach, R. (1981). On the nature and development of children's writing. In C.H. Frederiksen and J.F. Dominic (Eds.), *Writing: The nature, development, and teaching of written communication. Vol. 2, Writing: Process, development and communication* (pp. 133–51.) Hillsdale, NJ: Lawrence Erlbaum Associates.

Halliday, M.A.K. (1973). *Explorations in the functions of language.* London: Edward Arnold.

Langer, J. (1987). A sociocognitive perspective on literacy. In J. Langer (Ed.), *Language, literacy, and culture: Issues of society and schooling* (pp. 1–20). Norwood, NJ: Ablex.

Perera, K. (1984). *Children's writing and reading.* London: Basil Blackwell & Andre Deutsch.

Piaget, J. (1983). Piaget's theory. In P.H. Mussen (Ed.), *Handbook of child psychology: Vol. 1: History, theory and methods.* New York: Wiley.

Rogoff, B. (1990). *Apprenticeship in thinking.* New York: Oxford University Press.

Smith, F. (1977). The uses of language. *Language Arts, 54* (6), 638–44.

Stubbs, M. (1980). *Language and literacy: The sociolinguistics of reading and writing.* London: Routledge & Kegan Paul.

Tannen, D. (1985). Relative focus on involvement in oral and written discourse. In D. Olson, N. Torrance, and A. Hildyard (Eds.), *Literacy, language, and learning: The nature and consequences of reading and writing* (pp. 124–47). Cambridge, UK: Cambridge University Press.

Tough, J. (1976). *Listening to children talking: A guide to the appraisal of children's use of language.* London: Ward Lock Educational and Drake Educational Associates.

Vygotsky, L.S. (1978). *Mind in society.* (M. Cole, V. John-Steiner, S. Scribner, and E. Souberman, Eds.). Cambridge, MA: Harvard University Press.

Wells, G., and Chang-Wells, G.L. (1992). *Constructing knowledge together: Classrooms as centers of inquiry and literacy.* Portsmouth, NH: Heinemann.

CHAPTER 2

Learning and Teaching Writing: Weaving Principles into Practice

CHAPTER OBJECTIVES

To review current theoretical and research literature related to learning and teaching writing

To discuss a sociocognitive constructivist or transactional approach to teaching writing and how it relates to current theories and research

To develop guidelines for teaching writing based on research and the principles of writing established in Chapter 1

PERSONAL REFLECTION

My parents began my love affair with language. My father introduced me to the fascinating world of words and their meanings—I would pester him, "What does such-and-such a word mean, Daddy?" And he would explain, "It comes from the Greek this and the Latin that, so it means ..." My mother, who was very active in our local theatre company, has a wonderful way with words in a literary and dramatic sense. I could listen to her read and recite poetry for hours on end.

When I think back to my school experiences with writing, they begin with Mr. Allen in Grade 4. I don't remember anything about writing per se before that, although I do have some memories about reading and being read to. I'm not sure if it is a coincidence or not, but it seems that Mr. Allen made writing come alive for me. We did lots of writing in his class. One of my most vivid memories is of the day when Mr. Allen talked to us about "giving tired words a rest." He drew on the board several little "beds" and on each wrote a word. I remember "good" and "nice" were included—maybe there were others. We "brainstormed" (that's what we'd call it now, but I don't remember what we called it then) all the words our class could think of to use instead of "good" and "nice." (Mr. Allen must have used one of those grease pencils—I don't think they had felt pens forty years ago!) When he posted the list, it was so long that it reached all the way from the ceiling to the floor, so long that he had to cut the bottom part off and put it next to the long part of the chart. I also remember from that year that I "discovered" the thesaurus (I think now that Mr. Allen probably introduced it to us) and that I would spend hours and hours writing poems using lots of colour words. Many of my poems were about sunsets and I remember falling in love with some of the sumptuous names of colours. I don't remember much of anything else about writing in school until Grade 12!

Reflect on your own experiences in learning to write. Do you remember being able to write before you went to school? What are some of the positive experiences you remember about writing in school? Do you have any negative ones? What happened? How have they affected you? What have your experiences in teaching writing been like?

I began this chapter with a personal perspective on learning to write because it illustrates the impact of both parents and teachers on young writers. The school incidents I recall happened forty years ago, yet they made lasting impressions on me. I encourage you to reflect on your own experiences with writing because they are the starting point for your process of learning to teach writing. In this chapter I explore recent research and theories about learning and teaching writing. I start with a focus on development and learning since I believe that this understanding forms a foundation for talking about teaching. In a sense, this chapter is autobiographical, a personal timeline—it reflects the evolution in my own thinking over the past thirty years or so in teaching and researching writing.

An Emergent Literacy Perspective on Writing Development

Most people think of writing in the elementary school as the second of "the three Rs"—reading, 'riting, and 'rithmetic. This phrase places writing as "basic" and as secondary in importance to reading. Traditionally, learning to write was seen as starting in Grade 1, after children had been taught the alphabet. Learning letter names and how to print them were thought of as part of "reading readiness skills"—writing was really an afterthought to reading.

Now, learning to write is seen as part of a process of **emergent literacy**. Teale and Sulzby (1986, p. xviii) discuss the following key ideas about an emergent literacy perspective that are important for our discussion of learning and teaching writing:

1. Literacy development starts in early childhood long before children enter school. "Children are doing critical cognitive work in literacy development during the years from birth to age 6."
2. *Literacy development* is a more appropriate term than *reading readiness* because children develop as *writers/readers*. Furthermore, listening, speaking, reading, and writing abilities develop concurrently in an interrelated manner, rather than sequentially.
3. "Literacy develops in real-life settings for real-life activities in order to 'get things done.'" Thus, learning about the functions of literacy is as

much a part of learning about writing and reading during early childhood as is learning about form.

4. Children learn written language by actively engaging with their world through interactions with adults in writing and reading situations and exploring print on their own. Children benefit from the modelling of literacy by significant adults, particularly their parents.
5. "Although children's learning about literacy can be described in terms of generalized stages, children can pass through these stages in a variety of ways and at different ages. Any attempt to 'scope and sequence' instruction should take this developmental variation into account."

From an emergent literacy perspective, writing in the elementary school years can be seen as part of a continuum beginning at birth and continuing throughout life. Children's writing development is interrelated with other forms of communication, especially oral language and drawing (Dyson, 1986a, 1986b), and one of the important learning tasks for children is differentiating the unique aspects of written language (Sulzby, 1986). Figure 2.1 shows how young children weave drawing and writing as they compose.

An emergent literacy perspective addresses the dual personal/social nature of learning to write. Emergent literacy can be thought of as a process of cognitive development. However, while earlier research tried to identify patterns or stages of development in writing, the concept of emergent literacy is not one of "ages and stages" in the Piagetian sense. Rather than being an invariant sequence, research shows that there are individual differences among children who vary in their learning styles, abilities, and rates of development. Emergent literacy can also be thought of as a cultural process because of the diversity in children's writing in different contexts, from specific writing situations to sociocultural variations. According to Vygotsky (1978), a focus on the mechanics of writing has influenced the way we have thought about writing and the way we have approached teaching it:

> [P]sychology has conceived of writing as a complicated motor skill. It has paid remarkably little attention to the question of written language as such, that is, a particular system of symbols and signs whose mastery heralds a critical turning point in the entire cultural development of the child. (p. 106)

Learning to write is an *active process*. But what does "active learning" mean? Some people think of it in terms of physical activity—children have

Figure 2.1 This is Tyrannosaurus Rex

Something to think about

Compare and contrast the ways in which a "reading readiness" view and an "emergent literacy" perspective are the same and different.

freedom of movement rather than sitting at desks for prolonged periods, they manipulate objects in learning mathematics, they explore things in their environments through hands-on activities, and so on. But while physical movement is important to children's learning (as Piaget and Montessori, among others, have so clearly demonstrated), physical activity as an end unto itself misses the point. Rather, the most important aspect of active learning is *mental activity*, through which children are engaged and involved, and make connections with what they are learning. Learning is a result of mental action—it is "minds on" as well as "hands on." Traditionally, learning was seen as a process of transmitting knowledge from one person to another. Learners were

Young children weave drawing and writing to construct meaning.

thus placed in a rather passive role, as receivers of information. Today, however, we see learners as active creators of understanding and that learning is a process of *constructing knowledge* by integrating new information with what we already know. Because each learner's prior knowledge, experiences, interests, and abilities are unique, learning is highly personal.

But children live with other human beings, and their worlds are social as well as physical. Children learn by acting and *re*acting within their various social worlds, which includes, on an interpersonal level, their homes, their classrooms, and their communities, and in a broader social sphere, their cultures and societies. One aspect of children's social worlds is language, both oral and written, and children can be seen as younger members of discourse communities. Children are *socialized* into the ways of using language in all its forms by other members of their community from the time they are infants. And while they construct understandings about written language personally by seeking meaning and formulating hypotheses about the nature of writing, they do not do it alone; rather, they do this by interacting with literate others and by using the literacy artifacts created by people. Children learning to write can be thought of as *literacy apprentices* who adopt or appropriate their culture's ways of using written language through their mentors, more advanced members of their discourse communities, such as their parents, teachers, and older children (Bakhtin, 1986; Vygotsky, 1978).

Writing and Learning

Michael Halliday (1982) suggests that we think about language development as having three interrelated dimensions: children learn language, learn through language, and learn about language. These three things occur for the main part subconsciously through meaningful communication with others. Halliday's three-dimensional framework provides a useful starting point for a discussion of writing: learning to write, learning about writing, and learning through writing.

Something to think about

Brainstorm all the ideas you can think of related to "writing and learning."

Learning to Write

Recall from Chapter 1 that learning to write is a complex process that involves learning to coordinate and integrate composing, the construction of meaning, and encoding, the recording or representation of ideas in written symbols on the page. To do this, children need to learn much about written language—how writing changes in different contexts (pragmatics), meaningful vocabulary (semantics), a variety of sentence patterns (syntax), and how the notational system works (graphophonics). Anne Haas Dyson (1984), who has written extensively about young writers, suggests that we think about learning to write as solving a puzzle, and that children must solve the written language puzzle "by gradually differentiating its pieces and, at the same time, actively manipulating those pieces within the context of a meaningful whole" (p. 174).

Research indicates that while there are many individual differences when we look at children's growth in writing on a finer scale, there are some common patterns among children learning to write in English when we view writing from a very broad perspective. *All* children learn about writing before they come to school, whether they come from the mainstream or minority groups. As they gain experience with written language, their knowledge and understandings change both quantitatively (i.e., they come to know more) and qualitatively (i.e., their concepts change, usually becoming more conventional or precise). Thus, the process of writing development is not simply additive. Instead, it is a progression of refinement from more unconventional and gross *approximations* to more conventional and specific ones.

Qualitative changes in children's spelling in particular reveal their growing knowledge of the nature of written English. Preconventional writing is characterized by linear "scribbles" that resemble cursive writing and/or letter-like shapes; children do not yet understand the **alphabetic principle**, that there are relationships between particular letters and sounds. Next, in what is sometimes called an "emergent literacy stage," children's writing begins to reveal the development of insights into sound/symbol relationships. This begins with a **syllabic hypothesis** (Ferreiro, 1982), a specific form of one-to-one correspondence, in which children use one letter to represent one syllable. Later, children begin to use their knowledge of the names of the alphabet letters, par-

REFLECTION

We often think of invented spelling as something that children should "outgrow." However, the inventing of spellings is a useful strategy for getting ideas on paper without interrupting the flow of ideas. This approach, called "placeholder spelling," will be discussed in Chapter 6.

What strategies do you use for spelling words you are unsure of when you are composing?

ticularly consonants, to figure out spellings (Read, 1975). First, they usually represent words with initial consonants; gradually, they represent more and more speech sounds, or **phonemes**, in words and create phonetic or "invented" spellings (Beers, 1980), as shown in Figure 2.2. Children's invented spellings are particularly helpful to adults in assessing children's knowledge of the spelling system (Bissex, 1980). As children gain more experience with reading and writing, their writing becomes more conventional-looking, their fluency in putting ideas into words on a page increases, and they begin to use writing in more complex and sophisticated ways.

Because the development of children's spelling is particularly striking, it is often difficult to see beyond this aspect of writing to consider dimensions such as function, text structure, elaboration of ideas, and so on. Figure 2.3 shows, in broad brushstrokes, many of the common developmental trends in writing across the elementary years. It is important to remember in reading this chart, however, that writing is a multidimensional process that varies with context, interest, levels of confidence, experience, and abilities in particular aspects of writing, and that young writers are not "in a stage" in the Piagetian sense. An 8-year-old's writing may, for example, match the descriptors in the "Developing Writer" column when we look at graphophonics, and yet match the emergent writer's (ages 5–7) descriptors when we look at his or her genres or text structures. Genres, in particular, are influenced greatly by children's experiences and the contexts in which they have encountered writing. It is by looking across the age bands that we can appreciate children's writing progress over time.

Figure 2.2 Caitlin's Fuzzy Duckling Story

This is a duckling. Its name is Fuzzy. One day Fuzzy thought the moon fell in the lake. He called the farmer.

The farmer said, "What is it?"

"The moon fell in the lake."

The farmer said, "There is no moon in the lake. It is the reflection show. Now go to bed."

"Okay."

In the picture: Good night. [the moon]
Come quickly, the moon is in the lake.
Coming!

Learning about Writing

Learning about writing means becoming *aware* of the nature of written language, its forms and its functions—in other words, **metalinguistic awareness.**

Dyson (1984, p. 166) suggests that coming to understand written language involves learning about

- perceptual features (i.e., what writing looks like)
- the symbolic nature of writing (that writing refers to something else, i.e., a word or an idea)
- structural characteristics (e.g., elements of stories, how ideas are linked)
- discursive procedures (e.g., how to encode ideas on a page)
- its sociocognitive nature (i.e., that writing must be able to be interpreted independently from the specific context in which it was written)
- functional capacities (i.e., the uses of writing)

Children develop knowledge about writing primarily in the context of its purposeful use. Much of language and literacy awareness occurs through independent explorations of reading and writing. Krashen and Terrell (1983) refer to this as **acquisition**, a subconscious process on the part of the child, without formal teaching. Sometimes, though, awareness is a result of a parent or teacher having drawn explicit attention to a particular aspect of writing or providing an explanation about how and why something is written in a particular way. Krashen and Terrell refer to this process as **learning**, conscious knowledge gained through teaching that involves explanations and analysis. Clearly, knowledge about written language is a result of both acquisition and learning. Either way, both processes occur more meaningfully in context rather than in isolation.

As young children participate in their social worlds, they come to understand the symbolic nature of writing and that writing can be used to communicate messages that can be read and reread. Young children come to understand that talk can be written down and that talking and writing are similar in many ways. One important aspect of language awareness for primary children is understanding the **alphabetic principle,** that the sounds of spoken language can be represented by letters, and that combinations of sounds in spoken words are related to combinations of letters in written words. As children gain experience, they acquire knowledge of many conventional spellings, common spelling patterns, text structures, and so on.

Figure 2.3 Common Developmental Patterns in Writing

BEGINNING WRITER (approximate ages 2–5)	EMERGENT WRITER (approximate ages 5–7)	DEVELOPING WRITER (approximate ages 7–9)
• Views writing as something that people do; likes to play at writing	• Shows interest in letter-sound relationships and how to represent specific speech sounds	• Enjoys writing and sharing own writing with others; begins to develop a sense of audience
• Writes mainly for him/herself	• Is learning to share his/her writing with others	• Is increasingly able to share his/her writing and to respond to writing of others
• Combines drawing and "writing" but drawing conveys most of the meaning	• Combines writing and drawing to convey ideas	• May combine drawing and writing but writing can stand alone to convey meaning
• May be aware of print but may not be aware that the print contains the message; may ask "What does this say?" about his/her own writing	• May understand writing as "talk written down"	• Is beginning to understand writing as "ideas written down"
• Demonstrates increasing knowledge of writing, e.g., letter formation (capitals), the alphabet	• Demonstrates increasing knowledge of: – letter names – common sound/symbol relationships, especially consonants – functions of writing – some genres (e.g., labels, letters, stories, invitations)	• Demonstrates increasing knowledge of: – letter–sound relationships, including vowels – common spelling patterns – common writing terms (e.g., word, sentence, story) – a wider range of genres (e.g., poems, reports)
• Plays at writing and may produce "scribble writing," strings of capital letters or letter-like forms; single letters that represent a syllable (not phonemic); single letters that may represent an initial consonant (e.g., S = Snake; DD = Daddy)	• Produces increasingly conventional writing with mostly phonetic spellings; directionality emerging but often reverses letters or writes right to left; some punctuation marks (nonconventionally at first, e.g., periods at ends of lines)	• Produces increasingly conventional writing: many standard spellings, but uses placeholder spelling when drafting; writes left to right but may still reverse b and d; some punctuation marks conventional (e.g., periods, question marks)
• May produce some words in conventional spelling (e.g., own name, MOM, DAD) as well as other forms	• May produce: – labels to accompany drawings – single words or phrases – short sentences – a series of simple sentences – simple stories with one character; short letters	• May produce: – a series of connected ideas that make sense – stories with two or more characters – stories of a full page or more – reports, letters, poems, etc.

Figure 2.3: Common Developmental Patterns in Writing (cont.)

CONSOLIDATING WRITER (approximate ages 9–11)	EXPANDING WRITER (approximate ages 11–13)
• Enjoys giving feedback and receiving feedback about his/her own writing; shows an increasing awareness of audience	• Enjoys playing with words and ideas to create particular effects; shows an increasing awareness of the need to adjust writing to suit the particular context and audience
• Is learning to work collaboratively: as a peer editor to give feedback on ideas; as a proofreader to help check spelling and punctuation	• Continues to learn collaborative writing skills and processes for composing, peer editing, and proofreading
• Is able to write for an increasing range of purposes	• Writes for a wide range of purposes
• Understands writing as "ideas written down"	• Can convey increasingly complex and abstract ideas through writing
• Demonstrates increasing knowledge of most spelling patterns; writing terminology (e.g., paragraph, punctuation, editing); a wider range of genres (e.g., fables, legends); a wider range of representations across curriculum areas (e.g., graphs, Venn diagrams)	• Demonstrates increasing knowledge of spelling patterns; writing terminology (e.g., description, theme); parts of speech (but is not yet able to grasp intellectually many of the formal aspects of "grammar"); a wide range of genres (e.g., myth, legend); representations across curriculum areas (e.g., timelines, matrixes); strategies for revising and proofreading his/her own writing
• Produces increasingly conventional writing: – by about age 9, students spell approximately 92% of words conventionally; even the poorest spellers use 80% standard spellings – uses placeholder spelling while drafting but standard spelling for final draft – uses many punctuation marks conventionally (e.g., periods, question marks) but not others (e.g., commas, colons, quotation marks)	• Produces increasingly conventional writing: – 13-year-olds spell with about 97% accuracy – uses most punctuation marks conventionally but may still not yet control others (e.g., semicolon)
• May produce – stories with two or more characters – topics or ideas supported by relevant details – a series of ideas connected smoothly and logically – a variety of sentence structures and varied sentence lengths – more complex reports, letters, poems, etc.	• May produce – writing that is easily understood, fluent, logically organized, unified, and elaborated – writing that is becoming more sophisticated in style and more precise in word choice – more complex narratives with convincing settings and characters; more complex expository forms (e.g., elaborate reports)

REFLECTION

The Language Experience Approach was based on the idea that writing is written-down speech. We now realize that speaking and writing, while similar, are very different. We *can* write down talk, but writing differs from oral language in significant ways. As will be discussed in Chapter 7, in the early years, teachers emphasize the similarities between talking and writing; in the later grades, teachers address the differences.

In what ways are writing and speaking the same? How are they different?

As they interact with more advanced discourse community members, children become aware of metalanguage, language about language. Young children develop concepts such as "word" and "sentence," while older children may learn about adjectives, phrases, and clauses. Children also learn **metaliterate language**, language about writing and print; for example, "book," "write," "letter," and, later, "paragraph," "essay," and so on. Another important issue related to language awareness is usage (often confused with grammar), a subject of much debate that will be discussed in Chapter 6.

Another aspect of learning about writing involves what is often referred to as the writing process. This includes strategies for generating and developing ideas, drafting, revising to clarify meaning or to make stylistic improvements, and proofreading to address the conventions of writing, such as spelling and punctuation. Writing process strategies are a significant area of growth for young writers as they proceed through the elementary school years. While many children acquire strategies independently, most children benefit from instruction. Writing process strategies will be addressed in Chapters 6 and 7.

Learning through Writing

As children learn to write and learn about writing, they simultaneously learn through writing. Learning through writing can be considered in two different ways: first, as a form of language across the curriculum; and second, as a medium for constructing meaning and clarifying one's understanding. Traditionally, it was thought that children must first learn to write (in the kindergarten through Grade 3 years)—that is, print neatly and spell conventionally—before they could write to learn (in Grades 4 through 7, and above). It was also thought that children needed to acquire vocabulary orally before learning it in written form. More recent views are that writing-to-learn can occur long before children have "mastered" the conventions of print, and that oral and written vocabulary can be learned together in an integrated manner when embedded in learning activities across the curriculum. Writing should not be seen as an add-on, nor should it be relegated to the language arts period. To emphasize how interwoven writing and learning are, I often use the term *writing/learning activities* in this book—rather than separate activities, these are really two sides of the same coin.

Each curriculum area has related ways of using language, such as specific vocabulary items or particular meanings for words. While preschool children's vocabulary develops mainly from oral interactions, once children come to school it is written language that becomes the primary source of vocabulary development. Another aspect of language in relation to curriculum is that each discipline has specific forms, or genres, of writing and ways of representing information. For example, in mathematics, children learn to write and interpret number problems and various types of graphs. As children write in social studies and science, they learn both factual knowledge and how to communicate their knowledge in writing in a variety of expository forms, such as reports and essays.

Writing is used for many purposes. These can be classified into two broad categories: writing for communication and writing to facilitate thinking and learning. The latter is what Wells and Chang-Wells (1992) refer to as the **epistemic mode.** Crowhurst (1994) explains how writing assists thinking and learning:

> The three great values of writing as a means of learning are its *explicitness*, its relative *permanence,* and the fact that writing requires *active participation.* The act of committing ideas to paper forces us to be explicit, to find words, to express them in complete thoughts, and to arrange those thoughts more or less coherently. The permanence of writing allows us to work on our thoughts. (p. 234)

In addition to clarifying thinking in particular situations, using writing as a tool for learning helps develop an attitude of thoughtfulness and a **reflective** stance toward ideas. Thus, writing-to-learn is becoming increasingly valued at all levels of schooling and can be addressed throughout the elementary years and beyond. (In Chapter 3 I further discuss curriculum contexts for writing, and in Chapter 7 I explore ways of expanding students' writing repertoires in the language arts and across the curriculum.)

Learning and Teaching Writing: The Role of the Environment

According to Heap (1991), literacy results from three cultural conditions: something to read or write, a purpose for reading and writing, and a social context. Of particular importance to this discussion is the nature of the social context. What is the role of the classroom environment in relation to writing? And since the teacher is part of this context, what is the teacher's role?

> **Something to think about**
>
> What sorts of things about writing might children learn from their various environments, such as home, neighbourhood, school, shopping centre, sports, etc.?

All of our children learn some things about print simply by living in a literate society: they are exposed to environmental print such as signs, labels, and flyers, and they see people reading and writing. But to maximize written language development, children need a language- and literacy-rich environment, including access to print in a variety of forms and opportunities to participate in literacy activities with people in their discourse community. Emig (1981) refers to these as "enabling environments ... safe, structured, private, unobtrusive, and literate" that provide "frequent opportunities to practice writing, many of these playful" (p. 25). Learning to write involves experimenting and taking risks. Thus, children need psychologically safe environments where they can express their ideas in writing without concern for adult standards of correctness.

Cambourne (1988, p. 33) suggests that learning to write should occur as "naturally" as learning to talk under certain "key conditions," that is, when:

- Learners are *immersed* in texts in many forms.
- Learners have opportunities to see meaningful *demonstrations* of how texts are constructed and used.
- Adults *expect* them to learn to read and write and provide *support* to children where necessary.
- Learners are encouraged to assume *responsibility* for their own learning.
- Learners are provided with time and opportunities to use writing in *functional*, realistic ways.
- Learners are encouraged to *approximate* and make "mistakes."
- Learners receive *feedback* from more knowledgeable others, with response that is timely, readily available, and nonthreatening.
- Learners are able to *engage actively* in the process of writing.

These key conditions emphasize acquisition and the facilitative role of the environment. It is important for us to be aware, however, that some children require more than an enabling environment in order to become successful readers and writers.

Children need many opportunities to engage actively in the process of writing.

The Teacher's Role

Many would emphasize that an enabling environment includes adults who take an active role in children's literacy development, providing deliberate input and explicit assistance (Malicky, 1991; de la Reyes, 1992). Vygotsky's (1978) theory about the relationship between development and learning provides a framework for understanding the active nature of an adult–child interaction and its impact on children. According to Vygotsky, children have two levels of development:

1. **attained development**—their "can-do zones" or independent levels
2. **zones of proximal development**—or "learning zones," which are *just beyond their attained levels* (see Figure 2.4)

Thus, learning *precedes* development. Vygotsky viewed the primary role of the adult as one of **mediator**, one who guides the child's participation in a learning task by providing directives and cues. These actions provide a **scaffold** for learning—the adult observes what the child does, determines the degree and type of support needed, **guides** the child's participation, and gradually removes support to allow the learner to take on more of the task. For Vygotsky, learning to write is a social process because it involves interaction, and it is a cultural process because it occurs in a sociocultural context. An important part of teaching literacy is to socialize children into the culture's ways of using writing or, to paraphrase Vygotsky, to "cultivate" writing rather than "impose" it.

A Sociocultural Perspective

Luke, Baty, and Stehbens (1989) criticize Cambourne's notion of "natural" literacy development because they believe it ignores the cultural dimension. They applied Cambourne's key conditions to Heath's (1983) study in *Ways with Words*, conducted in three different communities in the southern United States, to demonstrate that language learning is culturally specific and also probably class- and gender-specific. They suggest that theories "of 'natural' learning, however progressive and child-centred in intent, may be alien for many children" (Luke, Baty, & Stehbens, 1989, p. 46). They believe that we should get to know children's "*actual*—not idealised or naturalised—uses and

Figure 2.4 Support for Independence

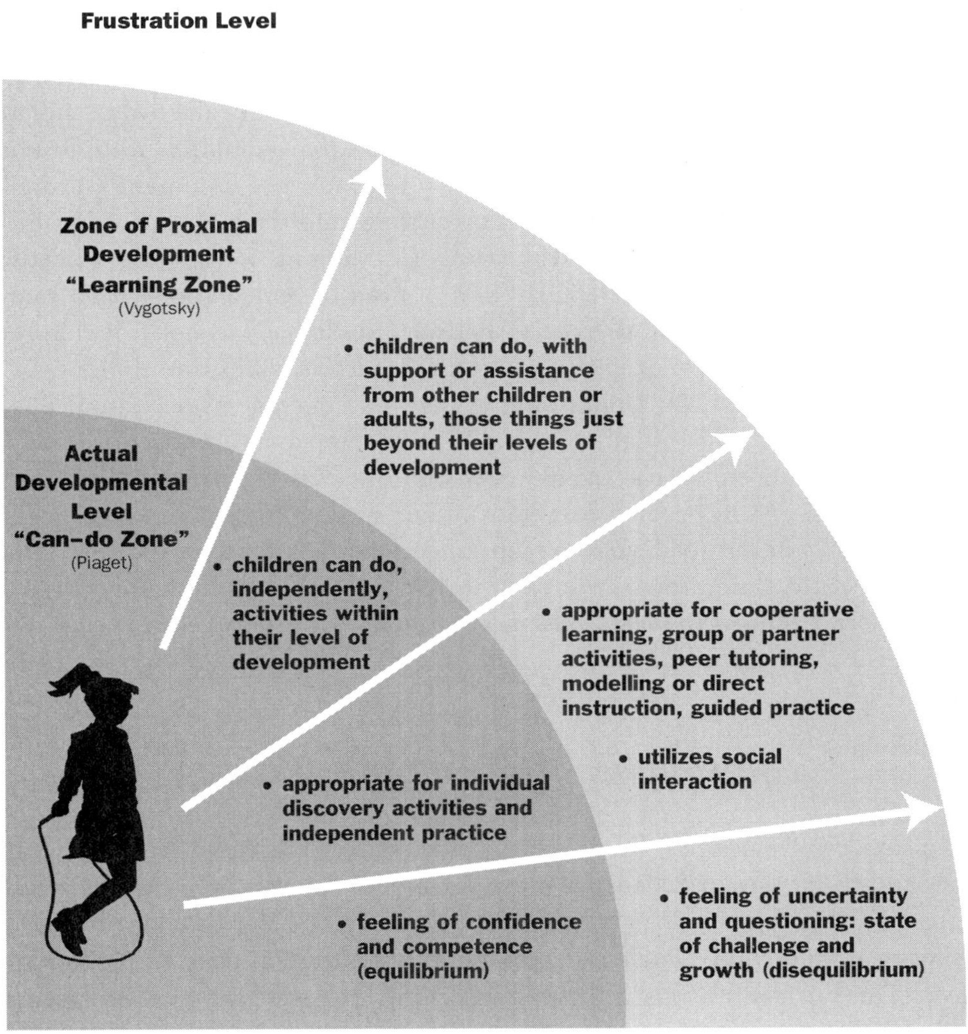

experiences with language, community textual and oral patterns" (pp. 46–47). This echoes Heath's conclusion that the varying ways of using language and literacy in the home and community differentially affect children's success in school.

In a later article, Luke (1991) argues that the notion that literacy is a natural process is a myth; there are many routes to literacy, all of which are artifices of culture. Luke and others (e.g., de la Reyes, 1992; Delpit, 1988) worry about the common misunderstanding that literacy is neutral; literacy is, in fact, enmeshed with the distribution of social and political power, and to think otherwise is naive. "Non-mainstream" children—children who do not belong to the dominant cultural group—often lack the dominant culture's ways of displaying knowledge, including writing, and their discourse features do not match the school's ways with words (McCollum, 1991). Until recently, these children were seen as deficient and in need of remediation rather than being culturally different. We need to understand "literacy as a set of cultural practices that people engage in ... rather than as skills or abilities ..." (Resnick, 1990, p. 170). Understanding written language as a cultural phenomenon, as opposed to a "natural" one, compels us both to become acquainted with children's actual ways of using writing in their discourse communities, and to become conscious of our own ethnocentrism if we want to help all children to develop competence in using written language. The issue, of critical importance with the increasingly multicultural diversity of our society, and how to create classrooms that are culturally sensitive and relevant, is explored in Chapters 3 and 4.

Approaches to Teaching Writing

To provide a framework for discussing various approaches to teaching writing, and to put into a broader context the model that I believe best incorporates the dual personal/social nature of learning, I have developed a grid (shown in Figure 2.5). Each axis symbolizes a continuum from active to passive. The horizontal axis represents teaching; the vertical axis represents learning. The intersection of the two divides the teaching–learning relationship into four general quadrants, which in reality encompass a range of approaches. Below the horizontal line, teaching is seen as a transmission process, with knowledge transmitted from teacher to student; above this line, the teaching–learning relationship is viewed as a constructive process.

"Transmission" Models

Let's begin with quadrant 1, the most familiar of the transmission approaches, the traditional model. This is what most of us experienced when we went to school. In the traditional approach, learners' prior knowledge, experiences, interests, and ideas are, for the most part, irrelevant. The teacher's role is to plan and provide instruction and then test students to see if they have learned what was taught. Learners have little say in what they learn, and education is something that is done *to* them. As a result, the most mentally active person in the classroom is often the teacher rather than the student. In a traditional model, written language is seen as a set of discrete skills that can be taught and drilled (Cook-Gumperz & Gumperz, 1992). A teacher has choices, but they are curriculum-driven; options include when and how to teach particular skills. The dominant technique is a direct or "presentational" (Hillocks, 1986) style of instruction.

At the other end of the continuum of transmission approaches is the delivery model (quadrant 2). Delivery approaches are based on the idea that teachers cannot or should not exert control over what, when, or how they teach. This may be either because the program developers consider teachers to be lacking in knowledge and skills, or because the topic is a political "hot potato." A salient feature of a delivery model is control external to the classroom and a lack of choice or influence by both teachers and students, so much so that teachers are required to read verbatim from scripts in teachers' manuals. Perhaps the best-known examples of the delivery model is *Distar* (Engelmann & Bruner, 1974), a program for teaching reading skills, and its complement for writing skills, which they refer to as "morphographic spelling" (Dixon & Engelmann, 1979).

Research studies indicate that transmission approaches have not been effective for teaching writing. In a meta-analysis of research in written composition, George Hillocks (1986) classified approaches to teaching writing into four modes: presentational (consistent with quadrants 1 and 2), natural process (represented in quadrant 3), individual (which could be approached from either a transmissive or a constructivist perspective), and environmental (synonymous with quadrant 4). Hillocks' meta-analysis determined that the presentational style of teaching writing was the least effective of the four. The

Figure 2.5 Approaches to Teaching Writing

Active student

3. *Cognitive Constructivist*
(Maturational)

The teacher is a *facilitator* who emphasizes personal development so students can develop at their own rates.

(e.g., some early "writing process" and "whole language" classrooms in which children did mostly personal writing and in which teachers used primarily indirect approaches to instruction with minimal "intervention.")

4. *Sociocognitive Constructivist*
(Transactional)

The teacher is a *mediator of learning* who employs both personal and social aspects of learning to promote growth.

(e.g., classrooms in which teacher and students actively share responsibility for learning; students work independently at their own levels and are provided with support and scaffolding to work in their zones of proximal development; learning is mediated through direct and indirect instruction.)

Passive teacher ⟷ **Active teacher**

2. *Delivery Model*
(Transmissive)

The teacher is a *technician* who delivers a program developed by outside "experts."

(e.g., some "direct instruction" or "mastery learning" programs, where the teacher and/or students work their way through a controlled sequence of materials that focus on discrete skills or concepts. What teachers and students do and how they do it is determined by those external to the classroom.)

1. *Traditional Model*
(Transmissive)

The teacher is an *instructor* who provides a program determined by curricula, textbooks, and/or basal series.

(e.g., classrooms in which teachers select from predetermined objectives and/or materials, guide students step by step to meet the objectives, and evaluate whether students have met them. The teacher may decide how to teach, but students have little or no input into what is learned and how.)

Passive student

inadequacy of transmission models has also been revealed by large-scale writing assessments. As Judith Langer (1991) remarked, "The results from the NAEP [National Association for Educational Progress, a large-scale assessment conducted in the United States] suggest that such [transmission] approaches have not been effective in teaching more thoughtful literacy skills" (p. 17).

> **Something to think about**
>
> Some educational programs are based on a delivery approach because of the concern for the need for sensitivity to particular issues and for "political correctness." Think about specific programs or issues that commonly use a delivery approach. In your opinion, when and why are transmission models an appropriate (or perhaps, best) type of program for teachers and students?

A Cognitive Constructivist Model

Theory and research in a variety of fields, such as cognitive and developmental psychology and psycholinguistics, have had a significant impact on the way we think about teaching and learning. Today we place more emphasis on learning and the learner. Interest in the process of writing began with examinations of the cognitive processes involved (e.g., Emig, 1971; Flower & Hayes, 1981; Graves, 1975). In other words, writing was looked upon primarily as an "in-the-head" phenomenon. Likewise, growth in writing focused on the cognitive dimension. Much of this work was based on Piaget's (1983) theory of development as a cognitive constructivist process involving assimilation and accommodation. A *cognitive constructivist* perspective, influenced greatly by Piaget:

- emphasizes development over learning
- proposes a general processing model to explain development; writing is thus part of a more general symbolic development
- de-emphasizes the social dimension of writing and the role of adults in writing development

Accompanying this focus on the learner, however, seems to have been a de-emphasis on the teacher's role. Some adherents of the model depicted in quadrant 3 believe that because learning is something that can be done only by the learner (individually), the teacher's role is primarily to create a conducive environment so that learners can learn by discovery. They believe that once the environmental stage is set, the teacher should "retreat to the wings" to get out of the learners' way. They recommend that teachers act as facilitators, that teaching should be indirect, and that interventions in the form of direct instruction should be discouraged. Because of a concern for inhibiting children and imposing on their writing, children in these classrooms do mostly personal and/or "free-writing." Teachers who adopt this philosophy also believe that since learning cannot be forced, teachers should let children develop at their own rates.

However, as mentioned in the discussion of natural learning, some critics of this approach suggest that while it may work for mainstream children of average ability and above, it is not helpful, and indeed may harm, children who belong to minority groups or who do not learn easily for a variety of reasons (Delpit, 1988). Other critics claim that "progressive" and "child-centred" education is inefficient and that it ignores the research on effective teaching (Nikiforuk, 1993). More importantly, research into the social aspects of learning suggests that emphasizing the individual learner fails to acknowledge the importance of other people, including the teacher, in the learning process.

A Sociocognitive Constructivist or Transactional Approach

In contrast to the cognitive constructivist perspective, if we were to apply a strictly social constructivist perspective on writing growth, we would emphasize the social dimension and ignore the cognitive. This would, in effect, be throwing out the baby with the bath water. Social constructivists propose that:

- Learning precedes and influences development.
- Development and learning are context-specific rather than general processes.
- The impact of the social context is significant; we need to examine the ways in which learning is facilitated by others, particularly the effect of adults and more able peers' interactions on children's writing.

An overemphasis on the social dimension could lead to the negation of the processes of acquisition—which we know make a significant contribution to children's development—and the misconception that children must be taught or guided through everything, that they will not learn anything unless we teach it to them. It is my belief that combining social and cognitive constructivist perspectives acknowledges the relative contributions of each. Sociocognitive constructivism acknowledges the interplay between cognitive and social constructivist perspectives. The term **transactional** is also used because learning is constructed through transactions between the individual and the community, between the personal and the social.

> **Something to think about**
>
> Janet Emig (1981) said that if we think there is a one-to-one correspondence between teaching and learning, then we're engaging in "magical thinking." Does teaching always result in learning? Does learning always result from teaching? How might you interpret Emig's comment?

As I discussed earlier, the influences of Vygotsky (1978) and Bakhtin (1986) have led to a reconceptualization of literacy development as a social and cultural process in which a child learns about written language by internalizing social action (Dyson, 1993; Pellegrini & Galda, 1993). From this perspective, children are socialized into literacy through participation in a kind of social dialogue: a child processes the words of others (both spoken and written) dialogically into his/her own words with the help of others' words (Bakhtin, 1986, p. 163). This is not a passive process of copying and imitation, however. Rather, young writers are actors who react to past and future actions (Bloome & Egan-Robertson, 1993), and as junior members of the discourse community they are literacy apprentices (Resnick, 1990; Rogoff, 1990; Vygotsky, 1978).

We can look at Piaget's notion of developmental levels and Vygotsky's theory of the zone of proximal development in tandem. The concept of dual levels has an important implication for teachers: we need to provide children with two kinds of experiences at *two levels.* When we want children to work independently, either to practise or apply something they have learned, or to engage in a discovery learning activity, we must ensure that the task is within their can-do or independent levels. In these instances, the teacher is a facilitator and instruction is indirect. However, it is important that children of *all* abilities are challenged to go beyond what they are capable of doing. Or, as Elizabeth Sulzby (1986) says, we give them a "developmental nudge." Since learning precedes development, learning means taking risks and venturing into the zone beyond the can-do's.

An appropriate level of difficulty for new learning is one which the child is able to meet with success when provided with support, guidance, demonstration, and/or instruction by an adult or a more capable peer. Vygotsky describes the teacher's major role as *mediator;* that is, one who enables children to make sense of their experiences, to make connections with the concrete world of the here and now and develop abstract concepts, and to integrate the new with the known. Through teacher-guided talk about their experiences, hands-on activity becomes minds-on learning. When children work at independent or collaborative activities, these should be followed by teacher-guided discussion (debriefing). When children work on teacher-guided activities, focused talk about the experiences should occur throughout.

The important point is that active learning does not imply passive teaching. A sociocognitive constructivist or transactional approach (quadrant 4) combines the active teaching of quadrant 1 and the active learning of quadrant 3. Hillocks' (1986) meta-analysis referred to earlier showed that the most effective form of writing, which he referred to as the "environmental approach" and which is represented in Figure 2.5 by quadrant 4, is the most effective approach to teaching writing. Yes, there are times when teachers do need to take a back seat and lead from behind, but this is only when children are working at their independent levels. Unless children are challenged to work at times within their zones of proximal development, to expand their repertoires by trying new functions and forms of writing with input from a teacher, learning is not optimal. We should aim for active teaching to enable active learning, the model represented by quadrant 4. Rather than focusing primarily on either learning or teaching, we need to see both as important. "There is a need for adult instruction in the process [of learning to write] and there is a need for children to have opportunities to play with the forms and functions of written language, just as they have had such opportunities in learning to speak" (Gundlach et al., 1985, p. 40).

Principles and Practice

In this book, I take a sociocognitive constructivist or transactional approach to teaching writing in the elementary school. I do so for a number of reasons, all of which reinforce one another. First, as I have discussed in this chapter, our current knowledge base in learning and teaching writing demonstrates that becoming a writer is a constructive process that is both individual and social in nature. A sociocognitive constructivist perspective combines both in a complementary way. Second, the research findings to date strongly support both acquisition and learning as factors in literacy growth. Third, if we reflect on the principles of writing developed in Chapter 1, we can see implications

Figure 2.6 From Principles of Writing to Practice

Principles of Writing	Implications and Guidelines for Practice
1. Writing is written language, a complex system of linguistic expression related to other forms of language such as speaking and reading.	1. Integrate writing with the other language arts: speaking, listening, reading, visual representation (e.g., drawing, drama, graphing), and viewing.
2. Communication and meaning-making are central to writing and should always be the primary focus.	2. Always emphasize communication and making meaning.
3. Conventions of print are a part of writing, not ends unto themselves.	3. Teach conventions of print purposefully, in a communicative context.
4. Writers compose meanings and encode them in writing in an integrated, simultaneous fashion.	4. Address various aspects of composing and encoding in an integrated, holistic way.
5. Writing involves many cognitive processes such as planning, generating, and organizing ideas; putting ideas into words; and reviewing for meaning and form.	5. Teach strategies to enhance students' writing processes, from prewriting to presenting.
6. Writing is a purposeful activity, and people use writing for a wide array of functions. Two major categories of writing functions are to communicate and to facilitate thinking and learning.	6. Have students write purposefully and incorporate a wide array of functions, including interpersonal communication and thinking and learning in all areas of the curriculum.
7. Writing is both an individual and a social activity.	7. Create opportunities for individual exploration, interaction, and collaboration, and instruction that is developmentally appropriate and culturally relevant.
8. Each sphere of activity has a language register, which includes vocabulary, syntax, and forms of discourse. Writers express their ideas in various forms of representation and genres, ways of using language to suit particular contexts and functions.	8. Cultivate writing by integrating it with every sphere of classroom activity—personal, interpersonal, and academic—and increase students' repertoires of forms of representation and genres.
9. Writing occurs in and is influenced by context, which is multidimensional. The immediate writing context is both social—embedded in a sphere of activity, community, and sociocultural context—and personal—part of an individual writer's life.	9. Teaching and evaluating writing should take into account the multiple dimensions of context, both social (the immediate situation, sphere of activity, community and sociocultural factors) and personal.
10. Writing is a product in many senses: a text containing a message, a document that reveals information about its writer, and a cultural artifact.	10. Use students' written products created in a variety of contexts as part of the process of assessing, evaluating, and documenting students' growth.

or guidelines for practice in teaching writing that support a transactional approach (see Figure 2.6).

In this chapter I have provided an overview of the research related to the learning and teaching of writing, and I have connected this to the principles of writing discussed in Chapter 1. In subsequent chapters, I demonstrate the specific how-to's and practical details of active teaching for active learning. The question of whether learning to write is "natural" or not is central to many of the great debates in literacy instruction. It translates into issues of whether or not children benefit from direct or explicit instruction. Of particular interest in writing are if, when, and how we should teach spelling, punctuation, and grammar. A related concern is the debate over process and genre approaches to composing. These issues are historical and, at least in part, also sociocultural, since some groups have different perspectives on the role of direct instruction. Rather than delve into the particulars here, I will discuss skills such as spelling and the related research in Chapter 6 and the process/genre debate in Chapter 7.

Reflections on the Chapter

Think about/talk about/write about:

Your Personal Writing History or Writing Autobiography

- Your own experiences in learning to write: are there any specific events that come to mind? Why are these significant or important to your understanding of writing development?
- What ways of using literacy were valued in your home? Your schools? Your community?
- Are there specific people who made particular contributions to your own writing development? How did they do this?

Your Understanding of Learning and Writing

- How has your understanding changed about writing development? What do you find most fascinating or interesting? What do you wonder about or want to know more about?

- Think of some more metalanguage and metaliterate vocabulary words, especially for the age level of children you teach or plan to teach.

Your Philosophy of Teaching

- Do you believe that learning to write is "natural"? Did it seem so for you personally? How much of your own writing development has been as natural as learning to talk?
- What approaches to teaching writing have you experienced as a student? How did these affect the way you think about writing today?
- If you have teaching experience, how would you characterize your approach to teaching writing? Has it changed over time? How and why has it changed?

REFERENCES AND FURTHER READING

Bakhtin, M.M. (1986). *Speech genres and other late essays.* (V.W. McGee, Trans., C. Emerson and M. Holquist, Eds.). Austin, TX: University of Texas Press. (Original work published 1979.)

Beers, J. (1980). Developmental strategies of spelling competence in primary school children. In E. Henderson and J. Beers (Eds.), *Developmental and cognitive aspects of learning to spell* (pp. 36–45). Newark, DE: International Reading Association.

Bissex, G. (1980). *Gnys at wrk: A child learns to write and read.* Cambridge, MA: Harvard University Press.

Bloome, D., and Egan-Robertson, A. (1993). The social construction of intertextuality in classroom reading and writing lessons. *Reading Research Quarterly, 28*(4), 305–33.

British Columbia Ministry of Education. (1990). *Primary program: Foundation document.* Victoria, BC: British Columbia Ministry of Education.

Cambourne, B. (1988). *The whole story: Natural learning and the acquisition of literacy in the classroom.* Auckland, NZ: Ashton Scholastic.

Cook-Gumperz, J., and Gumperz, J. (1992). Changing views of language in education: The implications for literacy research. In R. Beach, J. Green, M. Kamil, and

T. Shanahan (Eds.), *Multidisciplinary perspectives on literacy research* (pp. 89–109). Hillsdale, NJ: Lawrence Erlbaum Associates.

Crowhurst, M. (1994). *Language and learning across the curriculum*. Scarborough, ON: Allyn & Bacon.

de la Reyes, M. (1992). Challenging venerable assumptions: Literacy instruction for linguistically different students. *Harvard Educational Review, 62*(4), 427–46.

Delpit, L. (1988). The silenced dialogue: Power and pedagogy in educating other people's children. *Harvard Educational Review, 58*(2), 280–98.

Dixon, R., and Engelmann, S. (1979). *Corrective spelling through morphographs*. Chicago: Science Research Associates.

Dyson, A.H. (1984). Reading, writing, and language: Young children solving the written language puzzle. In J.M. Jensen (Ed.), *Composing and comprehending* (pp. 165–75). Urbana, IL: National Council of Teachers of English.

———. (1986a). The imaginary worlds of childhood: A multimedia presentation. *Language Arts, 63*(8), 799–808.

———. (1986b). Transitions and tensions: Interrelationships between the drawing, talking, and dictating of young children. *Research in the Teaching of English, 20*(4), 379–409.

———. (1993). *From invention to social action in early childhood literacy: A reconceptualization through dialogue about difference* (Tech. Rep. No. 67). Berkeley, CA: University of California, National Center for the Study of Writing.

Emig, J. (1971). *The composing processes of twelfth graders*. Urbana, IL: National Council of Teachers of English.

———. (1981). Non-magical thinking: Presenting writing developmentally in schools. In C.H. Frederiksen and S.F. Dominic (Eds.), *Writing: The nature, development, and teaching of written communication. Volume 2, Writing: Process, development and communication* (pp. 21–30). Hillsdale, NJ: Lawrence Erlbaum Associates.

Engelmann, S., and Bruner, C. (1974). *Distar reading I–II: An instructional system*. Chicago: Science Research Associates.

Ferreiro, E. (1982). The relationship between oral and written language: The children's viewpoints. In Y. Goodman, M. Haussler, and D. Strickland (Eds.), *Oral and written language development research: Impact on the schools* (pp. 47–56). Urbana, IL: National Council of Teachers of English.

Flower, L., and Hayes, J. (1981). A cognitive process theory of writing. *College Composition and Communication, 32*(4), 365–87.

Graves, D. (1975). An examination of the writing processes of seven year old children. *Research in the Teaching of English, 9*(3), 227–41.

Gundlach, R., McLane, J.B., Stott, F., and McNamee, G. (1985). The social foundations of children's early writing development. In M. Farr (Ed.), *Advances in writing research, Volume One: Children's early writing development* (pp. 1–58). Norwood, NJ: Ablex.

Halliday, M.A.K. (1982). Three aspects of children's language development: Learning language, learning through language, learning about language. In Y. Goodman, M. Haussler, and D. Strickland (Eds.), *Oral and written language development research: Impact on the schools* (pp. 7–19). Urbana, IL: National Council of Teachers of English.

Heap, J. (1991). Reading as cultural activities: Enabling reflective texts. *Curriculum Inquiry, 21*(1), 11–39.

Heath, S.B. (1983). *Ways with words: Language, life, and work in communities and classrooms.* Cambridge, NY: Cambridge University Press.

Hillocks, G. (1986). *Research on written composition.* Urbana, IL: National Conference on Research in English.

Krashen, S., and Terrell, T. (1983). *The natural approach: Language acquisition in the classroom.* Hayward, CA: Alemany Press.

Langer, J. (1991). Literacy and schooling: A sociocognitive perspective. In E.H. Hiebert (Ed.), *Literacy for a diverse society: Perspectives, practices, and policies* (pp. 9–27). New York: Teachers College Press.

Luke, A. (1991). Literacies as social practices. *English Education, 23*(3), 131–47.

Luke, A., Baty, A., and Stehbens, C. (1989). "Natural" conditions for language learning: A critique. *English in Australia, 89*, 36–49.

Malicky, G. (1991). Myths and assumptions of literacy education. *Alberta Journal of Educational Research, 37*(4), 333–47.

McCollum, P. (1991). Cross-cultural perspectives on classroom discourse and literacy. In E.H. Hiebert (Ed.), *Literacy for a diverse society: Perspectives, practices, and policies* (pp. 108–21). New York: Teachers College Press.

Nikiforuk, A. (1993). *School's out: The catastrophe in public education and what we can do about it.* Toronto: Macfarlane, Walter & Ross.

Pellegrini, A.D., and Galda, L. (1993). Ten years after: A reexamination of symbolic play and literacy research. *Reading Research Quarterly, 28*(2), 163–75.

Piaget, J. (1983). Piaget's theory. In P.H. Mussen (Ed.), *Handbook of child psychology: Volume. 1: History, theory and methods.* New York: Wiley.

Read, C. (1975). *Children's categorizations of speech sounds in English*. Urbana, IL: National Council of Teachers of English.

Resnick, L. (1990). Literacy in school and out. *Daedalus, 119*(2), 169–85.

Rogoff, B. (1990). *Apprenticeship in thinking*. New York: Oxford University Press.

Sulzby, E. (1986). Writing and reading: Signs of oral and written language organization in the young child. In W.H. Teale and E. Sulzby (Eds.), *Emergent literacy: Writing and reading* (pp. 50–89). Norwood, NJ: Ablex.

Teale, W., and Sulzby, E. (1986). Introduction. In W.H. Teale and E. Sulzby (Eds.), *Emergent literacy: Writing and reading* (pp. vii–xxv). Norwood, NJ: Ablex.

Vygotsky, L. (1978). *Mind in society: The development of higher psychological processes*. (M. Cole, V. John-Steiner, S. Scribner, and E. Souberman, Eds.). Cambridge, MA: Harvard University Press.

Wells, G., and Chang-Wells, G. (1992). *Constructing knowledge together: Classrooms as centers of inquiry and literacy*. Portsmouth, NH: Heinemann.

CHAPTER 3

Writing in the Fabric of Classroom Life

CHAPTER OBJECTIVES

To examine the teacher's roles as decision-maker and action researcher

To discuss features of classrooms that enable writing: the emotional, artistic/aesthetic, and intellectual climate; and the social dimension (the discourse community)

To explore the idea of creating contexts for writing and to discuss ways of using writing in these contexts (the classroom workplace, the language arts, and across the curriculum)

To discuss writing in kindergarten and to introduce Kindergarten Corner ideas

PERSONAL REFLECTION

I began Chapter 2 with a personal school vignette that was a positive learning experience for me. What a contrast between my Grade 4 year with Mr. Allen and my experience as an undergraduate at university in a composition course required for all prospective teachers. In this course, weekly essays were assigned and topics were given (no choices). Each week I wrote an essay (at home) that was returned graded the following week. During the first term, I received my first low mark on an essay—a D! I had never received less than a B in all of my years of schooling, and I recall the shock of seeing that D on the paper. The assignment had been "to argue for or against socialism." My instructor's political persuasion just happened to be the opposite of my own, and it appeared that he had given me a low grade because he did not agree with my politics. The instructor could not tell me what was wrong with my writing (other than that he disagreed with my point of view), nor how to improve it. He simply gave me a failing grade and wrote a derogatory remark. Although I hung in there and completed the course with a fair-to-middling grade (primarily because I became good at second-guessing what my instructor wanted), I became discouraged about my abilities as a writer and came to hate writing, so much so that I put off taking another university course for seven years, delaying completion of my baccalaureate degree. As a teacher of writing, I think about the contrast between these two learning experiences in terms of what each teacher did to encourage or inhibit my attitudes and abilities in writing.

As you ponder the issues discussed in this chapter about creating learning environments that enable writing, put yourself in a dual role: (1) draw upon your own experiences, both positive and negative, to put yourself in your students' shoes; and (2) think about your role as a teacher and the impact you have on students' learning in your classroom and in their lives.

The Role of the Teacher

As I discussed in Chapter 2, the role of the teacher has undergone a transformation from the traditional view of a dispenser of curriculum—teacher-centred learning—to a sociocognitive or transactional perspective—learner-centred teaching. This means that teachers are professionals who get to know their learners and who make decisions on an ongoing basis about what, who, when, and how to teach. They assume responsibility for the teaching and learning in their classrooms rather than letting outsiders such as curriculum planners, publishers, or administrators control what they do. To do this well, teachers first need to know themselves, their values and beliefs, strengths and limitations. At the same time, they must hold a willingness to continue to grow as professionals. As well, they need to reflect about what they do, to be both active participants in classroom life and observers of it. As well as being decision-makers, they are researchers into their own practice.

Teacher as Decision-Maker

Not only do teachers have to make multiple decisions daily about what to do, when and how to do it, and why, they need to be able to articulate their rationales for their decisions. One of the most important areas of decision-making is in designing the classroom learning environment. Just as the state of the ecological environment is partly a result of the actions and decisions people make about the way to treat the natural world, the classroom environment is created to a great extent by teachers' actions and decisions. Certainly, they start with the physical space and resources allocated to them and the groups of children who are assigned to their classes, but it is up to teachers to take responsibility for their classrooms by applying their knowledge (for example, principles of writing and guidelines for practice) and skills (for example, instructional strategies). And, of course, creating the classroom environment does not stop at the end of September with things in place for the year. Instead, constructing the learning environment is a dynamic, ongoing process of problem-solving and decision-making throughout the school year. There are so many factors that it is easy to get caught up in trivial pursuits, yet we must keep in mind our goals and the big picture we want to create.

Teacher as Researcher

One of the ways that teachers can focus on the larger picture and balance the various parts of their practice in relation to the whole is to become an **action researcher** in their own classrooms. This means assuming a dual role as a *participant-observer*—putting ideas into action and interacting with students and, at the same time, constantly observing what is happening and how—collecting data on the children and their learning in relation to the various writing/learning contexts in the classroom.

Research begins immediately with an initial assessment of what is, or a baseline. Teachers cannot do justice to their learners without knowing who they are—their experiential backgrounds (including sociocultural factors), not just as a group, but also as individuals (their learning styles, interests, and so on). Teachers can also take into account knowledge of the developmental characteristics of particular age groups and common developmental patterns in writing (Chapter 2, Figure 2.3). An initial assessment should also include examining curricular expectations and learning about the school context; for example, the values, beliefs, and approaches of our colleagues and the resources available. This assessment should also take into consideration the community context in which the school is situated. What are the students' families like? What values and beliefs do they hold, in learning generally and in relation to writing in particular? When teachers know how parents think and feel, teachers can facilitate children's transitions between home and school and help parents understand what is taught, how, and why.

Classroom research is ongoing as teachers continually observe their students in various learning contexts—their learning processes and the products they create, and as they engage in conferences and conversations with students to learn their perspectives. As I discuss in Chapter 8, these are the same data that teach-

REFLECTION

Hanci Ping (1995), a graduate student at Simon Fraser University in Vancouver, wrote "Chinese Attitudes Towards Learning and Reading," a chapter in a book I edited (Chapman & Anderson, 1995). In this chapter she explains how the Chinese education system reflects Confucian thought—being "good" through learning. This Confucian principle has led to a reverence for book learning and "the intensive reading method"—mastering a text through repeated reading and accumulating vocabulary through memorization and rote learning. It is no wonder that many new Chinese immigrants to Canada are dismayed with our child-centred educational practices.

How might we help parents understand what we are doing in our writing programs, and why?

ers use for evaluating children's learning and development. What changes is the focus. When information is interpreted in relation to individual children, it is a process of evaluation. When it is interpreted in relation to the class as a whole (or to particular groups of children) this information can inform us about our teaching. For example, if I try out a particular writing strategy (such as note-taking) and many of the children have difficulty, does this mean that those children have a learning problem or that I have a teaching problem? It is my firm belief that while it is important for learners to assume responsibility for their own learning, teachers hold primary responsibility for students' learning—that is the mandate given to teachers when they receive their teaching credentials, and it is the implicit mandate given to teachers by parents and the community. So, if the note-taking was not overly successful, I must formulate hypotheses about the source of the problem: Did the students have prerequisite skills? Did I demonstrate the activity clearly? Did I provide guided practice and scaffolding? Did I provide students with peer support through collaboration or cooperative learning before I expected them to work independently? Was the timing appropriate? and so on.

As well as engaging in self-reflection, it is also important, particularly as beginning teachers or teachers who are novices in a new approach, to seek support from the professional community—colleagues who are co-learners. Engaging in talk about teaching and learning, both in general and in relation to specific issues, provides us with opportunities to articulate our thinking (which is often helpful in itself) and can shed new insights into something we find challenging. Sometimes it is hard to find other classroom teachers who are interested in such "teacher talk." In these instances it is even more important to keep active in professional development through attending in-service sessions and workshops, belonging to professional associations (for example, the Canadian Council of Teachers of English Language Arts or a local affiliate of the International Reading Association), taking courses, and reading professional books and journals. In these ways, teachers become active members of their professional community of teacher-learners.

Cultivating Writing

As I discussed in Chapter 2, learning to write is both an individual and a sociocultural process, and an important role of the teacher is to "cultivate"

REFLECTION

What is a writer? When I ask this question, typical responses include comments such as "an author," "someone who writes books for a living," "someone who writes fiction," "someone who gets their writing (i.e., novels) published." Many school writing programs are based on these notions of writing as authorship, and they emphasize the creation of fiction and narrative forms. Yet very few people become writers in this sense, and even fewer are able to make their livelihoods as authors. Contrast this view with the fact that, in a literate society such as ours, almost everyone uses writing in the context of their daily personal lives, many of us use writing in our work, and some of us do the majority of our work through writing—but rarely in narrative.

If one of the functions of school is to socialize children into the culture's ways of writing, is an emphasis on authoring and the writing of narrative appropriate? Or should teachers be cultivating the many different functions and forms of writing in their cultures?

writing (Vygotsky, 1978). In this context, "cultivating," which is derived from the participle of Latin *colere,* to care for, means "to promote or improve growth by labor and attention; to develop or improve by education or training; to promote the growth or development of an art, science, etc.; to foster" (Webster's, 1989, p. 353). Just as a master weaver takes an active role in fostering the art of weaving, a teacher takes an active role in fostering writing. In this book I use the term "cultivating writing" as Vygotsky (1978) used it, to convey the active nature of the teacher's role in encouraging writing for a variety of personal and social purposes and promoting growth in students' writing abilities.

Classrooms that cultivate writing are created—created by teachers who make decisions, who act on their decisions, and who reflect on their actions. Writing is cultivated in classrooms that are multidimensional. These include what I call the climate—emotional, aesthetic/artistic, and intellectual; the discourse community—the social dimension; and organization—the physical dimension or ways of using time, resources, and space. You will notice that as I discuss environments that cultivate writing, I discuss concepts that apply throughout the school years. In some instances, I will also point out how a general idea is enacted in a primary classroom or with younger writers and what it might look like in a junior classroom or with older writers. Keep in mind, though, that grades are organizational structures that are quite arbitrary and that as we design our own classrooms, we must take into account our own learners and their needs. At the end of this chapter I will address the particulars of fostering writing in the kindergarten classroom.

The Classroom Climate

The aspects of the classroom that I am referring to as climate include those that are intangible yet very real. Sometimes the classroom climate is referred to as the "tone," "atmosphere," or "ethos" of the classroom. Perhaps the most important thing we need to keep in mind is that the classroom climate is not something that just happens. Instead, it is something that is created, and the person who holds primary responsibility for this is the classroom teacher. Teachers create an atmosphere that encourages writing through the things they do and the things they say. And as I have just discussed, teachers do not act willy-nilly; they choose to act in particular ways. I have approached this discussion of creating our classroom climate by focusing on the emotional, artistic/aesthetic, and intellectual dimensions. Please keep in mind, however, that these are abstract distinctions and in reality they are overlapping and integrated, not at all separate.

The Emotional Dimension

First, it is important to consider the emotional or affective dimension of the writing climate, for learners construct their attitudes toward writing and toward themselves as writers at the same time that they acquire knowledge and skills. So what do we want for our young writers? Positive climates, ones that Janet Emig (1981) refers to as "enabling environments." In such a learning climate, young writers develop confidence so that they can explore, take risks in their learning, and venture into new learning territories. One of the main reasons for not emphasizing correctness in the early stages, whether we are working with younger children or starting a new school year with older students, is that learning to write is a complex process. Writers are continually facing new challenges and solving new problems. To do so requires courage—and as my personal experience at the beginning of the chapter illustrates, we are never too old to become discouraged. Teachers create positive, enabling environments when they accept what children have attempted and acknowledge their efforts, accomplishments, and strengths, and when they convey a can-do attitude, a belief that *all* students can and will learn. When this happens, students are more open to learning and to suggestions for improving their writing.

In a classroom that is a safe place to take risks in one's learning, where confidentiality is respected, and where students are encouraged to engage in personal writing, students will develop an appreciation of writing as a vehicle for expressing feelings and opinions. From kindergarten on, students can be encouraged to write about themselves in journals, to write cards to family and friends, and so on. Personal writing can be continued throughout the junior years as a valued form of writing. Preadolescents and adolescents have particular emotional needs and benefit when they can express their feelings and opinions in a safe and appropriate manner; writing can play an important role in this regard.

The Artistic/Aesthetic Dimension

If we want students to use written language creatively and effectively, then we need to saturate our classrooms with a variety of models that embody the qualities of good writing; for example, a large number of well-written texts in both literary and expository forms. As well as making these available for students to read themselves, we need to provide opportunities for students to *hear* rich language. Kindergarten and primary children should be read to several times a day, and the practice of reading aloud should continue throughout the junior grades. Keep in mind that the literature we immerse children in should include texts from a variety of cultures, not just Western culture. And families who speak a language other than or in addition to English in their homes should be encouraged to maintain their native languages by reading to their children in their first language as well as in English, if they are able. We should also remember that effective writing is not limited to literary forms. If we want students to communicate with clarity and precision, which are also aesthetic qualities, then we need to provide them with good models of various forms of writing. This means widening our notion of "story time" to include other types of writing, including factual texts (Green & Green, 1991).

The classroom is a community of learners and writers.

Whatever forms and purposes we use, we should keep in mind Cambourne's (1988) principle of *immersion* (see Chapter 2), not only in literacy, but in aesthetically pleasing written language forms. To help children "stretch" aesthetically, we read to them quality written language that is beyond their independent reading levels and direct their attention to the way authors choose words for particular effects, such as sound patterns and images. We can also discuss in such contexts stylistic devices such as alliteration and metaphor. In this way we are developing children's aesthetic metalinguistic awareness.

The Intellectual Dimension

In our classrooms we also want to create an intellectual climate that emphasizes the development and expression of ideas rather than focusing on surface features or conventions of writing. Now, of course, we write *about something*, and so one of the intellectual foundations for writing is a wealth of experiences. Throughout the elementary years we want to provide students with many first-hand experiences. And we use talk as an important medium for helping students move from specific experiences to develop concepts and understandings about their world. While **language experience activities** are a common practice in kindergarten and primary classrooms, they are important throughout the elementary years—experiencing, thinking, and speaking are truly the basics of writing. For emergent writers, we can help them make connections by applying the adage: *If I can think it, I can say it; if I can say it, I can write it; if I can write it, I can read it.*

We should also keep in mind that for young children writing is very much related to other symbolic activities, such as drawing and dramatic play. These other symbolic forms also mediate children's thinking and are best thought of as integral to their writing processes, rather than merely as accompaniments. Thus, in our intellectually rich climate, we provide many ways for children to construct and convey meanings, and we situate writing within this multimedia context.

Emphasis is on experiencing, thinking, speaking, and representing in a variety of forms continues throughout the elementary school years. As children mature, however, they become increasingly able to differentiate their use of symbol systems for particular purposes. Thus, while we emphasize the similarities between oral and written language in the early years, when we work with older students we help them make distinctions between oral and written discourse forms and explore the ways in which writing is unique. Whatever the age of the children we teach, we want to engage them in much discussion about language in all its forms to develop their metalinguistic and metaliterate knowledge, their conscious awareness of language and literacy.

To my mind, an essential attribute in any intellectual pursuit is the element of *play*—of trying things out this way and that, exploring what happens when we try different techniques or arrangements. What effect does this arrangement create? Does it make sense? Does it sound right? Is there a better way to write it? Students need many opportunities to play with language in oral and written form, which is, I think, the essence of composing poetry. They also need opportunities to integrate writing with other forms of creative expression: drawing, painting, music, and movement. There are those who think that play belongs only in the preschool, kindergarten, and primary grades, but I am not one of them. Play is a hallmark of intellectual life; playing with words and ideas is the essence of writing.

Another attribute of the intellectual climate we want to cultivate is *reflection*. The way that we do this is by immersing students in talk—talk about their experiences, talk about ideas, talk about words—for it is through talk that we develop the ability to reflect. According to Vygotsky (1978), young children think out loud (talk to themselves) rather than in their heads. Then, at about the age of 7, children internalize this self-talk as **inner speech.** This is the main reason why talking is so important to children and why, if we want them to learn, we cannot deny them access to speech. And because children learn ways with words through interactions with others, if we want them to reflect on what they have learned (knowledge) and how they have learned (their learning processes), then we need to immerse them in talk. We wrap talk in, through, and around experiences to help them develop the ability to *reflect in action*, and we talk afterward (*debrief*) to develop the ability to *reflect on action.*

The Classroom Discourse Community

A community is not just a random collection of individuals. It is a group of people who come together around a central purpose; its members have many things in common, one of which is using language in particular ways in the various spheres of activity that are part of community life. A classroom is a special kind of community, a *community of learners*, that has three essential features central to our discussion: membership in the community, a focus on learning (which is the work of the classroom and its central purpose), and writing in the context of participation in the classroom.

Assigning students and a teacher (or teachers) does not a learning community make. Just as teachers create the climate in the classroom by the decisions they make and the actions they take, the teacher is the catalyst in creating a community of learners. I say "catalyst" because a community of this kind is not static or fixed; it is dynamic, continually evolving through the actions and interactions of its members. That said, what are the elements we want to work toward in our classrooms?

Membership in a Learning Community

Each member of a learning community is a learner and a teacher. While we have much to teach our students, we also learn much from them. So that we can work and learn together, we need to create within our classrooms a *social support system* that embodies interdependence and a cooperative spirit rather than individualism or competition. In order to achieve this, we need to be clear about what we *expect* from our students as members of our classroom community (and ourselves, too):

- We expect everyone to *participate actively* in all of the activities in our classroom community.
- We expect them to be *independent* to the degree that they are able when it is appropriate.
- We expect them to assume *individual responsibility* for their actions and to do their share (what David Suzuki refers to as "the power of one").
- We expect them to be *socially responsible*, to be considerate and to value and respect the community and all its members.
- We expect them to *share* their ideas, feelings, and opinions and to be *responsive* to one another.
- We expect them to *cooperate* and work together to achieve common goals.
- We expect them to *collaborate* by giving and receiving help when appropriate.

Apprenticeship: Learning through Community

Becoming a member of a classroom community involves socialization into the work of the community, that is, learning. For our purposes, this includes (simultaneously) learning to write, learning about writing, and learning through writing. We can think of this as a process of writing/learning apprenticeship. Apprentices do not sit on the sidelines and watch experts, nor do they sit and listen to lectures from masters. Rather, they are immersed in the community's work (learning and writing) and its accompanying ways with words (oral and written discourse); they are expected to participate in the work of the community in developmentally appropriate ways and to take responsibility for things within their capabilities. Older and more advanced members of the community act as role models and mentors. Naturally, this includes the teacher, but older, more able or advanced students can be mentors too. Mentors provide demonstrations of writing for a variety of purposes, in a variety of forms and in a range of contexts; provide assistance and guidance to apprentices; and talk about writing and learning in the context of meaningful activities.

Children learn much about literacy from interactions with other children

Something to think about

One of the functions of a mentor, and thus a teacher, is to serve as a role model. Students will value what we value—not just what we say, but what we do. A teacher who writes, who shares his or her writing with students, who can discuss his or her own writing accomplishments and struggles, demonstrates attitudes, skills, knowledge, and values of writing. When we are intentional and thoughtful about what we do, we become aware that much of what we want students to learn results from our ongoing actions rather than in particular instructional episodes.

While the teacher is not the only mentor in the classroom, he or she has been given responsibility for the apprentices' progress and achievements. Teachers in writing communities aim to help their students become writers who can be independent when it is appropriate and who can also be writing mentors to their classmates, in other words, interdependent. Teachers do this by providing support toward independence through

- *Ongoing assessment*—observing learners in the process of writing and learning, examining their writing products, and engaging in conversations with them
- *Evaluating* what learners can do (have learned) and what they are learning to do (learning in progress)
- *Making decisions* about what learners should learn next, the kind of support they need, how much, and how best to provide it

Sometimes teachers decide to take a more hands-off approach and design learning activities that will enable students to learn independently. Sometimes they decide to provide support to learners by having them work collaboratively with other students. Sometimes teachers take a facilitative role and provide indirect instruction; for example, through guiding participation, providing support yet encouraging students to assume responsibility for the things they can do, or through scaffolding with prompts, cues, and explanations. At other times teachers take a more direct approach by providing more explicit instruction and mediated learning activities.

Something to think about

My student teachers often ask me, "How will I know when to intervene and when to keep out of a learner's way?" One way is to listen to the children. If children say they don't want help (this is not unusual—they often want to try things on their own and be independent), then I stay away (keeping an eye on them, of course, in case they get frustrated; making eye contact and smiling at them, keeping an open invitation in case they change their minds). If a child asks for help, I will often respond, "How can I help you?" If a child seems frustrated, I might say, "How are you doing? Do you want some help?" Encourage children to seek help from one another as well. Some teachers use the motto: "Three before me" (ask three classmates for help before you seek help from me). Remember that our goals are independence and interdependence, not dependence. Children who want to be "helpers" need to know that helping does not mean taking over someone else's work.

Teachers choose collaborative and cooperative learning activities as ways not only to support less able students but also to provide opportunities for students to be mentors. As well, they provide opportunities for children to be an audience for one another's writing. From the beginning, we can encourage emergent writers to share their writing/drawing creations with one another and to engage in discussions about them. As writers mature, they become increasingly aware of audience as an important dimension of writing. In the junior years, students become increasingly oriented toward their peers, and teachers can either ignore this disposition or use it to enhance learning.

Classroom Contexts for Writing

Our discourse community engages in writing in various contexts as part of each day, all of which are the result of conscious decision-making on the part of the teacher. We can group these contexts for writing into three general spheres of activity: (1) classroom workplace literacy events that are part of ongoing classroom community life, (2) writing activities that are situated within a broader language arts context, and (3) writing/learning activities integrated across the curriculum. All three spheres of activity provide opportunities for children to learn to write, learn about writing, and learn through writing. In this chapter I explore ways of embedding writing in all aspects of classroom life. I approach this exploration from a functional perspective, and you may find it helpful to refer back to the Functions of Writing chart (Chapter 1, Figure 1.2) as you read. In subsequent chapters I build on concepts introduced here.

Because a classroom is a place where children gather to work, play and learn, we can think of the classroom as a *children's workplace*. Just as adults' workplaces contain particular forms and functions of writing that are job-specific, so does the classroom. In Chapter 5, I show how classroom workplace writing threads its way throughout the school day in primary and junior classrooms. The details of specific activities related to the other two spheres of writing, which are more "academic" in nature, are found in Chapters 6 and 7.

Classroom Workplace Literacy

People in literate societies use writing in their places of work to get things done. The classroom workplace provides children with many opportunities for writing. Many of these are for regulating or directing classroom life. Traditionally, much

Activity:
Our Class Rules and Expectations T-Charts

These expectations are very abstract. So how do we convey them to our students? It is very common for adults to tell children what *not* to do, but this isn't very effective. Instead, we can work *with* our students at the beginning of the year to develop charts that translate abstract ideas into actions that can be observed. One way to do this is to develop Our Class Rules, stated in terms of *what we do* in our class (not "what we don't do"); for instance:

- In our class we share ideas and help each other.
- In our class we listen to each other.

Another way is to make T-charts like the one shown in Figure 3.1. Keep in mind that one of the important aspects of both activities is involving the students—helping them think about their actions and make connections to their own understandings and language. Making new charts every year is necessary because they need to be made by each community if they are to be meaningful and relevant to its members.

Figure 3.1 Expectations T-Chart

of this writing has been done by the classroom teacher, but if we view the classroom as a place where children can learn about using writing in the contexts of their daily lives, then we will want our students to learn to accomplish these "administrative" tasks. The beginning of the school day, in particular, provides opportunities for writing: students can sign in when they come to school (signing out when they leave the room for various reasons, too), and they can help take attendance.

We often begin the school day by reconnecting with one another and looking ahead. Here, we can use writing as part of our morning news and making plans for the day that involve children in the process. Similarly, writing can be used to come to closure at various times: at the end of a lesson, before dismissal at recess or lunch, or at the end of the school day. Students can be asked to reflect on something that they learned by writing in a special notebook set aside for this purpose. This goes by a variety of names, including *learning journal* or *learning log*. A similar activity is the *exit slip*.

Activity:
Exit Slips

At the end of a period or the school day, students write a response on a small piece of paper that they hand in to the teacher before they leave (signed or unsigned, depending on your purpose). These serve as exit slips (Crowhurst, 1994) or "tickets out the door." Exit slips can be used in a variety of ways for students to reflect on their learning: an open or free response, a summary of the most important part of the lesson, one important or interesting idea that they learned, a question for the teacher (perhaps something they don't understand or need clarified), and so on. Sometimes I use exit slips to collect information to help me in lesson planning; for example, I might say to my student teachers, "Tomorrow we're going to be talking about spelling. What's your most burning question about spelling you'd like me to address?" I also use exit slips to do periodic "temperature checks," asking students how they are feeling about school in general, or in relation to a particular aspect of their learning. An adaptation of this last idea is to have students put a plus sign (+) on one side of their paper and a minus sign (–) on the other; on the plus side, they tell me something positive, and on the minus side they tell me something that they are struggling with or worrying about. Alternatively, they can write a P on one side (for positive comments) and S on the other side (for suggestions).

REFLECTION

Many purposeful and practical ideas for writing arise from problems that occur in the classroom. When I was a primary teacher, I invented a way to use writing in relation to children's behaviour—a method that would help me to maintain my sanity! The children in one particular class seemed to squabble an awful lot, and I got really tired of hearing tattletales. So I found a shoe box, sealed it with tape, put a slot in the top, and wrote on it "Teacher's Mailbox." I put the box on my desk and told the children that if they had any more complaints about recess and lunch-time behaviour (not counting injuries, of course) they were to write a note to me rather than talking to me about it and I would read the notes after school. I found this a good solution for many reasons: because I didn't pay a lot of attention to the tattling, the behaviour diminished drastically; we got off to a better start after recess and lunch (less time wasted); we had a more positive tone in the classroom (less negative talk); and children were able to get things off their chests if they wanted to. I figured if an incident didn't bother children enough for them to write it down, it wasn't important enough to take so much class time to solve the problem.

Activity:
Teacher's Mailbox

Handling children's written complaints is but one of the functions of a teacher's mailbox. I found it interesting that when I taught Grade 7, my students would *never* "tattle" as the primary children would do; instead, they adhered to a strict code of silence about matters relating to their peers. Students of all ages can use the mailbox for providing information or reminders about such things as after-school practices. They can also use it for making suggestions or voicing their opinions. Primary students often like to give "love notes" to their teachers. A mailbox is an effective communication vehicle for those students who are shy and for those "cool" junior students who don't want their classmates to think they are buttering up the teacher.

Students can assume responsibility for the writing that is part of many classroom routines such as recording book exchanges, keeping track of project work, writing reminders to the class, and recording important events in the classroom, such as decisions made in class meetings. We can write collaboratively with students when we plan events and in interpersonal situations, such as sending invitations and expressing thanks. We can also provide children with access to materials so they can write letters, notes, cards, and so on.

Students can be encouraged to use writing to help them manage collaborative and cooperative group work (making plans, recording procedures, keeping track of what needs to be done, negotiating who will do various tasks and how they will be done, giving directions, and so on). They can also be encouraged to use writing as a vehicle for reflection on and evaluation of their group's learning processes.

We should also encourage students to use writing instrumentally for their own purposes, such as letting us know when there is a problem or when they need something. They can write reminders to us. (I still have a note that says, "Ples Mrs. C cut sum mor book cuvrs"—Please Mrs. C., cut some more book covers.) They can write the reminders on the board: *Ashley has to leave at 2:30.* And they should also be encouraged to write reminders to themselves (for example, in their homework books).

Another way to use writing is in a disciplinary context. (I use "discipline" to mean the things we do to help children learn to make appropriate choices about their behaviour.) Earlier in the chapter, I showed how we can use writing proactively in making classroom rules and discussing what appropriate behaviour looks like and sounds like. We can also use writing in situations when students have made poor choices about how to behave.

Activity: Classroom Message Centre or Graffiti Board

Writing notes was a bad thing when I went to school, but as long as students write them appropriately (in terms of content and timing), I think they are a good idea. Why not have a message centre in your classroom for children to send notes and cards to one another? It can either be in the form of a **graffiti board** (a chalkboard, white board, or large pad of newsprint) or as mailboxes made of clean, stacked milk cartons taped together. Learners can write themselves reminders and put them in their own mailboxes. Notices can be delivered to them, and so on. You can write notes to them too—happy ones, of course! Remind students to check their mail and take it home daily.

When I worked as a vice-principal, it was often the case that students were sent to the office for inappropriate behaviour on the playground (and occasionally in the classroom, although I discouraged this practice except in dire circumstances). I often had students complete a Consequence Form (Figure 3.2), which is a type of epistemic writing that helps students to think about their behaviour,

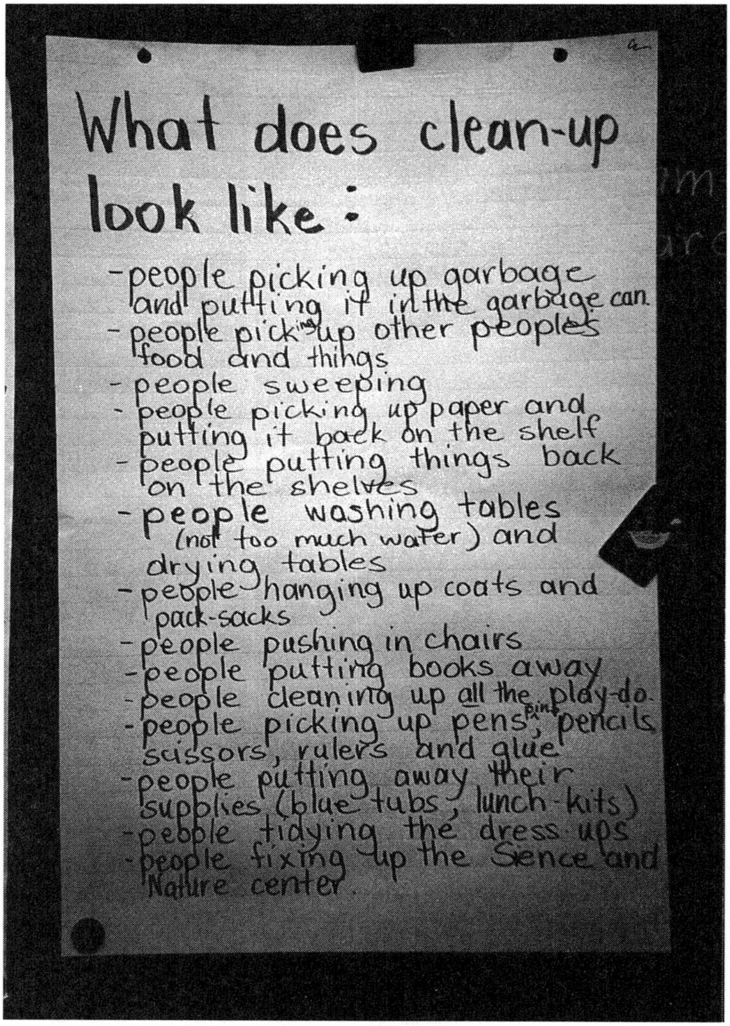

Writing is part of the classroom workplace.

to reflect on the consequences of their actions, and to consider better choices for their behaviour. With very young children, I read the form to them and had them tell me what to write. I have also used this form as a vehicle of communication between the office, the classroom teacher, and the parents, if we felt they should be informed. My staff came to like these forms, and many of them started to use them in their own classrooms.

Writing in the Language Arts

When I first began teaching, it was common to refer to "creative writing," which was taught as a separate subject—separate from other curriculum areas, separate from reading, and separate from other aspects of writing such as spelling. Now writing is viewed not as a discrete subject but as part of the language arts and part of learning across the curriculum.

Referring to writing as part of the language arts reflects more than an organizational shift; it reflects an understanding that writing is a thread in the web of language. Teachers integrate writing with listening, speaking, reading, viewing, representing, and drama. For example, they build learners' conceptual and linguistic knowledge and skills by reading aloud to them. They help learners make connections between oral and written language when they encourage students to talk and to represent their ideas in writing and by providing opportunities for students to share their writing with one another. Teachers connect writing to other forms of representation when they explore other means of communication such as video and live performances, two- and three-dimensional models, graphs and charts. They can integrate writing and drama by having students write in role, as if they were someone else.

A language arts context provides our students with opportunities to write for a variety of purposes. For example:

Personal/expressive writing

- In journals students can write to reflect on their experiences, to express their feelings and opinions, to extend their knowledge of themselves, to project into others' experiences, and so on.
- In reader-response journals they can respond emotionally and express their opinions about what they have read, they can project into the experiences of real people and fictional characters they read about, and so on.

Figure 3.2 Consequence Form*

______________________________ Elementary School

Consequence Form

Name ______________________ Division ____________

Date ______________ Time ___________ Place ____________

Please complete this form, have it signed, and return to: ____________

What happened? ______________________________

____

Why did it happen? ______________________________

____

____

How did your actions affect the situation? ______________________

____

____

In a similar situation, what are three things you might choose to do instead?

1. ______________________________
2. ______________________________
3. ______________________________

What can you do to make the school a better place for everyone?

____

____

Your signature ______________________________

Teacher's signature ______________________________

Parent's signature ______________________________

Principal's/Vice-Principal's signature ______________________

*This is a two-page form that is to be printed back-to-back on a single sheet.

____ Elementary School

Consequence Form

Dear Parents:

We believe that when the home and school work together, children's learning is enhanced. This applies both to academics and to behaviour. This **Consequence Form** is intended to serve several functions:

1. As a learning tool—To encourage students to reflect on their behaviour and to think about making better choices in behaviour; to help students take responsibility for their own actions.
2. As a communication tool—To inform all parties (parents, teachers, and administrators) about a student's behaviour, when that behaviour is inappropriate.
3. As a recording device—To serve as a written record of inappropriate behaviour. This record is kept for the remainder of the school year and then destroyed. It is used to keep track of behaviour during the year and to determine behaviour patterns. It is not kept in the student's permanent file, nor is it forwarded to another school.

We request that you take some time with your child to read and discuss the **Consequence Form** comments written (or dictated) by your child, to discuss appropriate behaviour and making wise choices. You may wish to add a comment to the form in the Parent's Comment section. Please sign the form and return it to the school.

Thank you

Teacher's Comment: ____

____

____

____

Parent's Comment: ____

____

____

Informative writing

- In reading notebooks students can write to retell what they have read in their own words, summarize a sequence of events or main ideas, identify elements of a story such as the characters, setting, initiating and resolving events, and so on.
- They can integrate writing with graphic representations such as story maps and story webs to show their understanding of what they have read.

Recording ideas and events

- Students can keep track of their own reading in a reading log.
- They can write notes about possibilities for their writing in a writer's notebook.
- They can keep track of various parts of project work.
- They can take notes from what they have read or viewed.

Imagining/creating

- Students can write original stories, poems, and plays.
- They can compose sequels or alternative endings.
- They can create original characters and settings.

Divertive/entertaining writing

- Students can engage in word play.
- They can make up jokes and riddles.
- They can create funny characters or situations.

Another important purpose of writing in the language arts is to use writing epistemically to enhance learning. Here teachers use writing *before*, *during*, and *after* engaging students in a variety of language processes. For example, we can have students write before they speak (to generate ideas and to allow less spontaneous students and second-language learners time to think); before they listen to, read, or view something (to make predictions and access prior knowledge); and in prewriting activities (for example, to generate ideas). We can ask students to stop and write at appropriate times in the middle of a language activity, to review, to explore a current idea, to evaluate several different ideas, to clarify something, and to anticipate what might come next. We can also use writing after language activities to review; to reflect on the experience; to analyze, interpret, and evaluate ideas and information; to identify themes and main ideas; and so on. These short writing activities can be done in a learning log (which keeps them organized), on scrap pieces of paper, or on small chalkboards.

Something to think about

Do you ever worry about all those trees that get cut down because of the paper we consume in our classrooms? Why not borrow an idea from the one-room school: the slate? Most school districts will, on request, recycle old chalkboards for classroom use by cutting them into individual chalkboards of approximately 30 cm x 45 cm. Students can bring an old sock (recycling again) to use as an eraser and to store their pieces of chalk. Students can sit cross-legged on the floor with the chalkboards in their laps, hold the chalk in their writing hand, and slip the sock on the other hand. The sock can also store the students' chalk. These slates can be used in a multitude of ways—you can walk around and see what students have written, if you wish, or have students turn their boards to show you.

Something to think about

When we ask students to write in journals, reading logs, learning logs, writer's notebooks, exit slips, and so on, it is really important to keep in mind that the writers' thoughts and feelings are what's important. We want to encourage students to write freely without worrying about spelling and such. *Marking errors and making corrections are not appropriate in these contexts* (more about this in Chapter 6). I want parents to be aware that I read these for the messages and ideas they contain and that I deliberately choose not to "correct" them. However, I do make note of things I think students need to learn about writing; for example, I use these forms of writing as a source of generating words for individualized spelling. To inform parents of the purposes of these books and how we use them, I include an explanatory letter at the front of the book (I paste it inside the front cover). An example of this type of letter is shown in Figure 3.3. (A similar letter can be included in your students' journals.)

Figure 3.3 Letter to Parents

Dear Parents:

This notebook is your child's **Learning Log.** The purpose of this log is to encourage your child to participate actively in learning situations and to use writing as a tool for thinking and learning. A log is a form of journal; the focus is on IDEAS. Research shows that students who use writing as an aid to thinking and learning, who can write for themselves rather than worrying about correctness all of the time, become more effective learners than those students who focus only on spelling, handwriting, and so on. It is not that spelling and handwriting are unimportant, but rather that correctness and neatness are important when the focus of the writing is to communicate with others. (For example, when we write a letter to someone, we want to be sure that they can read and understand what we have written.) Because the audience of the learning log is oneself, and the focus is on ideas, the learning logs will not be corrected. Instead, the learning logs will be used as follows:

1. Students will share their ideas in group discussions.
2. I will read the logs and respond to the children's ideas by making a written comment.
3. I will assess the children's understanding and use the information to plan instruction (for example, to reteach a concept that students do not understand).
4. From time to time, students will bring home their learning logs to share with their parents.

The learning log is a useful way for me to assess and address your child's learning needs.

Yours truly,

In the next chapter, I discuss ways of organizing the language arts program to provide opportunities for integrating writing with other language processes. In Chapter 4 I also explain a workshop approach to writing and learning. Teaching various forms of writing applicable for a language arts context is elaborated in Chapter 7.

Integrating Writing across the Curriculum

Each discipline has its own variety of language or **register.** This includes specific vocabulary (or specific meanings of more generally used words), characteristic grammatical structures, forms of representation (ways of communicating information), and genres (ways of writing texts to suit particular functions and contexts). For example, the register of mathematics includes mathematical terminology and particular phrase and sentence patterns. It includes forms of representation such as equations and graphs, and it has unique genres such as story problems. All curricula are inherently integrated because thinking and language are interwoven into every discipline. And so, writing is more than part of the language arts; it is part of learning in every curriculum area. (In Chapter 7 I explore how to expand young writers' repertoires of genres and forms of representation across the curriculum.)

From a functional perspective, writing can be used in a variety of ways in all curriculum areas:

- *To direct*—for example, to explain procedures for an experiment, to keep track of work on a social studies project.
- *To respond personally*—for example, to formulate opinions about whether or not the West Coast fishery should be reduced, to project into the experiences of people who live in communities different from one's own.
- *To imagine*—for example, to consider what life might be like on the moon, to write a journal entry in role as a forestry conservation officer.
- *To inform*—for example, to write a report about insects, to label the parts of a lever and explain how it works.
- *To record*—for example, to take notes from reading about mammals, to record observations in science.
- *To learn*—for example, to formulate hypotheses about why dinosaurs became extinct, to explore the different perspectives on whaling.

REFLECTION

As we move from an interpersonal context to the wider social realm, the teacher's role as mentor takes on an expanding significance, for we all convey beliefs and values about writing that we are not consciously aware of. To a great extent, these are socially constructed within and by the various cultural groups to which we belong (for example, economic, ethnic, and gender groups). It is important for us to become aware of the values we may be implicitly conveying to our students, especially those that conflict with the things we believe at a conscious level. For example, researchers are becoming aware of the gender biases in writing that perpetuate notions about the suitability of particular genres and topics for boys and for girls.

We need to encourage both boys and girls to write for many purposes, in a variety of forms and about a wide range of topics. We also need to broaden our cultural horizons to consider the various forms of writing emphasized by different cultural groups (ethnic and economic) different from our own rather than perpetuating only those types of writing with which we are familiar.

Writing can also be integrated across the curriculum as a strategy for constructing meaning. Writing in learning logs, on exit slips, on individual chalkboards, and so on, is as much a part of learning in the various academic disciplines as it is in the language arts. So, too, is the use of epistemic writing before, during, and after learning activities in various subjects. For example, we can engage students in writing before viewing a film on a social studies topic, before conducting a science experiment, or before a field trip. We can stop and write at various points during lessons to review and to clarify ideas. And we can have students write at the end of lessons to reflect on their learning.

Fostering Writing in Kindergarten

There are many different perspectives on writing in kindergarten. Some people believe that kindergarten should be like playschool and that kindergarten children should not be doing anything academic. At the other extreme, there are those who believe that kindergarten should be more academic and include formal lessons in printing and so on. In my view, neither of these views is appropriate. I reject the playschool image of kindergarten because I believe that children at this age are eager to learn and curious about written language and there is no reason to deny them opportunities to engage in literacy activities that involve writing. On the other hand, I do fear that some kindergartens are more like watered-down Grade 1 programs, and this is really inappropriate.

An emergent literacy perspective suggests that kindergarten children should have many opportunities to interact with their teacher and classmates in reading and writing situations and to explore writing on their own. Because we know that learning to write is an emergent process, we encourage children to write in ways that are appropriate to them and do not stress correctness. Sometimes little ones will say, "But I don't know how to spell such-and-such," or they might refuse to write because they are afraid of being wrong. Children often construct such notions about the importance of correctness in conventions of writing at home because this is what their parents emphasize. (In some cultures, correct form is very highly valued, and children are not encouraged to do something unless it is done correctly.) I think it is important to reassure children that we don't expect them to write like grown-ups. After all, we don't expect them to go to work, drive cars, do the grocery shopping, and so on, so why would we expect them to write like adults? It is very important to encourage children to represent their ideas in their own ways; for example, to combine drawing and writing. And their attempts should always be celebrated, just as their first steps and their first words were. (For examples of emergent writing behaviours, see Chapter 2, Figure 2.3.)

Above all, the tone of the kindergarten classroom should be an encouraging one rather than one that imposes or forces writing. Many of the learning/writing

KINDERGARTEN CORNER

Integrating writing and play

Kindergarten and primary teachers often have various centres in the classroom where children can create things (for example, an Imagination Centre filled with recyclable materials, the Blocks Centre, the Construction Centre) and engage in dramatic play (for example, a playhouse, an office, or a store). Writing materials should always be provided in these centres so that children can integrate writing into their play activities. They can make labels and signs for their creations, and they can write grocery lists, take telephone messages, write cheques, take orders, and so on.

ideas that I have discussed in this chapter can be adapted to kindergarten. Classroom workplace literacy experiences are particularly important because they demonstrate that writing is something people do in the contexts of their daily lives.

Kindergarten classrooms are unique in some ways, and so while many of the ideas I present in this book apply as equally to kindergarten as they do to Grades 1 to 7, there are often times when ideas need to be adapted. To address the particular needs of kindergarten teachers, I have devised special idea boxes I call **Kindergarten Corners**. Other primary teachers may also find these ideas applicable to their classrooms.

Reflections on the Chapter

Think about/talk about/write about:

Principles into Practice

- Use Figure 2.6, From Principles of Writing to Practice, to find examples in this chapter of each principle as it is put into practice.

The Role of the Teacher

- How many decisions do you think a classroom teacher makes about teaching written language on a typical school day? What kinds of decisions do you think he or she makes about teaching writing?

The Classroom Climate

- Think about two very different classroom climates that you have experienced. Compare and contrast them in relation to the emotional, aesthetic/artistic, intellectual, and social dimensions discussed in this chapter. How did each of these classroom climates affect your attitudes toward and abilities in writing?
- Compare your experiences of the effects of classroom climate on your writing and yourself as a writer with someone else's experiences.
- How do you feel about play, particularly as it relates to writing? Is it something you consider suitable only for children?

The Classroom as a Discourse Community

- In what ways does your own classroom (either the one you teach in or one you are a student in) reflect dimensions of a discourse community?

- What discourse communities are you a member of? How do you use writing in these different discourse communities?

Writing in kindergarten

- What is your view of writing in kindergarten?
- Compare your point of view with someone else's.

REFERENCES AND FURTHER READING

Cambourne, B. (1988). *The whole story: Natural learning and the acquisition of literacy in the classroom*. Auckland, NZ: Ashton Scholastic.

Chapman, M., and Anderson, J. (1995). *Thinking globally about language education*. Vancouver: Research and Development in Global Studies, Centre for the Study of Curriculum and Instruction, University of British Columbia.

Crowhurst, M. (1994). *Language and learning across the curriculum*. Scarborough, ON: Allyn & Bacon.

Emig, J. (1981). Non-magical thinking: Presenting writing developmentally in schools. In C.H. Frederiksen and S.F. Dominic (Eds.), *Writing: The nature, development, and teaching of written communication. Volume 2, Writing: Process, development and communication* (pp. 21–30). Hillsdale, NJ: Lawrence Erlbaum Associates.

Green, P., and Green, M. (1991). Introducing factual texts. In E. Furniss and P. Green (Eds.), *The literacy connection: Language and learning across the curriculum* (pp. 33–57). Armidale, Australia: Eleanor Curtain Publishing (distributed in Canada by Peguis Publishers, Winnipeg).

Ping, H. (1995). Chinese attitudes towards learning and reading. In M.L. Chapman and J. Anderson (Eds.), *Thinking globally about language education* (pp. 35–48). Vancouver: Research and Development in Global Studies, Centre for the Study of Curriculum and Instruction, University of British Columbia.

Vygotsky, L. (1978). *Mind in society: The development of higher psychological processes*. (M. Cole, V. John-Steiner, S. Scribner, and E. Souberman, Eds.). Cambridge, MA: Harvard University Press.

Webster's encyclopedic unabridged dictionary of the English language. (1989). New York: Gramercy Books.

CHAPTER 4

Designs for Learning and Writing

CHAPTER OBJECTIVES

To explore ways of addressing student diversity in writing and learning

To suggest ways of increasing students' writing knowledge through a variety of instructional experiences

To develop criteria for designing appropriate writing/learning activities

To discuss ways of supporting young writers and encouraging collaboration and independence

To describe planning processes and organizational strategies for teaching writing

PERSONAL REFLECTION

Like weaving and writing, teaching is a creative process. This is probably why we can stay excited and energized in our daily work, even after many years of teaching. Of course, we could make it a rote activity by following someone else's ideas and plans, but then we would be as bored by this as our learners (perhaps even more, since at least they would only have to experience the program once, while we would repeat it over and over). How wonderful to have an opportunity to create and re-create designs for learning. Like a weaver, we use our available resources and materials and weave them together in interesting ways. We refine our craftsmanship by drawing on our constantly expanding knowledge and repertoires of skills. Sometimes we learn from observing and interacting with others—we see what they do, and ask them to demonstrate and explain to us what they do, how they do it, and why. But most importantly we need to engage in meaningful practice of our craft, experimenting, practising, and playing with new techniques, doing as best we can yet at the same time giving ourselves permission to be learners—to make mistakes and not to worry about being experts in the early stages. We reflect on our learning processes as we try out new strategies and skills and think about how we might adapt them to our particular learning styles. We also reflect on the various parts of our creations and how they contribute to the design as a whole. Sometimes we are pleased with the effect; at other times we find particular parts don't make sense in the context of the whole design, so we unravel them. So, too, teaching is a dynamic, integrated learning process.

What do teachers need to know to create designs for learning and writing that will enable all students to be successful?

In the last chapter, I talked about the decision-making processes that teachers go through as they create classrooms that cultivate writing. Creating a classroom setting that acts as a stage or backdrop for the individual teacher and student "actors" is important, but it is just the beginning. Other important aspects of fostering writing are devising learning opportunities and designing writing/learning activities to meet our students' needs. Classroom communities consist of students who have varying abilities, skills, and backgrounds; it is the teacher's job to provide opportunities that will enable all of them to be successful learners and writers. Planning and organizing learning experiences to address this diversity are complex, dynamic processes. It is these processes that are the focus of this chapter.

Addressing Diversity

REFLECTION

Terms such as "Grade 1" and "Grade 6" somehow imply that there is a sameness to the children in a particular classroom. Although there are similarities among children of about the same age, there are also vast differences, and it has probably always been so, despite the nostalgic longings some people have for the good old days of traditional schools. I remember my last Grade 3 class—twenty-eight children whose reading and writing abilities varied enormously. I had four students who were excellent readers. Their favourite novel that year was *The Chrysalids* by John Wyndham, a book that was, I later discovered, on British Columbia's novel list for Grade 11! All four of these children were very verbal and avid writers and readers. Their spelling abilities ranged from adult-like to what I thought of as typical Grade 3 spelling. I also had a little girl in that class who reminded me of the illustrations in *Ramona the Pest* by Beverly Cleary. She did not yet use vowels in her invented spellings when she wrote, and the only things she could read with confidence were the language experience stories that she had dictated to me. And, of course, I had students at various levels between these two extremes. The children in this class came from similar cultural and economic backgrounds, so many people would have thought they might be homogeneous in some way, yet they had diverse learning needs.

Why do you think there has been a search for the one best way to teach—and to teach writing? Think back to the discussion of Hillocks' (1986) research (Chapter 2). What did he find out about effective and noneffective approaches to teaching writing?

One of the benefits of the increasing diversity in our schools today, as communities become more culturally varied and as more children who have special learning needs are mainstreamed, is that schools are forced to come out of the closet and acknowledge the truth that there is no "grade level learner."

Every classroom is, in reality, a multilevel classroom, and there is no one-size-fits-all program. We can't even pretend that traditional approaches to teaching and learning are suitable for all or most children. The pressing issue for teachers is how to address the diversity within our classrooms and still have time for personal and family lives, and how to cultivate writing in all of our students without having individualized educational programs for each of them. (Of course, totally individualized instruction would not capitalize on what is known about the social dimension of learning.)

Some of the keys to addressing diversity in our classrooms are to build on students' existing literacy knowledge and extend their writing/learning repertoires, to provide support in ways that will help them to become independent and interdependent learners, and to design appropriate writing/learning activities.

Increasing Young Writers' Repertoires

One of the most important goals in teaching writing is to build on students' existing knowledge and skills and increase their writing/learning repertoires. A sociocognitive constructivist or transactional approach to teaching writing values two ways of building this repertoire: acquisition (i.e., indirectly through immersion, demonstration, and discovery) and learning (i.e, through explicit teaching and guided activities). Writing teachers can provide for both through shared experiences that involve writing and through teaching literacy lessons to the whole class and small groups. Because everyone in the class is both a learner and a teacher, it is important to create situations that incorporate collaboration and cooperative learning and also include opportunities for students to learn and write individually.

Shared Experiences

Sometimes teachers engage children in whole-group classroom-workplace activities that help to create a feeling of community and belonging, such as making decisions about life in the classroom community, planing events that involve everyone, and celebrating special events. In whole-class contexts, writing is usually linked to lots of talking and listening. Sometimes the teacher or particular students will act as recorders of ideas that are discussed orally. At other times, teachers will ask students to write their own ideas first, before discussion, so that everyone has an opportunity to be engaged in the learning,

Activity:
Think, Pair, Share

Some people speak to think; other people think to speak. The problem is that the first type of learners can overwhelm or dominate others. An effective sequence that enhances the learning of both types of people is: (1) give students an opportunity to *think* for a minute or two and to *represent their thinking* in whatever way they choose (make a list or a web, free-write, draw, etc.) using a piece of paper, a learning log, or a chalkboard; (2) then have them discuss their ideas with a *partner* (or with a *small group* if they sit together); and (3) finally, *share* and discuss these ideas with the whole class. This approach is also very helpful for shy children, children with learning difficulties, and students for whom English is a second language or second dialect. It is an effective way to provide "wait time" and encourages spontaneous students to be more reflective.

not just those students who are spontaneous in talking. Teachers can also take time for whole-class sharing and reflection after students have worked individually or in collaborative and cooperative learning groups. An example of this is **Authors' Circle,** which will be elaborated in Chapter 6.

REFLECTION

One of education's biggest mistakes has been the use of fixed ability groupings in an attempt to meet different learning needs in the classroom. Many teachers have heard about the problems with ability grouping and, as a result, now believe that any kind of small-group teaching is poor practice. It is beyond the scope of this book to deal with this issue in depth (for an in-depth treatment, see my article in the October 1995 issue of *Language Arts* [Chapman, 1995]). The keys to using groupings appropriately are *purpose, variety,* and *flexibility*. In other words, we use a variety of groupings in flexible ways to meet particular purposes, and we avoid at all costs static groupings of students into high-, middle-, and low-ability groups.

How do we decide when to teach the whole class and when to work with small groups?

Literacy Lessons and Mini-Lessons

To introduce something, be it a new strategy (using webbing for prewriting, for example), a new genre (such as the legend), or a new form of representation (for example, a story-line map), it is often appropriate to teach a lesson to the whole class. I refer to these kinds of shared experiences as *literacy lessons* because, although the focus may be writing, they often incorporate reading (and invariably, listening and speaking too).

At other times you may want to take only ten minutes or so to teach or review a specific strategy (COPS: capitals, omissions, punctuation, spelling) or skill (for example, using commas to separate items in a list) in a *mini-lesson* with the class as a whole. At other times, it may be more appropriate to teach a mini-lesson to a small group of students, for instance:

- To address a *common need* of a group of students. For example, if you have only a few students who write run-on sentences, why not pull that group of students together and work at it with them?
- To provide additional *guided practice* to students who need it. Suppose you have introduced story maps and most of the class is meeting success but you have a few children who are struggling. You could bring them together around a table and give them some help.

Teachers can mediate children's learning through literacy lessons and mini-lessons.

Support for Independence

All growth involves challenge—taking risks and venturing beyond the "can-do" zone. In addition to providing learning/writing opportunities through shared experiences, lessons, and mini-lessons, teachers provide varying degrees of support so that learners can become independent.

- *Maximum support* is important in the early stages of new learning; begin with teacher-led literacy lessons or carefully designed cooperative learning experiences.
- *Moderate support* is helpful when using small-group or partner activities to extend students' learning or provide guided practice. Some students may need continued teacher support in small-group or individual mini-lessons; student tutors, teaching assistants, and parent aides may help out too.
- *Minimal support* is provided as appropriate as learners make the transition to independence; sometimes encouragement and feedback are all that is needed.

Collaboration

Peer collaboration is central to a writing community. Whether classmates work collaboratively on a single piece of writing or each child creates an individual piece, they can support and help one another. Sometimes a group of students may have a common interest (for example, I had a group of Grade 3 girls who were into writing novels); they can create their own group for sharing ideas and giving feedback to one another. Teachers can initiate this by having group writing conferences or Writing Clubs so that students learn how to respond and give feedback. After a few weeks of teacher-led writing clubs, encourage students to start their own informal writing clubs. Often, students form these on the basis of friendship. Sometimes a writing club comes into being because a teacher has shared his or her observations with the class. For example, a Horse Club developed in my class when I said that I noticed several people seemed to be interested in horses. These students (a group of Grades 3 and 4 girls) formed a group that read horse stories and wrote horse stories, poems, and reports. In my Grade 1–2 class I had a similar group who were interested in dinosaurs.

Another way to use peer groups is for collaborative editing and proofreading. Now, this isn't simply a matter of putting kids into groups; to be effective, young writers first need some direction or guidance from the

Activity:
Spotlight on Writing Groups

Here is a way to focus on a particular aspect of writing with a mini-lesson for a group of up to eight students: spotlight on writing groups. At the beginning of the day or the language arts period, announce to your class that today you will be doing a writing lesson, "Spotlight on (quotation marks, haiku poetry, letters, etc.—you fill in the blank)." Students sign up (and if there are particular children you think would especially benefit from this mini-lesson, encourage them to join—privately and unobtrusively, of course). Spotlight on writing groups can be used for review, for extra practice, for enrichment and extension, for introducing new forms of writing, and so on. Be sure to have mini-lessons to attract students of all ability levels and interests because you don't want these sessions to be perceived as being remedial (older students are especially sensitive to this). Spotlight groups help students increase their writing knowledge and improve their skills. You can combine this with the snowball writing activity described a little further on in the chapter.

Activity:
Writing Clubs

Group conferences or Writing Clubs provide opportunities for children to share their writing with a small peer group and the teacher. Four to six students take turns reading aloud to the group something they have written. The group gives comments and feedback to the writers on their work. On Monday, put up a sign-up sheet for the week so students can group themselves into approximately equal groups for each weekday. I used to have reading clubs as well (each student had a different book, something she or he had read and wanted to share with others) and alternated writing clubs and reading clubs on a weekly basis. Reading and writing clubs provide an audience for reading and writing, and opportunities for children to interact and share ideas and enthusiasm and to learn appropriate ways of responding and giving feedback. They also provide an effective vehicle for assessment. The primary classroom described in the next chapter incorporates Writing Clubs.

teacher. For example, suppose you have a junior class and you want to work on editing sections of social studies research reports. You might begin with a whole-class lesson or mini-lesson and then have students do peer editing with a partner or in small groups of up to four students. Usually not everyone in the class is ready for this instruction at the same time. A better approach in this instance is to have a Spotlight on Editing mini-lesson with those students who are ready. You could do this over and over until everyone has had this lesson. Or, you could use a snowball technique—teach the mini-lesson to the students who are ready, and then have each of those students teach the others. This can be done either as an "each-one-teach-one" process (which works like a relay race) or by using the first group as team leaders. In either case, you will want to develop a chart, checklist, or some other kind of teaching aid for the peer coaches to refer to.

Sometimes teachers have students work collaboratively with partners or younger and older buddies. Partnering children provides opportunities for mentoring and tutoring as well as working collaboratively on a writing task.

REFLECTION

In one of my research projects I was looking at ways children learn from one another. I was particularly interested in collaboration in writing. On one of my three-day visits to a classroom, I videotaped three boys writing a collaborative story. They were really involved in their writing, and I ended up with about three hours of videotape. As I watched the tape and transcribed their talk, I came to realize that one of the boys directed the group's efforts, did a lot of drawing, contributed a few ideas to the story, but never wrote anything down. I decided to watch my other videotapes of him and, to my dismay, discovered that Michael had always chosen to write with other boys, at least during the last year during my visits. In each instance I had on videotape, he acted as a group director and never did any encoding or recording of ideas. After discussing my concerns with the teacher, we decided to do some individual assessments with him. We found that he was really struggling with writing and was not nearly as able a writer as we had thought. And to think how much time had gone by before we made this discovery!

Are there times when collaboration in writing is not a good thing to encourage? Are some students disadvantaged if we allow them to work collaboratively all or most of the time? When? Why?

Sometimes children like to choose their own partners; at other times it is a better idea for the teacher to make the decision. This is particularly the case when it is desirable to have varying abilities between the partners.

As well as collaboration, teachers also encourage children to work individually. Some students really prefer to work on their own, and this provides an opportunity for them to do so. Many students like to work in groups some of the time, but need time out for individual writing and reflection (has this ever happened to you?). Sometimes I feel the need to ask students to work individually because there is so much collaboration in my classes that I am not always sure what a student knows or is able to do independently. And unless I know what a student can do on his or her own, it is hard to make the best decisions about his or her learning needs. This might be one of the rare occasions when I ask all students to do the same thing. This gives me a sense of what each student is able to do and the range of abilities in my class, keeping in mind, of course, that this is only one kind of writing in a specific context. (More about this in Chapter 8.)

Activity
Snowball Groups

A cooperative learning activity, snowball groups provide an opportunity for students to teach and learn from one another. First, teach a small group of students, who become "experts" in the strategy or skill. Each of these students then becomes a group leader and teaches three or four others.

Individualized Instruction

There are also times when teachers provide individual instruction, but these are usually not the norm since this approach misses out on the benefits of group interaction. Individual instruction is usually brief and very specific. For example, as students are working on individual and collaborative writing activities, teachers monitor by walking around to see how children are doing. They often stop and engage in a conversation or mini-conference with a child about his or her writing or do a mini-lesson one-on-one. Often this kind of teaching is the most meaningful for a student and the most effective.

Occasionally teachers will set up a more formal individualized lesson or conference to discuss a student's writing.

Designing Writing/Learning Activities

My intention here as I discuss the nature of learning activities that cultivate writing is to introduce some important criteria that will thread through subsequent chapters. You will see these criteria applied, for example, in the vignettes of primary and junior classrooms in Chapter 5 and in the specific suggestions for writing activities in Chapters 6 and 7. The principles of writing (Chapter 1) and guidelines for learning and teaching (Chapter 2) provide direction in developing criteria for writing/learning activities. It is important to try to design writing activities that are

Something to think about

A colleague and friend of mine, Colleen Politano, says: "Every time I ask all the kids to do the same thing in the same way at the same time, I am asking for trouble!" Are there times in writing when it is appropriate to have all students do the same thing at the same time in the same way? When? Why?

- *Purposeful*—in other words, done for real reasons rather than as dummy runs or practice exercises. Purposeful writing can serve a variety of functions, but central to all of these is constructing meaning. And often what gives writing its purpose is that it is meant to be, and is, read—and not just by the teacher.
- *Holistic*—so that students will always realize that communication and meaning are the central purposes of writing. Learning holistically provides a context for specific objectives and promotes more effective learning of the various aspects of written language, whether they be processes, strategies, genres, or skills.
- *Integrated*—so that writing is connected to the other language arts and integrated across the curriculum. Like holism, integration contextualizes writing and promotes learning that is deep and lasting rather than superficial and short-lived.

- *Open-ended*—so that students can put to use their knowledge and skills in ways appropriate to their varying abilities. This is particularly important whenever teachers want all children to do the same thing at the same time since open-ended activities are by nature flexible and multilevelled. Open-ended activities also make teaching easier because students are more motivated, spend more time on task, and are more engaged with their learning; as a result, they need fewer interventions and reminders about their behaviour. Open-endedness can be achieved by allowing students some choice and control over the content, process, and/or form of the activity.

In situations where teachers want students to engage in a whole-class writing activity, it is really important to think through the ways of addressing learners' diversity and ensure that all children can be successful. It is particularly important in these contexts that the learning activities be open-ended and flexible.

Something to think about

In her award-winning Ph.D. dissertation, Julianne Turner (1993) investigated children's motivation in literacy situations in traditional and integrated language arts classrooms. She found that children in integrated language arts classrooms were more motivated in their learning and used more learning strategies, which to a great extent was attributed to more frequent use of open-ended activities. Turner found that regardless of the teaching approach used, open-ended activities and tasks resulted in

> more opportunities for students to mould activities to their interests, to select strategies and determine outcomes, to calibrate challenge to developing understandings and skills, to use higher order thinking skills, and to use errors diagnostically. Because students were engaged in more meaningful activities, they were more willing to apply effort and remain engaged if they had difficulty. (p. 289)

Turner concludes that the kinds of learning activities and tasks we select have "motivational implications; at the same time, greater effort and persistence facilitate strategic thinking and cognitive engagement" (p. 289).

In order to lead healthy lives people need balance between work and play, exercise and rest, solitude and socialization. They also need to eat a healthy and balanced diet to meet their body's various needs—healthy in that it includes nutritious, high-quality foods and balanced in that it incorporates a variety of foods from different food groups. Likewise, students need a healthy diet of writing/learning activities. To continue the analogy, this means making choices from a menu of writing functions, forms, and contexts. In writing/learning activities this means

- including a variety of forms:
  - genres such as labels, personal narratives, suspense stories, poems, research reports, and so on
  - representations such as webs, charts, role-plays, and models
- allowing students some choice, for example:
  - choosing whether to write independently or collaboratively
  - selecting from a range of options determined by the teacher
  - choosing how to respond to a shared experience
  - free choice—deciding what to write about (their own topics) and how to communicate their ideas (what forms to use)

Including a variety of forms ensures that young writers' repertoires continue to grow rather than being restricted to a narrow range of writing forms. It also precludes boredom and lack of interest in writing. (See Chapter 7 for an in-depth discussion of genres and forms of representation and a wide range of examples.) Providing some choice does not mean that students get to do whatever they want, however. For example, sometimes students might enjoy a particular kind of writing so much that that is all they want to do, day after day. *One of our major aims is to get kids hooked on writing*, so there are times when we might decide that it is fine to allow them to follow their passions. In other circumstances, though, we might think it is important to encourage or request that students have a more balanced writing diet and to do other kinds of writing for a change. There will also be times when we want all students to do specific things; for example, if you have just introduced Venn diagrams, you will likely want everyone to have a try at using this form. However, it is important to allow students to make some decisions and choices about their writing as well as to request that they meet particular requirements or complete "must-do" assignments. It is our responsibility as teachers to ensure that there is a balance in our students' writing/learning activities.

Enabling English-as-a-Second-Language and Second-Dialect Writers

Today many classrooms include students whose first language is other than English (English as a second language, or ESL) or who speak a second dialect (English as a second dialect, or ESD). This varies from one or two students in a class to schools that are made up almost entirely of ESL or nonmainstream speakers of English. During the 1980s the dominant approach to teaching ESL was a communicative approach, which was based on the idea that children will learn English mostly by interacting with English-speaking peers. While this is true for the most part when it comes to basic interpersonal language acquisition, it does not appear to be so for much of the cognitive and academic language children need to be successful in school.

Although "linguists are clear that no dialect is superior to another linguistically or logically" (Ward, 1997, p. 61), the ability to use Standard English is still required for easy access to higher education and to social power. Because the standard dialect of English is more like its written form than nonstandard dialects, children who speak a form of English that differs from Standard English also have particular needs when it comes to developing cognitive and academic language proficiency. (For an in-depth discussion of language variation, including dialect and Standard English, see Angela Ward's *Classroom Conversations* [1997], which is a companion book in this series.)

While an in-depth discussion of teaching writing to ESL or ESD students is beyond the scope of this book, keep in mind that the ideas included in this chapter—increasing writers' repertoires, supporting learners through collaboration and cooperative learning, and designing appropriate learning activities—are all essential components in meeting the needs of ESL and ESD writers. As well, current knowledge about teaching bilingual or multilingual students can provide some key ideas that can act as guidelines for teaching writing to ESL and ESD students. These include

- *Holding developmentally and culturally appropriate expectations*—Learning a second language occurs over a much longer period of time than previously thought, and although second-language acquisition is similar in some ways to learning a first language, it is not an identical process.

Second-language (L2) development is not uniform; for example, ESL writers may seem to pick up vocabulary quite quickly and yet use English words with grammatical structures from their first language (L1). This is an example of what is called "L1 interference," and it reveals that the writer is sorting out the linguistic systems of both languages. Like all writers, ESL and ESD students' development is a series of approximations that reveals their emerging understanding of written language.

- *Building on what they know*—Although ESL and ESD students may not yet be proficient in Standard English, this does not mean that they know nothing about language and literacy. Traditionally ESL and ESD students were viewed as deficient and in need of remediation; now they are seen as linguistically and culturally different, bringing with them their existing knowledge and skills from their first language or dialect. ESL and ESD students are not generic—just as native speakers of English have varying abilities and background experiences in writing, so too do ESL and ESD students. Most ESD students are Canadian-born; some ESL students are Canadian-born while others are new immigrants. Some ESL and ESD students come from literacy-rich homes; some can read and write in another language; some cannot. Some come from well-to-do homes; others are impoverished. All of these factors need to be taken into account, while keeping in mind that no ESL or ESD student is a blank slate.
- *Making connections*—Like all writers, ESL and ESD students need to make connections—connections with their prior knowledge and experiences, connections among the language arts, and connections across the curriculum. Integrated and holistic writing experiences are essential for these learners since they provide opportunities for building vocabulary in the context of meaningful activities. Teachers can also help these students make connections by allowing them to use their first languages or dialects, a practice that used to be discouraged. Research now indicates that using L1 benefits students in many ways, and access to it should not be denied them. Learning English should in no way diminish a child's first language—English should be an additional language rather than a replacement for the first. Likewise, Standard English should be seen as a particular form of English that should not supplant a person's first dialect.
- *Providing support*—Support is essential for ESL and ESD students. Of particular benefit is reducing language demands by using visual and nonverbal forms of representation. Open-ended learning activities are also important, as they allow students to be successful in whatever ways they are able.

Likewise, collaboration and cooperative learning are important ways of supporting ESL and ESD learners. Interaction with Standard English speakers is the best vehicle for acquiring interpersonal communication skills.

- *Providing more explicit instruction*—While native speakers may acquire much literacy knowledge through immersion and indirect forms of instruction, ESL and ESD school-age learners appear to benefit from more explicit forms of instruction. This does not mean that skill-and-drill exercises or decontextualized learning activities are appropriate, since these do not allow students to make essential connections. What it does mean is that teachers need to be explicit in pointing out particular things to ESL and ESD students rather than assuming that they will learn by osmosis. Another consideration to keep in mind is that some cultures use what we might consider very traditional forms of teaching. Students who have had previous school experiences in another country may often be more familiar and at ease with explicit forms of instruction than with discovery approaches. On the other hand, just because a student (or more likely his or her parents) believes in rote learning, skill exercises, and so on, this does not mean we should change to a traditional model (as you may recall from the discussion of teaching models in Chapter 2).
- *Addressing academic language and writing*—All students, but particularly ESL and ESD students, need to learn academic language—the registers of the various disciplines. While interpersonal communication is acquired primarily through interaction, **cognitive academic language proficiency** (CALP) takes longer to develop and needs to be addressed specifically. Whenever we teach content, we also teach language (oral and written). Writing across the curriculum is an important component of a writing program for all students, perhaps even more so for ESL and ESD learners.

Planning Processes

I often hear comments about certain classes being "very structured" and other classes having "no structure." *All* classrooms have *structure*. A classroom's structure is like its skeleton: it provides a framework, learning experiences and activities "flesh" it out, and the teacher and students breathe life into it. Just as our bodies' skeletal systems provide support yet allow for *flexibility*, classroom structures should be enabling frameworks rather than being restrictive and limiting.

Teachers need to plan to allow for flexibility. Let's be clear what the function of planning is—it's a decision-making process that includes discovering possibilities for teaching and learning, exploring territory described in official curriculum documents, making judgments about what we think is valuable, determining priorities (what we consider to be essential, what we think is desirable, and what we will do if we have time), and making choices about what to include and what to exclude—because we can't teach everything! These decisions provide teachers with goals and directions.

While some teachers believe it is best to be spontaneous and pursue children's current interests, it seems to me that if we have no sense of direction, then we have no sense of purpose and no "big picture" to work toward. On the other hand, if we get too attached to what *we* plan to do, we can end up being *inflexible* and unable to respond to emergent interests and needs of our students. And we may miss out on some potential powerful opportunities for learning. So, if we think of planning as exploring, then plans can be starting points from which to involve learners and to be open to new possibilities. Remember, too, that learning is more like a dance than a route march: teachers need to respond to learners' needs by stepping back to review or reteach, by moving sideways to try a different approach, by slowing down or speeding up to adapt to their learners' paces. There is no point in going ahead or keeping to a teaching plan if learners are not with you.

Sometimes unexpected incidents occur that teachers perceive as interruptions to their plans, yet the reality of classroom life is that these incidents must be dealt with. Some of these seem serendipitous because they provide teachable moments, but others are challenging and more like problems to be solved. (As I discussed in the previous chapter, even "problem" situations can be used purposefully.)

Because life is experienced in time, which is linear, teachers need to consider how they will sequence learning experiences and activities to best suit their particular classroom community's needs. To develop a balanced design it is helpful to plan at several levels, beginning with the largest unit of time, the school year, and then proceeding to smaller units of time: monthly, weekly, and, finally, daily. In this way, specific learning activities and experiences are contextualized rather than being thought of as isolated, separate lessons. More importantly, we are able to put individual writing and learning experiences into perspective as part of a bigger picture instead of a trivial pursuit.

Yearly Planning

First, sketch or draft out in broad brushstrokes a yearly overview that will enable you to develop your big picture. Think globally, in large learning units. How can you apply what you know about the ebb and flow of the school year to help you decide when certain things make the most sense? For example, I like to begin the school year by getting to know my students, so some sort of All About Me theme and personal writing makes sense at this time. Look at the various official curricula such as science and social studies. Are there topics that might lend themselves to particular themes through which you could develop integrated units? Do these curriculum possibilities suit certain times of the year better than others? If I am going to teach a science unit on growing things, for example, I like to do it in the spring.

Thinking about the school year in this global way can help provide a sense of direction, remembering, of course, that this yearly plan is a *draft* that will be revised as we live our classroom lives. Once you have a draft overview of the year, look at it to see the range of writing/learning experiences it provides and the balance between different kinds of writing. The Functions of Writing chart (Chapter 1, Figure 1.2) can be used to cross-check the range and balance of purposes for writing.

Monthly/Unit Planning

Second, focus on learning units that extend over a period of a month or so. At this level, plans start to become more specific and focused. Consider relevant learning goals and outcomes, and generate focus questions that will lead to particular kinds of learning inquiries and form a framework for integrating the curriculum and weaving in writing. In writing, specifically, think about the different functions and genres that will make sense and be purposeful within the context of the unit and the processes and skills you want students to develop. Once again, these plans are flexible and fluid so that learning activities can unfold rather than become a strict regimen that must be adhered to.

Activity:
All About Me

An important part of yearly planning is to find out about your students so that you can consider their particular needs and interests. In September, engage the children in some getting-to-know-you writing activities. You can do this in a single activity—make an all-about-me web—or choose each of the suggestions below as the focus for a single writing activity (responses can be written in a journal or learning log):

- Things I know a lot about/I'm an expert on ...
- Things I'm good at ...
- Things I wonder about ...
- Things I want to learn more about ...
- Things I want to get better at ...
- Things I can help with and things I need help with ...
- Things I like to read/write ...

REFLECTION

Sometimes flexible planning means changing the topic of a unit you planned to teach. For example, Jan Johnston, a teacher in Delta, British Columbia, had planned to teach a unit on rabbits when the children returned from spring break. On the first day back, the class was greeted with a surprise—right outside the classroom window was a bird's nest with some eggs in it. The Grades 1 and 2 children were so excited and full of questions that Jan realized it was important to capitalize on this interest rather than proceeding with her original plan. Jan was able to use many of the same ideas and activities she had planned simply by switching the topic from rabbits to birds. One of the activities included research on birds and writing bird reports.

A sociocognitive approach blends student-led and teacher-led activities. How might we decide when to follow students' interests? How do we integrate curriculum goals and objectives in planning and also be student-centred?

There are many ways to learn more about integrated unit planning. You can attend workshops at in-service days or at professional conferences. You can take university courses. You can read professional books such as *Making Themes Work* (Davies, Politano, & Cameron, 1993). You can also watch videos. With my student teachers I use an excellent video resource, featuring Heidi Hayes Jacobs (1993), that develops an inquiry-based approach to integration: *Integrating the Curriculum, Video Journal of Education.*

Weekly Planning

I have found that weekly planning helps make an effective transition from unit to day plans. Weekly plans are built on a general weekly timetable that is developed at the beginning of the school year. The weekly timetable is based on large blocks of time (to enable flexibility) and incorporates use of the gymnasium, teacher preparation periods, and so on. (In some cases, teachers have to allocate time to specific subjects because of official directives. I find that this is easy to work around because I include integrated periods that combine various curriculum areas.) Making weekly plans makes it easier to focus on the connections between the daily learning activities and the process of learning. I use a large calendar that shows the period of time I plan to allocate (usually about a month) and plot out how I think learning experiences and activities should progress. Even after all this time (I hate to admit how long) I still find that I plan more than I am usually able to accomplish. This is partly because I value process and I want to provide whatever time is needed for students to talk about their learning, and also because I want to pursue things in more depth when the desire arises. A workable solution for me has been to plan fully for four weekdays. Then I can use Fridays to round things out and come to closure on the week's learning activities. (I dislike having to start a new week by working on unfinished business.) If, by chance, I end up with unplanned time available, I either allow students to pursue something of their own interest (they love this!)—within the boundaries that we negotiate, of course—or have them work on activities that extend their learning in directions beyond what I had initially planned.

Daily Planning

Finally, it's time to fine-tune your daily plans. I find this easy to do because I have three sets of planning in place already and now I am just weaving them together and working out the details. I use my specific weekly plan and a day plan template (Figure 4.1) that reflects the shape of the day (discussed further in this chapter). The template incorporates the daily routines and rituals (such as opening activities and regularly scheduled activities) and provides a flexible structure within which to work. I do the template on my computer and organize it so there is one full page for the morning and one for the afternoon. I photocopy these back-to-back and punch holes on the right side of the morning pages so that when I put the pages in a binder, a full-page spread shows the entire day, with the morning on the left side and the afternoon on the right. (The template also, by the way, ensures that I don't omit things inadvertently, and it saves a lot of repetitive work.)

I have found that regardless of whether I am teaching young children or university students, we work more effectively when we have a structure that becomes familiar to us, when we have established routines or ritual ways of doing things that occur on a regular basis, and when we have the flexibility and freedom to vary these when it seems appropriate and desirable. My daily plan is my working document (and, of course, it provides invaluable information for my replacement if I am absent). From my day plan I make a daily agenda for the class so that my students know what to expect for the day. This can be written either on the chalkboard or on a chart; always put it in the same place (near your meeting area) so students will know where to look for it. (For examples of primary and junior grade agendas, see Chapter 5.)

REFLECTION

Imagine it's the end of the school day. The children have all gone, they've helped you straighten things out for the most part, but here you sit ... staring at the pile on your desk. It's been a good day but a busy one. You've been on the go all day and your energy level is at its lowest ebb. Now all you want to do is have a rest, a cup of tea, and a snack. But your day plan for tomorrow is blank! How can you plan when your brain has little fuel? How can you think clearly, never mind creatively?

When you view your day plan as "something to be filled," it can be daunting at the end of the day. On the other hand, if you see it as part of an ongoing writing/planning process, you rarely, if ever, are faced with a blank page. The planning sequence I suggest here is not only pedagogically sound, it is very practical. No more day plan blues!

Figure 4.1 Day Plan Template

Date: ______________________________ MORNING

9:00 Group Meeting (at Group Meeting Centre. See chart for names of today's special helpers.)
Attendance (Messenger does attendance and takes completed form to office with a partner)
Calendar (see bulletin board—led by Calendar Helper)
Announcements and reminders for the children:
____
News (from the children and teacher)
Agenda (on board): Read together and discuss plans for the day

9:15 Language Arts (start at Group Meeting Centre)
Mystery Message and COPS (Capitals, Omissions, Punctuation, Spelling—on board/chart)
Shared Experience/Lesson:
____
____
____
____

Independent and/or Collaborative Work:
MUST DO's ______________________________
____
____
____

Reading Writing Workshop:
MAY DO's: ______________________________
____
____
____

• Respond to shared experience by:
____
____
or brainstorm ideas with children before beginning
• Or any language/literacy-related activity such as: journal, listening/ library/ writing/publishing centres

Group/Individual(s) with Teacher:
as circled/indicated from the list below:
• Reading Club (see sign-up sheet):
____
• Writing Club (see sign-up sheet):
____
• Literature Circle:
____
____
____
• Small-group skill lesson: ______________
____
____
____
• Individual reading/writing conferences:
____

10:15 Clean-Up followed by Sharing (Children share activities from Reading/Writing Workshop.)
10:30 Recess
10:45 Storytime (at Group Meeting Centre), read to the children:
____
11:10 Mon./Wed.—P.E.; Tues./Thurs.—Free Exploration/Centres; Fri.—Class Meeting
____
____
11:45 Music
____
____
12:00 Lunch (Children may not go out to play before 12:15)

Date: ____ AFTERNOON

1:00 Sustained Silent Reading (SSR) (Children read independently. Teacher reads too.)

1:10 Shared Reading (Children share books/read with a buddy or in small groups or continue SSR.)

1:20 Mathematics

Opening Activity:

____

____

Shared Experience/Lesson:

____

____

____

____

____

Individual and/or Collaborative Work:
MUST DOs: ____________________
____
____
MAY DO's: ____________________
____
____
____

Group/Individual(s) with Teacher:
____
____
____
____
____
____
____

2:00 Mon.–Thurs.—Theme Time (Integrated Activities/Centres) OR _______ Fri.—P.E.

____

____

____

____

____

____

____

____

____

____

2:40 Clean-up followed by sharing and group reflection (May share activities from Theme Time.)

3:00 Dismissal (Bus students leave promptly!)

REMINDERS

- * To leave the room, children must go in pairs and sign out.
- * In addition, to go to library or computer lab, children must use a pass.
- * Supervision: ______________________________
- * Meeting: ______________________________
- * Other: ______________________________

Shape of the Day

Each school day provides opportunities for three kinds of writing/learning experiences: (1) classroom workplace writing activities that are embedded in the ongoing life of the classroom, (2) writing in the context of language arts, and (3) writing in other curriculum areas. In Chapter 3, I discussed workplace literacy in depth, so I will not repeat it here. What I intend to do now is to look at the *structures* or ways of organizing what is often called the language arts period and how to shape the school day to allow for integration of writing across the curriculum. (Chapters 6 and 7 will provide the details of specific writing/learning activities and forms of writing.)

Integrated Language Arts

In the language arts period we want to provide opportunities for a variety of experiences: whole-class shared experiences, literacy lessons and mini-lessons, collaborative and cooperative writing/learning activities, and individual writing opportunities. A **shared experience/individual response** structure is a way to embrace all of these. The period begins with a whole-class shared experience or literacy lesson, for example:

- *Reading* the same story, poem, or chapter in a novel; shared reading of a big book, a poem on a chart, or a newspaper item on an overhead transparency; engaging in a collaborative reading activity such as ReQuest (Reciprocal Questioning) or Reading Like a Writer (Brownlie, Close, & Wingren, 1988).
- *Listening* to a story or poem read aloud, to a guest speaker, to a storytelling or readers' theatre performance, to a classmate share his or her own writing.
- *Speaking* about an experience (shared or individual), sharing ideas related to a particular topic, participating in a discussion with a classroom guest, participating in the composing of a language experience story.
- *Viewing* a film or live performance.
- *Engaging in a drama* such as a story drama or a role-play.

During (if appropriate) and immediately after this shared experience, engage the students in discussion. Sometimes in the context of this discussion a teacher (or a student helper) may write words and ideas on the chalkboard or a chart; in this way, the shared experience acts as a **prewriting** activity.

This is followed by independent and/or collaborative writing and/or reading. There are several options at this point:

1. Allow free choice for these activities and consider the shared experience as an invitation to read or write.
2. Provide a specific follow-up activity that you have designed and that all students are to do (in this case, it is particularly important that it be open-ended).
3. Provide several options for follow-up activities and allow students to choose among them.
4. Request that all students respond to the shared experience, but allow them to choose the way in which they respond. If you choose this last option, it is a good idea to brainstorm some possibilities first. (An example of this is shown in the primary classroom vignette in the following chapter.)

Sometimes I want to engage students in an ongoing activity that takes place over several days, or even longer. In these instances, I plan an introductory shared experience at the beginning of the project and smaller, more focused ones at the beginning of each new period or day. Sometimes these take the form of mini-lessons.

Writing Workshop

The shared experience and/or mini-lesson flows into a workshop period in which students are actively engaged in literacy. Some teachers have a Writing Workshop with all students involved in writing in one way or another (the Grade 5 teacher in Chapter 5 does this). Other teachers (like the primary teacher in Chapter 5) use a Reading/Writing Workshop approach; here, students are involved in various kinds of reading and writing.

A workshop setting for writing implies the following:

- Everyone participates in the work of the community, in this case, learning and writing (and, often, related language activities).
- Everyone works collaboratively to improve their craft (sharing ideas, helping one another, and doing their part).
- Everyone is a learner and a teacher (learning with and from one another).
- Everyone shares responsibility for learning and writing.

What this translates into is student engagement in a variety of writing/learning activities. While this is occurring, it is important to observe and monitor what and how students are doing and to interact with them to provide feedback, assistance, mini-lessons, and so on. Because students are actively engaged and can support one another, the teacher is freed up to work with small groups of students for a variety of purposes; for example, participating in a Writing Club or teaching a Spotlight on Writing mini-lesson. In the next few chapters you will have an opportunity to see what all of this looks like in the classroom, read about some specific language arts–related writing activities, and learn strategies for a process approach to writing.

Integrating Writing across the Curriculum

Writing does not occur only in language arts periods, but throughout the day. It can be incorporated into subject-area lessons in a variety of forms. Sometimes writing is used to facilitate learning concepts and skills; for example, using a learning log in mathematics (this is illustrated in the junior classroom vignette in the next chapter).

Sometimes writing is more central to the subject-area lesson. As discussed in the previous chapter, each discipline has its own register (ways of using language) and genres (forms of discourse related to particular contexts), and part of learning to write in schools is learning the writing of mathematics, social studies, science, and so on. For example, in science students learn not only science concepts but also how to "write science" in the form of experiments, charts, and expository reports. In the next three chapters I will further develop ideas about writing across the curriculum: Chapter 5 will show a primary class learning to write science reports and a junior class writing in role in social studies; Chapter 6 will introduce a process approach to writing that will be applied to specific genres across the curriculum in Chapter 7.

Organizing the Physical Environment for Writing and Learning

To many of us, organizing the physical environment is the first thing we think about when we get our first classroom or when we start a new school year, yet I have left talking about it until the end of this chapter because the physical environment is important but not an end unto itself. It serves a variety of functions. Not only do we want our environment to be aesthetically pleasing and language- and literacy-rich, we want it to enable the various kinds of learning experiences we design for our students.

Materials and Resources

Learning to write is a hands-on/minds-on process. We saturate the classroom with functional environmental print not just for the sake of displaying words, but to demonstrate that writing is part of what people do. While some of these materials may be purchased, an alphabet for example, to be meaningful and useful most of these should be made *with* the students. Although I and many other teachers have spent a lot of time making pretty charts, the students don't really use them. What they do refer to are the charts that are made within the context of an activity—charts that incorporate their own words and ideas, and are written to serve a particular purpose. And of course it is also essential to bring a multitude of books, magazines, and other reading materials into the classroom.

Provide many different materials for writing too: paper in all colours and sizes, lined and unlined, newsprint, bond, and art paper—lots of *blank* paper so students can represent their ideas in a variety of ways, as opposed to using worksheets and photocopied activity pages. (And just think of the money you'll save by doing this—money to buy more books, for example!) A class set of individual chalkboards is useful, especially for primary children. You may want each child to have a journal and/or learning log, writing folders or large envelopes for drafts, a scrapbook or portfolio for finished pieces of writing. You can also use a variety of writing implements: pens, pencils, markers, chalk, and perhaps one or more typewriters or computers. Consider also materials for publishing students' writing: cloth, cardboard, and dry mount (available at photography supply stores) for cloth-covered books; bookbinding tape; large ring-clasps for class books; coil bindings; plastic covers; and of course staplers (heavy-duty and long-arm as well as standard staplers) and staples.

Remember to provide writers' resources such as dictionaries and thesauri of various kinds. Some of these may be traditional published materials; some may be in electronic form, such as CD-ROM; others may be class-made books, charts, or checklists (described in Chapter 6).

Computers are being used increasingly in classroom writing centres.

Places and Spaces

Classrooms need places to store materials and resources and spaces for various kinds of activities. Storage areas need to be arranged so that students can access materials and resources easily and take responsibility for keeping them in order. If not, either students won't use them or there will be a mess to clean up at the end of the day. Many teachers have a *writing centre* for storing and organizing all the writing materials.

You need spaces of various sizes to suit a variety of writing/learning activities:

- A space large enough for the whole class to meet; if you want students to sit on the floor, it should be carpeted (in fact, you can bring in a carpet that also acts as a way of defining the area).
- A place for small-group conferences and lessons, such as a table and chairs for up to six or eight students; ideally, this should be round or oval to allow for more equal participation.

- Places for students to work collaboratively; rows of desks are not conducive to collaboration or cooperative learning, so if you do not have tables, consider arranging desks in pods of four to six.
- Places for students to write individually; find a way to provide a few quiet, private spaces for students to work.
- A place for the writing centre that is easily accessible, yet not in the middle of a traffic path; if you have one or more computers, you will need to keep in mind access to electrical outlets as well.

Finally, remember that materials, resources, places, and spaces for writing do not stop at the classroom door. Take your class to the school library and computer lab often. Establish routines and expectations, and encourage your students to visit the library and computer lab for writing too—they will do so enthusiastically and responsibly!

PERSONAL REFLECTION

I remember the excitement of having my first classroom. I spent countless hours finding resources, arranging and rearranging furniture, and decorating my room to make it beautiful. How wonderful it was to have my own room! Every new school year was always an exciting new beginning. Even now, at the university, I have arranged to have my own teaching space—my own room. I managed to get tables and chairs (instead of those horrible chairs with deskette arms), dragged in an old carpet and my teaching "stuff"—pocket charts, books, etc.

Why do you think the physical environment is important to so many teachers? Is it important to you personally? Why or why not?

Reflections on the Chapter

Think about/talk about/write about:

Principles into Practice

- Use Figure 2.6, From Principles of Writing to Practice, to find specific examples in this chapter of each principle as it is put into practice.

Diversity in the Writing Classroom

- What have you noticed about the learners in your own (or your practicum) classroom? Consider the ways in which your class is diverse.
- What do you know about the linguistic, cultural, and socioeconomic backgrounds of your students?

Collaboration

- Think about experiences you have had with collaborative writing. What was it like for you? How did your group work? What could have made it better? Are there times when you prefer collaborative writing to individual writing?
- Think about experiences you have had with individual writing. What was it like for you? What could have made it better? Are there times when you prefer individual writing to collaborative writing?

Planning Writing Activities

- Design a writing activity that meets the criteria outlined in this chapter. Think about how you would sequence a lesson for this activity.
- What are the pros and cons of the planning process discussed in this chapter?

The Physical Environment

- Draw a picture, make a map, or build a three-dimensional model of a classroom you would like to teach in. What would you include in it? How would you arrange it? Why?
- Compare and contrast your design with someone else's design.

REFERENCES AND FURTHER READING

Brownlie, F., Close, S., and Wingren, L. (1988). *Reaching for higher thought: Reading, writing, thinking strategies*. Edmonton: Arnold Publishing.

Chapman, M.L. (1995). Designing literacy learning experiences in a multi-age classroom. *Language Arts, 72*(6), 416–28.

Davies, A., Politano, C., and Cameron, C. (1993). *Making themes work*. Winnipeg: Peguis.

Hillocks, G. (1986). *Research on written composition*. Urbana, IL: National Conference on Research in English.

Jacobs, H. (1993). Integrating the curriculum (video recording). *Video journal of education*. Fountain Hills, AZ: Linton Productions in association with The National Center for Outcome Based Education.

Turner, J. (1993). Situated motivation in literacy instruction. *Reading Research Quarterly, 28*(4), 288–89.

Ward, A. (1997). *Classroom conversations: Talking and learning in elementary school*. Scarborough, ON: ITP Nelson.

CHAPTER 5

Weaving Writing throughout the School Day: Primary and Junior Classrooms

CHAPTER OBJECTIVES

To illustrate through two classroom vignettes (one primary, one junior) how a school day can provide many contexts for learning and writing

To demonstrate how different writing/learning activities can be woven throughout a school day in primary and junior classrooms

To explain two teachers' decision-making processes about how best to put principles into practice

PERSONAL REFLECTION

When I think back over my years of professional involvement in education, I realize that in addition to the years I have spent teaching my own classes, I have been in literally hundreds of other classrooms. Over the years I have not only put into practice in my own classroom most of the things I advocate in this book, but I also witnessed in other classrooms many of the methods that I consider to be best practice in writing instruction. So, you see, these ideas are not "newfangled" or "experimental."

As you read the two classroom vignettes in this chapter, think about the classrooms you've been in yourself and whether you have seen in action some of the things I describe here.

The two teachers you are about to meet in this chapter—Lena Chan and Dave Mitchell—are fictional. However, what you are about to see as you visit their classrooms are vignettes that incorporate many real experiences that have occurred in my own classroom and those I have visited. The purpose of these descriptions is to provide you with a sense of what a day in two classrooms, one primary and the other junior, might look like when teachers adopt a sociocognitive constructivist or transactional approach to writing.

We begin by visiting Ms. Chan and her class of twenty-four Grade 2 children; we then join Mr. Mitchell and his class of thirty Grade 5 students. Both classes might be thought of as typical in that the children demonstrate a wide range of abilities and are at different points along a developmental continuum in the various curriculum areas. As with most public school classrooms, the students come from a variety of home backgrounds socioeconomically, culturally, and linguistically. These are factors that we need to consider as we establish an appropriate climate and create a classroom discourse community. In Chapters 1 and 2, I developed a set of principles about writing and guidelines for learning and teaching writing. Ms. Chan's and Mr. Mitchell's teaching practices embody these principles as well as demonstrate specific strategies and suggestions discussed elsewhere in this book. To highlight the key points in learning and teaching writing, I have made annotations alongside the descriptions of each of the activities.

I also provide you with the day's agenda for each classroom to give you an overview of each day. I use the agenda in my teaching and have found it to be a valuable tool for various age groups. It provides learners with a visual representation of the day, which is of benefit to many learners but especially ESL students (Early, 1989). The agenda also imparts a sense of structure that is important in all classrooms, regardless of the age of the students or the teaching approach used, and demonstrates functional use of reading and writing. You might consider adopting (or adapting) the agenda for your own classroom use.

Writing in the Primary Years (Kindergarten–Grade 3)

We used to think that the primary grades should concentrate on learning to write and that the junior grades should focus on writing to learn. That dichotomy has now been refuted since we realize that learning to write is part of an emergent literacy process that extends throughout our lives. And now that we have begun to put the conventions of writing into a more appropriate context and to appreciate the value of writing as a tool for learning, we see that writing-to-learn in school can, and indeed should, begin in kindergarten. All of the principles and guidelines established in the first two chapters and the features of the classroom and learning activities laid out in Chapters 3 and 4 apply to the primary program.

Ms. Lena Chan, our primary teacher, is in her fifth year of teaching. The children in her class and the school's teaching staff reflect the multicultural nature of her urban school community. Ms. Chan is a third-generation Canadian of Chinese descent. She sees her background as advantageous for her particular teaching situation, since it has helped her understand the values and beliefs both of the Canadian education system and of the parents of many of her students who have come to Canada from Hong Kong. Her dual heritage has enabled her to realize that belief systems are not neutral, but culturally constructed. As a result, Ms. Chan communicates with her students' parents from the beginning of the school year, listening to and talking with them about learning and teaching as well as discussing their children's progress.

Ms. Chan uses an integrated, thematic approach to teaching, as do many primary teachers. Each theme lasts about a month. She chooses topics for her themes that emphasize science, social studies, and literature so that she can weave the language arts throughout the curriculum. She also finds that by having a variety of themes she can incorporate differing interests of all the children and provide balance among a variety of forms of representation and different genres for reading and writing. She has found the notion that boys like scientific topics and girls prefer narrative and fiction to be a stereotype rather than real, at least among the children she has taught. Ms. Chan also believes that all children should experience all types of written language. She has found that she feels better organized and the children are more focused when she has only one major project going on at a time. This month the class is working on an animal theme, and the ongoing projects are animal reports that involve reading in science and writing in an expository genre. The report-writing process is a lengthy one involving many processes and skills. You will find an in-depth treatment of report writing in Chapter 7.

KINDERGARTEN CORNER

No Better Place to Start Writing

Kindergarten children should be nudged—but not pushed—into writing. Many of the writing activities described in this chapter, such as the Classroom Workplace uses of writing, are very appropriate for kindergarten children. I have been in classrooms where kindergarten children, including those who were not yet fluent English speakers, have participated in Writing Workshop and have engaged in researching and writing a factual class book. The important thing in the kindergarten classroom is to encourage children to participate and to represent their thinking in whatever ways they are able.

A classroom discourse community has many uses of writing for a regulatory function—*classroom workplace literacy.* Many of these occur near the beginning of the school day.

A Day in a Grade 2 Classroom

9:00–9:25 Group Meeting (Opening Activities)

Ms. Chan begins the day with a series of informal activities that are designed to provide opportunities for the children to meet and greet one another and to attend to administrative details such as attendance:

Figure 5.1 Primary Classroom Agenda

Tuesday, March 12, 1997

Agenda

Group Meeting
Story
Reading and Writing Time
- Reading and Writing Workshop
- Writing Club

Sharing
Recess ————
P.E.
Math
Lunch ————
Quiet Reading
Shared Reading
Science
Centres
Learning Logs
Group Meeting
Hop on Home

Sign In. As the children enter the classroom they put away their outdoor clothing and snacks, then take their name tags from the Our Class chart by the classroom door and hang them on the Who Is Here Today? chart in the group meeting area. Before sitting down on the carpet for opening activities, they return their books from their Take Home Reading Envelopes and select new books to take home to read with their parents. Then they record the date and titles of the new books on a sheet attached to the envelope they use for transporting their books.

The teacher encourages parental involvement in literacy.

The teacher helps the children gradually take more and more responsibility for running the classroom, and for regulatory writing.

Attendance. Ms. Chan treats attendance-taking as a collaborative problem-solving activity that integrates the language arts and mathematics, reading and counting the name tags on the two charts with the children to help them discover how many children are present and who is away. Once the children have determined who is absent and why, Reena, the Attendance Helper, completes the form and takes it to the office. The others focus their attention on the calendar.

Calendar. Margriet, the Calendar Helper, is assisted by Ms. Chan and the other children in figuring out the day and date and selecting from preprinted cards to complete the following chart:

> Yesterday was (Monday) (March) (11).
> Today is (Tuesday) (March) (12).
> Tomorrow will be (Wednesday) (March) (13).

Writing is integrated with mathematics: children learn a variety of notational systems and forms of representation.

The children read the chart in unison. Ms. Chan then asks the children which of the three dates she should print on the top of the Today's News chart. Next, Margriet adds a stroke to a tally chart and the children figure out how many days they have been in school. Margriet prints the appropriate numeral on the Days in School chart. Ms. Chan has incorporated many of the calendar activities suggested in *Mathematics Their Way* (Baratta-Lorton, 1976), a program based on sociocognitive constructivist principles.

Mystery Message. Ms. Chan has written on a chart a message to the children. The first half is written in a format with missing letters, and the second half is written with nonstandard spellings and punctuation. Today's message is:

Graphophonics is addressed within a meaningful, communicative context.

K _ _'s m _ _ is _ __ ing t _ _ mou _ _ to _ _ _ _ _ _ .
[Kim's mom is bringing the mouse today.]

we wll nd to thnk ov sum rulz for mows safe
[We will need to think of some rules for mouse safety.]

There is a lot of animated excitement as the children solve the Mystery Message. Ms. Chan actively involves all the children; for example, she asks Parminder to volunteer beginning letters for words and asks David to spell the word "safety." After the Mystery Message, Ms. Chan talks with the children about the handling of pet mice and the class develops a set of rules, which Ms. Chan records on a chart.

Peer collaboration and teacher scaffolding support children in their learning.

Agenda. Once this is done, Ms. Chan draws the children's attention to today's agenda, which is printed on large chart paper (Figure 5.1). Ms. Chan and the children read the agenda aloud together and discuss plans for the day. In the context of this shared reading activity, Ms. Chan encourages the children to make predictions about some of the words on the agenda chart and to share their thinking of how they figured the words out.

Talking about written language in the context of a meaningful activity helps students develop metalinguistic awareness.

News. Sharing of special news follows next. Ms. Chan encourages the children to talk about interesting things that have happened in their lives and news items from television or the newspaper. Today Adelle has brought in a clipping from the local newspaper about her older sister's soccer tournament. In the context of the discussion, the class composes Today's News, which Ms. Chan records on a chart (Figure 5.2). While the focus of this activity is on meaning, Ms. Chan thinks aloud as she writes; for example, "I'll start this sentence with a capital letter," and involves the children in the process by asking them to predict how some of the words might be spelled, confirming their predictions and explaining spelling conventions as appropriate. For example, she asks Singh, who has been speaking English for only two years, "How do you think 'going' starts?" while to Cameron, a very capable 8-year-old, she says "Cameron, how do you think we might spell 'exciting'?" Ms. Chan and the children discuss the news chart and read it aloud together. Ms. Chan reminds the children that they may write other personal news in their journals later on

The teacher helps the children make many connections: experiencing, thinking, talking, reading, and writing.

The teacher provides demonstrations of writing in the context of a purposeful activity.

The teacher has developmentally appropriate expectations that vary for different children.

Figure 5.2 Today's News Chart

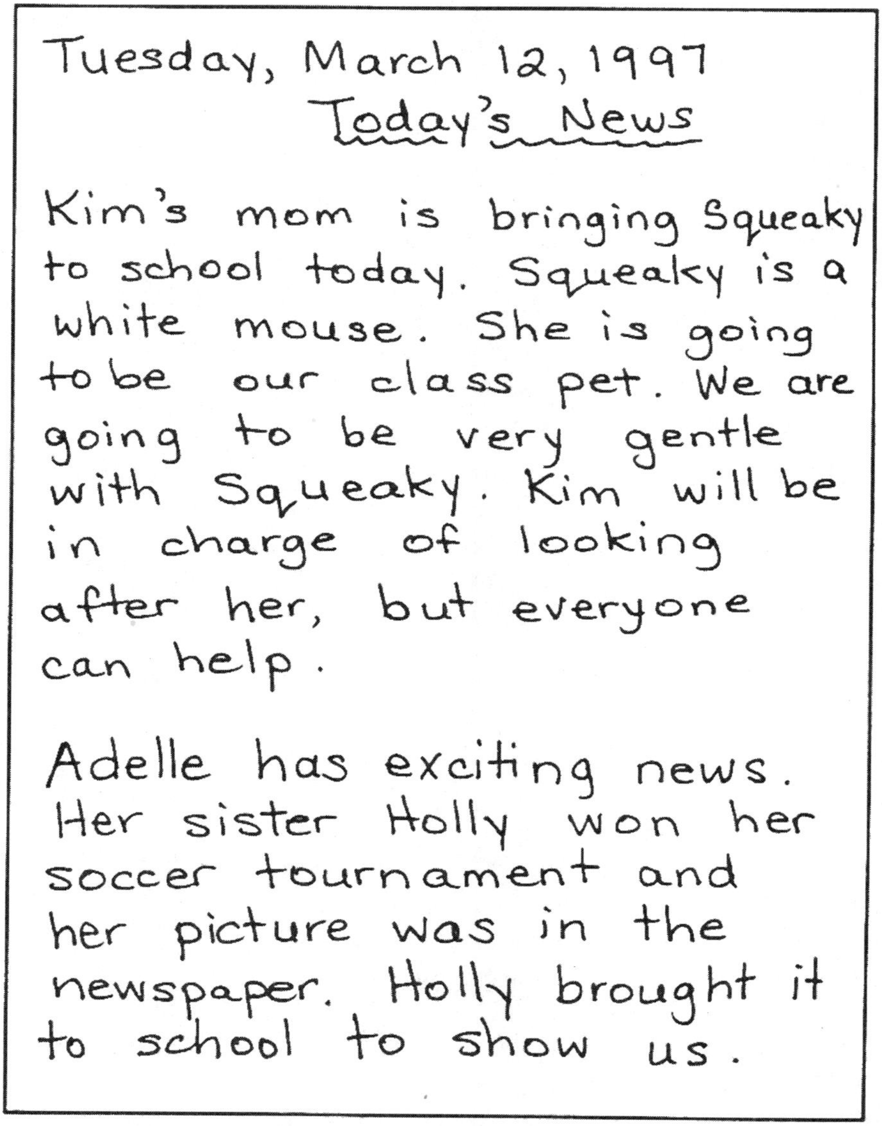

Tuesday, March 12, 1997

Today's News

Kim's mom is bringing Squeaky to school today. Squeaky is a white mouse. She is going to be our class pet. We are going to be very gentle with Squeaky. Kim will be in charge of looking after her, but everyone can help.

Adelle has exciting news. Her sister Holly won her soccer tournament and her picture was in the newspaper. Holly brought it to school to show us.

(during Reading and Writing Workshop or Centres Time).

9:25–9:45 Storytime/Prewriting (Whole Class)

As well as helping children connect writing to their own experiences and to oral language, Ms. Chan knows that children need to have many opportunities to hear written language in a variety of forms. Because a mouse is coming to school today, she has chosen to read Edna Miller's (1967) *Mousekin Finds a Friend.*

Prereading. First, Ms. Chan points out the title of the book as she reads it aloud. She encourages the children to make predictions about the book both from its title and from the illustration on the cover. As well as having the children predict the content of the book, Ms. Chan draws attention to the type of illustration, in this case a drawing, to encourage the children to think about whether the book might be factual or fiction. Next, she prints the word MICE in the centre of a large piece of chart paper. The children brainstorm what they know about mice, and Ms. Chan records the ideas as a web (Figure 5.3). In the context of the web-building, there is discussion about whether a particular idea is true or not. The mouse on the cover of the book is brown, and one of the children asks whether all mice are brown. Kim says that her mouse is white. Since the class wonders about what other colours mice could be, Ms. Chan writes "What colours are mice?" with a red pen and puts a large red question mark beside it. She then adds "brown" and "white." She suggests that some of the children might be interested in visiting the classroom and/or school library to find a book about mice that may help them find out the answers to the questions indicated on the web or to find out other interesting things about mice that can be added to the web. They may do this during Reading and Writing Workshop.

Discussion and collaborative writing are prewriting experiences that help children generate ideas for their own writing.

Reading to children is one of the best ways to help them develop concepts about written language.

Reading and talking about books helps children access prior knowledge and generate ideas for writing.

Webbing is a prewriting strategy that allows ideas and language to "flow" freely.

Inquiring and researching to acquire information are useful for building a knowledge base. They are also other types of prewriting activities.

Figure 5.3 Mice Web

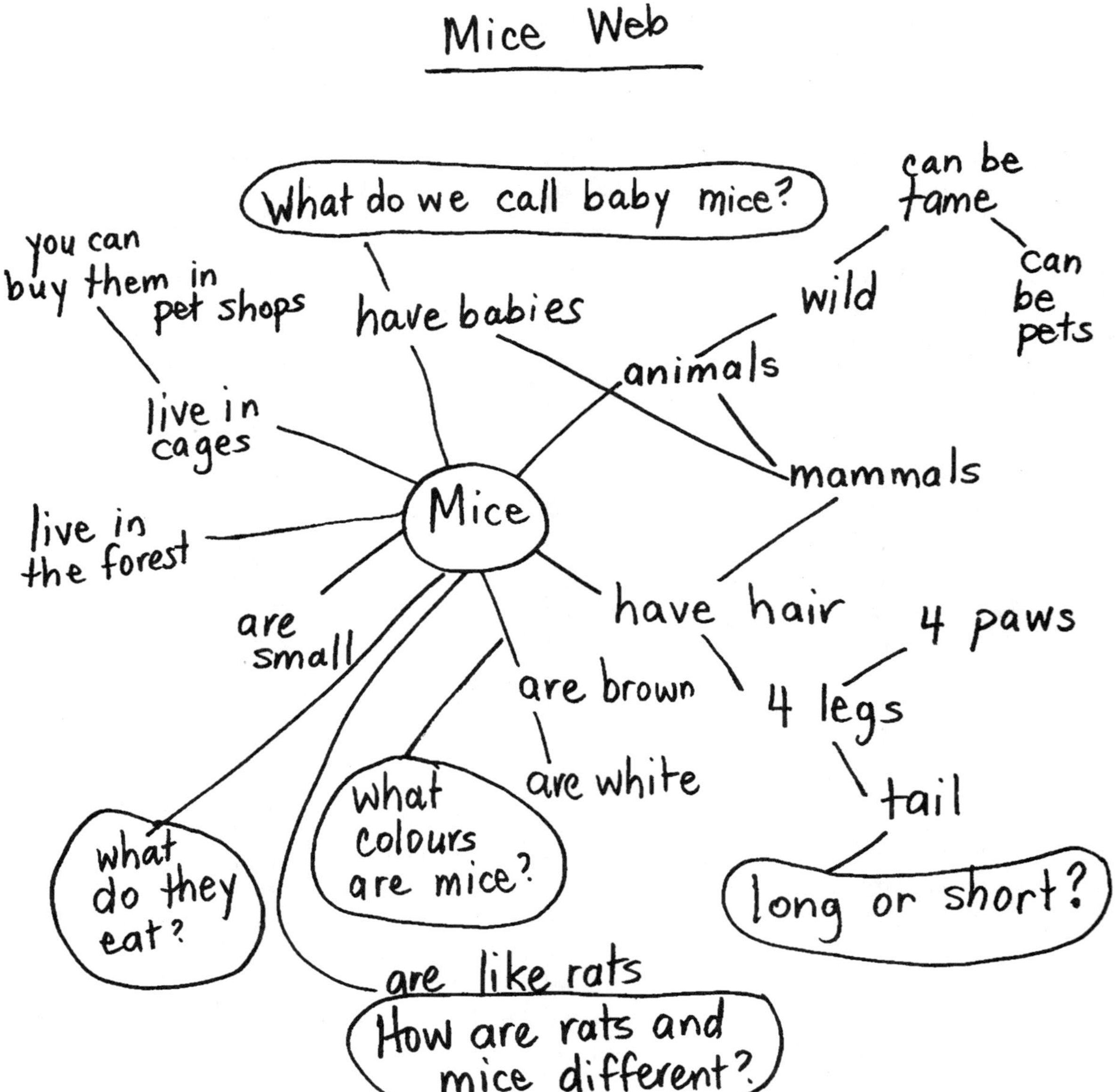

Reading the Story. The prereading activity is followed by Ms. Chan's reading of the book. She encourages the children to be active participants in the reading, asking them to make predictions and to respond to the story.

Reading to children is an excellent prewriting activity. It activates their prior knowledge and provides a starting point for discussion.

Reading to children is an excellent prewriting activity.

After Reading. The reading is followed by discussion of the children's responses. Next, Ms. Chan directs the children's attention back to the MICE web, and more ideas are added.

Children benefit from opportunities to choose the content and form of their writing.

Many children benefit from discussing writing possibilities before they start to write.

Students need guidance in generating purposes for reading and writing.

Recording ideas helps demonstrate a useful purpose for writing and provides structure for the children.

Introducing children to a variety of forms of representations helps build a repertoire of writing forms they can draw on.

Many conventions of writing can be taught in teachable moments.

Preparing for Reading/Writing Time. Rather than providing a specific writing activity for today, Ms. Chan wants the children to choose what to read and write. The children will be engaged in Reading/Writing Workshop activities until recess while she plans to have a small-group writing conference she calls Writing Club. Rather than leaving children to fend for themselves, she leads a discussion of possibilities for reading and writing activities.

When she says, "Boys and girls, in Reading/Writing Workshop today I'd like you to choose what you'd like to do. It must be some kind of reading and writing. One of the things you could do is write in your journal. Sometimes our morning news gives us ideas for our journals. What are some things you could write about today?" Adelle suggests soccer, so Ms. Chan writes on the board:

Today's Choices

Writing: journals – soccer
– other sports
– your own idea

Ms. Chan continues, "What else might you like to write about?" Lindsey says, "Mice." "What kinds of things about mice?" asks Ms. Chan. The children come up with a variety of ideas: a story about Mousekin, a story about Kim's mouse, facts about mice from books, a picture of a mouse with labels, a Venn diagram comparing mice and rats, and a script for a play. Ms. Chan records all of the children's ideas on the board. She also seizes the opportunity to show the children how a script is written (character names, followed by a colon) for those children who are interested. She reminds the children that they can visit the Writing Centre for ideas too. Then she points out to the children that they can choose to read today as well. She adds to the chart:

Reading:
- books about mice
- *Mousekin Finds a Friend*
- other Mousekin stories
- your own choice

Classroom workplace literacy is in effect, and children are assuming some responsibility for their classroom community.

To organize for the Writing Club, Ms. Chan and the children check the Writing Club Sign-Up sheet to see whose turn it is today. Early in the school year, she made the sign-up forms herself. Now the children have taken over this responsibility. Philomena made this week's sign-up sheet (Figure 5.4) and posted it on the chalkboard next to the meeting area.

Figure 5.4 Sign-Up Sheet for Writing Club

M	T	W	Th	F
Philomena	Parm	KANW-AR	Michele	Lindsey
RISHMA	Kim	Cameron	Singh	Colleen
Holly	Margriet	Sean	Gino	Leah
Adelle	Carlos	DAN	Jacob	Cathy
AMy	Marie-Claude	JoJo	DANICA	

"Before you leave the carpet, think about what you are going to do in Reading/Writing Time. Think about what you will need. Paper? Books? Who's ready to work? Tell me what you plan to do." The children raise their hands as they finalize their decisions, and Ms. Chan dismisses them a few at a time as they tell her what their choices are.

Children are encouraged to take responsibility and be self-directed.

9:45–10:20 Reading/Writing Time

Following the whole-class activities, Ms. Chan structures experiences for children to work individually or in small groups. Sometimes she tells the children there is something they first must do (such as respond to a new story they have read together) before they choose from a variety of language activities. Today it is Children's Choice from Reading and Writing Workshop activities:

Provide a balance between teacher-directed and self-selected activities.

Children need opportunities for independent and collaborative writing with peers as well as teacher-directed experiences.

Reading and Writing Workshop. This block of time is structured to ensure children are actively engaged in literacy through:

- *Reading*—rereading books (including big books) from a shared reading experience, visiting the Book Corner or the animal book display in the Science Centre to select a book to read, reading classroom charts (including Today's News and the MICE web) or class-made books in the Classroom Authors Centre, or visiting the library to find out more about mice.
- *Listening*—Visiting the listening centre to hear a taped story and follow the accompanying text.
- *Writing*—Writing in their journals, visiting the Writing Centre to start or continue a story of their own or write a letter (ideas are provided in a book *Free Stuff for Kids* [Peers, 1995], which is updated regularly).

Publishing children's writing, individually or in class books, shows that we value their efforts and provides motivation to write.

Choosing to write is an option within a variety of language arts activities.

Journals and other forms of personal writing should be an option, and not the only writing activity.

- *Puppetry*—Visiting the puppet centre to re-enact the morning story or another familiar story, or to create an original puppet play.
- *Science*—Working on their note-taking for their animal science projects (explained later in this section).

While the children set to work and today's Writing Club group gets ready, Ms. Chan circulates about the room observing the children, talking to them informally about what they are doing, and recording her observations. Today she notes that Carlos began by writing right away. This is the first time that she has observed Carlos working in this way; previously, Carlos has started by drawing and then adding writing. Ms. Chan records her observation in anecdotal form on an At-a-Glance Observation Sheet (see Chapter 8, Figure 8.5).

Writing Club. Once the children settle into the various activities just described, Ms. Chan begins a small-group writing conference or Writing Club. She uses a combination of group and individual conferences for reading and writing, depending on her purpose. Writing Club allows the children to share their own writing with their teacher and a small group of classmates and enables Ms. Chan to interact with the children, record her observations, and assess their progress. In reading and Writing Clubs the children practise oral reading meaningfully as they read their own writing. Interacting with other children enables them to learn from one another and to share their ideas and enthusiasm. Today, Ms. Chan is meeting with Carlos, Parminder, Margriet, Marie-Claude, and Kim.

By now all of the children know the routine: they bring their writing folders, journals, and a piece of their writing to read to the group. Some of the children will read up to three journal entries (if they are short), while those who are writing longer pieces will read one (or just a selection, if the piece is quite long). While the rest

Writing is integrated across the curriculum.

Observing children in the process of writing provides important information about their development and learning.

Recording observations in a variety of contexts over time helps teachers document children's development and evaluate their progress.

Teachers use multiple sources of information for assessment and evaluation.

Children benefit from sharing their writing with one another and their teacher.

Group writing conferences (Writing Clubs) are a useful way to collect data to assess children's writing.

of the children in the class continue with their Reading and Writing Workshop activities, Ms. Chan meets the Writing Club at the Conference Centre, bringing with her conference record sheets for the five children (see Chapter 8, Figure 8.6).

Children need an audience for their writing so they can see that writing is a form of communication.

The children each take a turn reading aloud (two or three minutes), and then the rest of the group makes comments and asks questions about the writing. Meanwhile, Ms. Chan records her observations on the conference record sheets. Let's listen to some of the discussion:

Talking about writing is important for members of a writing community.

Margriet: *... So Princess Katrina said to the knight, if you ever come back to my castle, you better not sneak in, just ring the doorbell.*

Young writers benefit from giving and receiving feedback on their writing.

Parminder: *That was funny. I liked when the princess kicked the knight off the cloud.*

Carlos: *I like the part when the knight climbed up the giant tree.*

Literacy-rich environments enable children to make *intertextual* connections among reading, literature, and writing.

Ms. Chan: *Margriet, I notice that the princess is really strong and brave. She reminds me of the Paper Bag Princess.*

Margriet: *Well, that's kinda what she's like. But she's beautiful too.*

Marie-Claude: *I think that knight got what he deserved. He shouldn't sneak around like that.*

Ms. Chan: *I notice you have some really interesting characters and unique ideas. How did you get the idea to have a castle in the clouds?*

In Writing Club, the focus is on ideas and use of language. These discussions help children share their knowledge and learn from one another.

Margriet: *Well, at first, I was going to have her live in a tower, but then I thought, well, I want to make this a really* different *fairy tale ...*

At the end of Writing Club, the children who have participated join the rest of the class to work on

Reading and Writing Workshop activities. Meanwhile, Ms. Chan puts on her Do Not Disturb hat (to signal to the children that she needs time for thinking) and takes about five minutes to complete her anecdotal notes on the children who participated in the group. Afterward, she circulates among the children at work, observing and interacting with them.

10:15–10:30 Closure and Preparation for Recess

Ms. Chan gives the children a signal to finish what they are doing, put their things away, and come to the carpet, bringing with them whatever they want to share. Rather than conducting a large-group sharing session (which takes a lot of time, but more importantly, does not actively involve all the children), the children form groups of two to four and share something they worked on during the morning; for example, reading to their friends something that they have written or talking about what they have read. Once the children have had a chance to share, they get ready for recess and go out to play.

10:30–10:45 Recess

10:45–11:20 Physical Education

After recess, the children hang up their outdoor clothes, put on their indoor runners, and line up for physical education. Ms. Chan takes the children to the gym and spends the period preparing materials for the afternoon activities.

11:20–12:00 Mathematics (Attribution and Graphing)

The mathematics lesson is a continuation of the previous day's. Ms. Chan reviews what the children know about attributes (e.g., colour, shape, size) referring to the chart they made the day before. To further develop the concept of attribution, she involves the children in a People Sort activity (Baratta-Lorton, 1976) where the children sort themselves into groups according to the

Recording ideas helps make them "concrete" so we can revisit them.

A variety of forms of representation—charts, graphs, and so on—integrate writing into content areas such as mathematics.

colour of the shirt or top they are wearing. In the sorting process there is much discussion of problems, such as tops with more than one colour. Once the children are grouped, the numbers for each colour category are counted and recorded on the board.

When teachers introduce new concepts and forms of representation, they provide children with models, demonstrate how writing works, and guide children's participation.

Ms. Chan wants to introduce the idea of representing mathematical ideas in different ways. Today she introduces graphing as a way of representing the classification of a set of objects by an attribute (colour). She guides the children through the concept and together the class makes several kinds of graphs using concrete objects, pictures, and stickers. Just as they are finishing, Kim's mother brings the mouse (in a cage) to school, so Ms. Chan quickly brings the math lesson to a close and the children are introduced to Squeaky. (There is a lot of squeaking from the children too.)

12:00–1:00 Lunch

Reading a variety of materials is important in developing children's repertoires of writing discourse forms, or genres.

1:00–1:15 Quiet Reading Time

As the children enter the classroom, they put their outdoor things away and find something to read. Ms. Chan has established a routine so that as the children return from lunch, they take from their desks the books they had begun to read earlier, visit the Book Corner to select a book, or find something to read from the Science Centre; for example, *Chickadee,* a science magazine. Ms. Chan reads too.

Involving children in self-directed and collaborative activities frees the teacher to interact with individual children and conduct informal assessments.

1:15–1:30 Shared Reading Time

After fifteen minutes of independent reading, Ms. Chan tells the children that they can find one or more classmates to share reading with. Ms. Chan uses this time as an opportunity to have individual reading or writing conferences with some of the children at the Conference Centre. She first asks David to read to her, and then confers with Ashley about the draft she completed yesterday. After about ten minutes of shared reading, Ms. Chan asks the children to put away their books and come to the carpet. Informal discussion of what the children have been reading today occurs as the group that has gathered waits for the others to join them.

Thematic units provide a vehicle for integrating the language arts across the curriculum. They can also provide for a balance between *informative* and *imaginative* purposes for writing.

1:30–2:10 Science

Like many primary teachers, Ms. Chan selects a science or social studies topic as a general theme through which to integrate the curriculum areas. The class is currently studying the theme Animals in Our World and writing a class big book report about different animals. (The details of this activity are provided in Chapter 7.)

When children read and write in the content areas, they learn content knowledge and literacy at the same time.

Earlier, the class had learned about birds, and Ms. Chan used that unit as a vehicle for developing informational reading and writing skills through a shared topic and writing a class book about birds. Now the children are collaborating on a big book, working in pairs to research and write about different animals. In the birds unit, Ms. Chan taught the children how to gather information by observing real birds, examining pictures of birds, and reading about birds. She also modelled how to record information in note form and to write a draft from notes. Ms. Chan showed the children how to fold paper into Idea Boxes, record ideas (a separate idea in each box), and then cut the boxes apart and sequence the ideas in a logical order. The children have finished collecting information on the animals they selected and now they are ready to cut apart the Idea Boxes and sequence them. Ms. Chan brings out the large chart paper with the ideas they collected and organized in the bird unit and reviews the sequencing process before they begin. Once it is clear that the children know what to do, they join their partners, get their notes from their project folders, and settle down to work. Ms. Chan uses the opportunity to observe and record how the children are working and to provide assistance where needed.

The teacher provides demonstrations and guided practice in finding and recording information.

Prewriting strategies vary with the function and form of writing undertaken.

Report writing is an important genre in academic settings. It should be introduced in the primary years, using developmentally appropriate instruction.

2:10–2:40 Centres

As the children finish their science writing activity, they put away their materials and move into Centres Time. Since they finish their writing at different times, the start of Centres Time is staggered. The children have learned to take out their Centres Folder first and check to see what they have already done before they decide what to work on today. Next, they go to the Choosing Board and put their name tags on the hook next to the centre they have chosen. They then record in their folder the name of the centre they are attending today. Ms. Chan goes to the Choosing Board to help anyone who needs it.

Collaboration provides support for children in their learning.

Classroom workplace literacy occurs purposefully.

At the present time the children may select from a number of different centres, some of which are ongoing (for example, the Writing Centre and the Book Corner), some of which are ongoing but with a new activity each week (for example, the Art Centre and the Listening Centre), some of which are brought in at various times of the year for a period of time and replaced and reintroduced as interests change (for example, the Puppetry Centre or Dress-Up Centre), and some of which are related specifically to the theme being studied (for example, the Animal Science Centre). Writing is an integral part of many of the centres (see Chapter 3). During Centres Time, Ms. Chan circulates and assists, talks with the children about their activities, poses challenges, and so on. She also records her observations of how the children are working.

Writing is integrated in many activities in the classroom, including learning centres.

2:40–2:55 Clean-up Followed by Learning Logs

At the close of Centres Time, Ms. Chan puts on the "clean-up music," which gives children the signal to put things away and to get their learning logs. The learning logs provide the children with quiet reflection time so that they can think about what they learned today. Ms. Chan has jokingly told the children that the learning

Writing in the epistemic mode is an important function of writing in schools.

logs can help them to tell their parents about what they have been learning in school so that they don't need to say "Oh, nothing" when their parents ask them what they did in school that day. This year, Ms. Chan is trying out a new idea with the learning logs: she sends them home once a week so that the parents can write a response to their child. Ms. Chan tries to incorporate many different ways of informing parents about their children's progress, and she finds that the learning log provides an interesting and informal opportunity for this. (She has discovered that Friday is not the best day for the learning logs to go home though, since the children often forget to bring them back on Monday.)

Learning logs provide a vehicle for students to use writing to reflect on their learning.

Teachers can use writing as a way of encouraging parents to become involved with their children's literacy and learning.

After the children have finished writing in their learning logs, they find at least one friend to share with before putting the logs away. Next, each child gets his or her Take Home Reading Envelope with today's new book and brings it to the carpet.

2:55–3:00 Group Meeting (Closing Activities)

Today there is a notice to go home with the children, so Ms. Chan reads it to them, reminds them to bring back the attached form the next day, and then asks Michael to hand out the notices. The children put the notices in their Take Home Reading Envelopes. The bell rings, Ms. Chan and the children say their good-byes, and the children chat with one another and their teacher as they put on their coats and head for home.

Writing in the Junior Grades (Grades 4–7)

Next, we'll look at what a day of writing in a junior classroom might look like. But first, let me introduce you to the Grade 5 teacher, Dave Mitchell. Mr. Mitchell is a veteran who has been teaching for seventeen years. He started out as a "pretty traditional teacher" (his phrase) but has continued to evolve professionally by attending workshops on topics such as cooperative learning and whole language. He is currently working on his master's degree, which he finds is giving him the confidence to refine his practice and implement an even greater variety of teaching strategies. Mr. Mitchell teaches in a suburban setting that has undergone a cultural revolution with an influx of new immigrants. In his graduate work he has learned to understand the social, cultural, and political dimensions of education, and this has helped him to appreciate and value the cultural changes to his community and classroom. Mr. Mitchell can also identify on a personal level with students who are newcomers to Canada since he immigrated to Canada from Britain when he was 10 years old. While he did not have to face the challenge of learning a new language, he remembers being teased about his accent and worrying about fitting in and being accepted by his classmates.

As with the previous description, I begin by providing an agenda to show the shape of the day. While there are some similarities between the two classrooms, there are also some differences that reflect the differing needs of the two age groups. Mr. Mitchell is well aware of the characteristics of preadolescents and adolescents: the need to interact with peers, the ability to work more independently, and the willingness to accept increasing responsibility and leadership. You will notice how he deliberately creates a learning environment that capitalizes on the needs and abilities of young people of this age.

Like Ms. Chan, Mr. Mitchell strives for curriculum integration. He finds that not everything can be integrated meaningfully, so rather than using a thematic approach, he alternates science and social studies topics and integrates the language arts and other subjects whenever possible. Alternating science and social studies allows him to focus in more depth on a topic and to build vocabulary, which is very important for the many ESL students in his class. This month, his class is studying a social studies unit on the forest. His Grade 5 students have also been writing storybooks for younger children. Like Ms. Chan, Mr. Mitchell finds that one major project at a time works best for him and for his students. He has selected the storybook project because it provides his students with an opportunity to write for a younger audience, encourages them to take pride in their work, and fosters success for his ESL students. Mr. Mitchell's class will be sharing the storybooks with their Grade 2 buddies, whose names are used for characters in the stories. Mr. Mitchell's students will be publishing three copies of their stories in book form—one for themselves, one for their buddies, and one for the School Authors section of the school library.

Writing in social studies and science becomes increasingly important in the junior grades.

Figure 5.5 Junior Classroom Agenda

Tuesday, March 12, 1997

<u>Agenda</u>

Opening Activities
News
Writing Mini-lesson
- Planning page layouts for books

Writing Workshop
- Progress check
- Work on storybooks

Recess————————
SSR
Math—Review and Learning Logs
Announcements
Lunch————————
Social Studies—Forest Unit
- Video—Preserving Our Forests
- Writing—Writer's RAFT

Art—illustrating storybooks
Wind-up
Homework books

A Day in a Grade 5 Classroom

9:00–9:20 Opening and News

Administrative tasks provide authentic opportunities for students to use writing in real-life workplace literacy events.

In most classrooms a fair amount of time is taken up by administrative procedures. Many teachers like to attend to such matters at the beginning of the school day. In Mr. Mitchell's class, students are responsible for many of these tasks. First, Sean takes attendance. After this is done, Maria makes a series of announcements, including reminders about overdue library books and soliciting volunteer helpers for the report card interviews. To conclude this portion of the morning, Kwan-Sui collects the orders for the book club. At lunch time, she will help Mr. Mitchell count the money and prepare the class order to forward to the publisher. Initially, the opening activities took very close monitoring and supervision on Mr. Mitchell's part, but with guidance, most students can take on such roles with increasing sophistication and learn many important skills. Mr. Mitchell continues to monitor the opening activities, explaining the rationale for procedures and ensuring that things proceed as they should. He also likes to take five to ten minutes each morning for students to share news from the class, the school, or the community, or from the province, the nation, or the world.

Using the newspaper creates an opportunity for students to read for information and to expand their knowledge of genres, for example, exposition and argument.

9:20–9:40 Writing Mini-Lesson

Audience is an important concept in writing. Students in the junior grades can learn to adapt their writing for different audiences.

Mr. Mitchell's class has been working for several weeks on storybooks for primary children. The students are working at various stages in the writing process. At this time, all of the students have written their first drafts and are now working on editing and proofreading. They worked in pairs to give and receive feedback and to make suggestions to make their stories more interesting and appropriate for a younger audience. Some students are still working on editing to incorporate these ideas, while others have proceeded to proofread their work to check for mechanics. Mr. Mitchell has decided at this point to talk to the whole class about organizing their stories into sections. Since the stories will be published in a picture book format, the students will need to decide approximately how much print would be appropriate on one page and where to make logical page breaks. Mr. Mitchell has prepared a mini-lesson using a transparency made from a students' story, "Water Rat's Adventure," written the previous year. (The entire story has been typed on one page.) He also has a large selection of picture books for the students to examine.

To begin, Mr. Mitchell reminds the students that they have already taken the initial steps in publishing their stories: in their last art lesson they designed and began work on the covers for the books they are writing; today they will complete the book covers and start to work on the illustrations. He asks students to look at the picture books he has distributed to examine the way the books are organized and the various formats used. On large chart paper, he writes: Format of Picture Books. He then elicits ideas from the students and records them on the chart. Several students contribute ideas, such as brightly illustrated covers, the cover illustrations sometimes wrap around the front and back of the book, an "about the author" section on the back of the book, a title page, author's and illustrator's names, copyright date, and so on.

Mr. Mitchell asks the students to look at the print in the books. Rosa points out that there are just a few sentences on each page and that much of the page is taken up by pictures. Ramon comments that the print is large and widely spaced. Mr. Mitchell asks students to think about why this format is used, to help them understand that the format is designed to help make the reading easier for young children.

A process approach is an effective way to help students learn the craft of writing.

Learning to give and receive feedback helps young writers focus on ideas and learn to write with clarity.

Strategies and skills are most effectively learned in the context of the writing process.

Writing and art can be integrated purposefully through publishing.

Students need to understand the purpose of particular editing and proofreading tasks.

Modelling and collaborative problem solving engages students actively in learning to write.

As he puts the prepared transparency on the overhead projector, Mr. Mitchell says, "Let's look at this story someone wrote last year. Compare how it looks to the picture books." Lotte suggests that the story needs to be divided up and each part printed on a separate page.

Having students generate criteria within the context of meaningful activity is an effective form of instruction.

"Let's look at "Water Rat's Adventure" and see how we might break it up." The class works through the story together. With a coloured pen, Mr. Mitchell marks the transparency to reflect students' suggestions for page breaks. He prods them to think about why each place would be an appropriate break, leading to the establishment of these criteria: make page breaks between sentences, make breaks at logical places, think about the pictures you could draw and make the breaks so the story parts will match the pictures. Mr. Mitchell adds these criteria to the Format of Picture Books chart.

Students need to develop metacognitive awareness about writing in addition to learning strategies and skills.

When students generate criteria, they more easily internalize them and apply them to their own writing than if criteria are provided to them.

9:40–10:20 Writing Workshop

The writing mini-lesson switches into a check of students' progress. Directing students' attention to the Picture Book Process chart the class developed earlier, Mr. Mitchell points out that everyone is working on some aspect of editing or proofreading. He tells students that making page breaks can be done once they have finished making editorial changes. They can decide on the page breaks before or after proofreading, but this must be done before they start to work on their published copy. He also suggests that it would be a good idea to work with a partner.

A Writing Workshop approach enables students to work at various stages of the writing process.

Working with partners provides support and makes success more likely.

At the close of the progress check, students move into various grouping arrangements for writing workshop. Mr. Mitchell has established a routine in his classroom so that during writing workshop, students go to their writing folders and pick up from where they left off last day. Today, for example, Bernadette,

Students need opportunities to engage in extended writing activities.

Eduardo, Natane, and Lotte are still working on revising their pieces. At another table, Lesley and Xiaoping have exchanged their work and are engaged in peer proofreading. Lesley and Xiaoping have already read each other's work to check punctuation and they are now concentrating on spelling. Mr. Mitchell realizes that young writers need guidance in editing and proofreading each other's work, so he has posted on the wall the editing and proofreading charts he used in various mini-lessons. (Ideas for these charts are provided in Chapter 6.)

Editing and proofreading are important parts of the writing process in the junior grades.

Guidance can be provided through charts and checklists. These should be introduced to students in lessons before they are expected to use them on their own.

Like Ms. Chan, the primary teacher, Mr. Mitchell circulates around the classroom to observe students at work and provide help where needed. Today he is also checking to see which students are writing in run-on sentences. He has noticed that Lindsey and Sean could do with a little extra help on this, so he is looking to see if anyone else should join the "spotlight on sentences" group lesson he is planning for tomorrow.

Ongoing observation is necessary for formative evaluation. It provides important information for planning instruction.

10:20–10:30 Closure and Progress Check

Shortly before recess, Mr. Mitchell signals to the class that it is time to wind up the morning's writing workshop activities. Students put away their materials, check off completed work on the Picture Book Process chart, and prepare for recess.

Writing can be used for regulatory purposes such as keeping track.

10:30–10:45 Recess

10:45–11:05 Sustained Silent Reading (SSR)

Like many students of this age, Mr. Mitchell's class enjoys socializing at recess time. To help them unwind and settle back to work, Mr. Mitchell has scheduled sustained silent reading immediately after recess. Students enter the room and immediately take out their reading materials. Many students are reading novels. Others enjoy reading magazines that Mr. Mitchell has brought into the classroom. Some of these magazines

Encouraging students to read in a variety of genres widens their repertoires of literacy knowledge.

come from the school library and some from Mr. Mitchell's own collection. He uses silent reading time to catch up on his personal reading; doing so is personally enjoyable for himself and is also important in modelling reading for his students.

Mr. Mitchell often finds that he and his students become so engrossed in their reading that the time slips by quickly. He looks up from his page and glances at the clock, realizing that it is time for mathematics. He puts his bookmark in his magazine and asks students to put away what they are reading and get ready for math.

The learning log serves two purposes: students can use writing to clarify their thinking (the epistemic function) and to demonstrate their understanding (an informative function).

11:00–11:55 Mathematics (Review and Learning Logs)

Over the last few weeks, Mr. Mitchell's class has been learning about the associative, distributive, and commutative principles. This unit is beginning to wind down, but before starting something new, Mr. Mitchell wants to ensure that all students understand the three principles and are able to distinguish them from one another. In their learning logs, students use their own words to express their understanding. In this way, the learning log acts as a window on children's mathematical thinking.

Mr. Mitchell begins, "We've been learning about three different principles in math, and it seems most people understand what they are, but I want to make sure everyone does before we start on a new unit. Let's start with the names of the three principles."

Natane volunteers, "Commutative." Xiaoping and Raj add "Associative" and "Distributive," and Mr. Mitchell writes the three words on the board.

When students express their understanding in their own words, teachers have a better understanding of students' conceptualization.

"Right. Commutative, associative, and distributive. Now it's also important to know what these three principles mean and to be able to distinguish one from the other. What I'd like you to do is to take out your learning logs. Write today's date and the subject: Math.

Then think about how you would explain these three principles in your own words to someone who doesn't know what they are. I'll give you about five minutes to do that, and more if you need it. Now, it's really important for me to know what each of you knows, so this is time for independent writing and no talking."

The students take out their learning logs and proceed as requested. They have been writing in their learning logs throughout the year, and they know the focus is on ideas rather than on mechanics. After about ten minutes, Mr. Mitchell interrupts them. He has been walking around as they write and sees that most students are finishing up. "I think some people need about a minute more. If you haven't started writing about one of the principles yet, jot some notes down—don't worry about sentences—and we'll get ready to talk."

Ideas, not mechanics, are important in personal and epistemic writing.

Expressing thoughts can take a variety of forms.

Writing before sharing provides an opportunity for all students to be actively engaged and to have something to say in a discussion.

After a minute or so, Mr. Mitchell asks the students to form trios and share what they have written, each student in the group explaining a different principle. Next he leads a whole-class discussion. Let's listen in on some of the conversation:

Mr. Mitchell: *So, Lindsey, how do you remember that the commutative principle means that the order of the numbers in addition and multiplication doesn't affect the answer?*

Lindsey: Well, when people go to work in the city, they commute. They go back and forth to work. They start at home and they go to work and they leave work and they go home. It's back and forth and forth and back, but it's the same distance.

Teachers can learn from students as well as the other way around.

Mr. Mitchell: *Mm, that's a good way to remember, Lindsey. I'll have to remember that idea when I teach Grade 5 again next year.*

Students' thinking processes are important, not just right answers.

Talking about thinking can help develop metacognition, awareness of one's thinking.

> *So, everyone, think of an equation that shows the commutative principle.*

Notice Mr. Mitchell's response. Even though Lindsey has arrived at the correct answer, Mr. Mitchell still probes to see how she was able to remember what the commutative principle means. This provides the teacher with insight into Lindsey's thinking processes and also models her thinking strategies for the other students.

11:55–12:00 Announcements and Preparation for Lunch

As in many schools, the morning is brought to a close with noon-hour announcements broadcast over the public address system. As the announcements are made, Mr. Mitchell records key information on the chalkboard. Before the bell rings, the students put away their supplies and prepare for lunch. Several students leave to go to primary classrooms where they act as lunch monitors.

12:00–1:00 Lunch

1:00–1:50 Social Studies (The Forest)

Writing can be an effective tool for learning concepts in different curriculum areas.

In social studies, Mr. Mitchell's class has been working on a forests unit. One of the focal points of the unit has been to explore the relationships between people and forests, including the contributions forests make to people's lives and the various perspectives different groups of people have toward forests. This focus involves understanding multiple points of view, and Mr. Mitchell is sensitive to the fact that students need to understand the complexity of the issue.

Viewing can provide a stimulus for writing.

Mr. Mitchell has decided to begin today's lesson with a video on forest preservation. He integrates writing in various ways within this lesson, using it as a vehicle for students to make connections to what they already know and to understand the varying points of view on forest preservation. He realizes that viewing can be a passive activity if students are shown a film or video without preparation and thoughtful follow-up. Just as a reading lesson involves prereading and postreading, he plans previewing and postviewing activities.

Writing can be used to generate ideas before viewing and reading.

First, Mr. Mitchell asks students to make a web individually, putting the word FORESTS in the centre and recording all thoughts that come to mind. This is followed by a brief sharing with questions such as: "Who has something on their web they think other people have too?" Who has something on their web that they think is a unique idea?" and so on. Mr. Mitchell suggests that students add ideas to the web during the viewing, if they wish, but that they will have time afterward to do so as well.

Ideas can be recorded in a variety of forms.

To make viewing a more active process, students can be directed to record their ideas during and after viewing.

The students view the video, after which they are given about five minutes to record other ideas. Next, Mr. Mitchell asks them to share the ideas from their webs in small groups of about four students. This is followed by a whole-class discussion of ideas that developed in response to the video. In the process, Mr. Mitchell scaffolds the conversation so that students will see that different people have different perspectives on preserving the forest. He has prepared four charts. On the first, he writes "Roles" and records ideas students suggest, such as logger, hiker, sawmill worker, builder, and so on. On the next chart, he writes the word "Topics" and with prompts, elicits ideas from students (scaffolding to express ideas in sentences), for example: forests should be preserved for future generations; forests provide work for people, forests provide lumber for people's homes.

Writing ideas individually before sharing produces more ideas than when students brainstorm together.

Teachers can use writing to record ideas and to scaffold students' responses.

"Now suppose," says Mr. Mitchell, "that there is an argument between two groups of people about whether or not logging should be allowed in a particular area. Which people do you think would be for logging, and

Learning to write effective arguments is a challenge for students in the junior grades. Writing in role has a powerful effect on this form of writing.

which ones would be against it? And suppose that you were one of these people and you believed very much in your own point of view. How could you convince someone who disagrees with you of your point of view?"

The students animatedly suggest protest marches, sit-ins, chaining oneself to a tree, and so on. Mr. Mitchell nods at all of these ideas, but then adds, "But suppose you couldn't do any of these things, you could only use words, then how would you persuade them?"

Before students engage in writing, they need to understand the purpose of the activity.

As the students suggest writing letters to the premier, making a speech on television, composing protest songs, and so on, Mr. Mitchell records these ideas on another chart that he first labels "Forms."

Writing in role helps students learn to write from a perspective other than their own.

"Now what I would like you to do today is to become one of these people (points to the Roles chart)—a forester, a hiker, or whatever—choose whomever you want to be. And think about how that person feels and how he or she could express personal ideas and feelings to someone else. Think about who would be your audience—it could be one of the people here [points to the charts] or someone else. Today, I want you to think seriously about this and get started on your plan. You won't have time to finish today, but you should be able to get a good start. You might want to start by making another web, or you might want to look at the web you have already made and add some more ideas to that. After you have thought of some ideas on your own, you may want to get together with someone else to share ideas. Some of you may have time today to start a draft. We'll also spend some time drafting tomorrow, and then we'll do some role-play so you can try your ideas out with each other."

In the early stages, students need to be in a state of relaxed attentiveness so that they can focus on generating ideas.

Teachers need to allow for different learning and thinking styles.

There is a buzz of excitement as students set to work. Some students start writing down ideas right away. Others sit and think, but Mr. Mitchell knows that allowing ideas to percolate is an important part of writing. He

Some students need more scaffolding before they write, especially ESL students.

also knows, however, that some students may need more talk time before they write, so he circulates around the room, paying particular attention to those students who are not yet fluent in English, to provide more help and encouragement if needed.

Near the end of the period, Mr. Mitchell signals that social studies time is almost over. He does a quick spot check to see how students are progressing and then asks them to take the next few minutes to finish up and prepare for art.

1:50–2:50 Art (Illustrating Storybooks)

The students began work on their art projects in the last art lesson, so as soon as they finish the social studies and writing activity, they go to the art storage area and retrieve their projects. Although each student is creating an individual book, they are working in groups to share materials and help one another.

Audience is an important concept in both art and writing.

To help students gain a sense of audience by becoming aware of what appeals to young children, Mr. Mitchell had brought in a number of quality children's books representing various genres. The class read the books and through discussion identified the characteristics of quality children's literature. These characteristics were recorded on chart paper, which was posted so that students could refer back to it as they needed. Mr. Mitchell then brought in books featuring a number of respected illustrators of children's books that represented different media and techniques. The students were familiar with most of the techniques (e.g., watercolour painting and line drawing), but not with Barbara Reid's use of modelling clay as depicted in *The New Baby Calf* (Chase, 1984), so Mr. Mitchell had students work on a clay pictures project before they selected the media for the illustrations of their books.

Writing down ideas makes them concrete so that they can be revisited and reviewed.

Writing and art are logically integrated through children's literature.

Kwan-Sui, Raj, Lotte, and Manjit are using a collage technique similar to that used by author/illustrator Ezra Jack Keats (1962) in *A Snowy Day.* Steve and his group are shaping modelling clay, busily put the finishing touches on an illustration. They will use a Polaroid camera to photograph the illustrations and then paste the photographs on the cover of their books. Meanwhile, two groups—Ramon's and Maria's—are using watercolour paints and felt pens to create scenes similar to Ted Harrison's bright colours and curved lines in *A Northern Alphabet* (Harrison, 1982). Amy and her group have chosen line drawings for their books, while the students in Eduardo's group are creating pictures with coloured pencils, similar to those done by Stephen Gammell in *The Relatives Came* (Rylant, 1985).

Many of the principles for effective writing instruction apply equally to teaching art.

While the students work on their projects, Mr. Mitchell circulates from group to group, monitoring progress and offering encouragement and suggestions. While he has previously demonstrated each of the techniques being used today, he also reteaches concepts or techniques when needed. He notices that several students in Amy's group are not using shadows to give their illustrations a three-dimensional look, so he again demonstrates how to achieve this effect.

Writing can be used for regulatory purposes. The classroom workplace provides many opportunities for regulatory writing.

2:50–3:00 Closure and Homework Books

Before the students leave for home, Mr. Mitchell reviews the day with them. Students talk about the best part of the day and how they are progressing with their writing and illustrating of the storybooks. Finally, Mr. Mitchell reminds the students to take out their homework books and record the homework and home study assignments that are written on the board and to make sure that they take whatever textbooks, and so on, they need to do their homework. As the school day draws to a close, students pack up their belongings, organize their homework materials, and get ready to go home.

Keeping a homework book is an example of regulatory writing. It is also a form of communication with parents.

Teacher Decision-Making

Each day in each classroom is unique, yet there are commonalities in what each teacher is trying to achieve. Every day teachers make hundreds of decisions about what to do in their classrooms; Lena Chan and Dave Mitchell base their decisions on the principles of writing and guidelines for practice established in Chapters 1 and 2 and on the concepts described in Chapters 3 and 4.

An important aspect of the teacher's decision-making is the *integration of curriculum*. However, it is important to realize that not everything can be integrated in a pedagogically sound manner. Likewise, not all curriculum areas can be included in a given day. Because language in its various forms is central to learning, I have shown examples of using language, and writing in particular, in the context of the classroom workplace, in language arts, and across the curriculum. None of the purposes of writing demonstrated here were superfluous or contrived; they were all authentic and integral to the learning situation.

Teachers need to plan their days yet allow for *flexibility*. Sometimes unexpected incidents occur that the teacher perceives as an interruption to the plan, yet the reality of classroom life is that these incidents must be dealt with. For example, when a group of children become involved in a conflict during recess, time often needs to be taken to help them resolve their differences. Writing can be used even at these times, as discussed in Chapter 3. Whatever the level we teach, we should strive for *balance* and *variety*. I have tried to demonstrate how teachers can structure opportunities for learning so that students have chances to work independently, in pairs, in small groups, and in large groups. Notice too that the children in both classes experienced opportunities for choice in their writing as well as having to meet particular requirements or "must-do's." Often the best way to manage this is to allow children choices within a range of options. For example, Lena Chan's students choose what reading and writing activities to do in Reading and Writing Time, but they do not have a choice of not reading or writing. As we move up the grades, the pressure of covering curriculum content increases, and this often results in teachers denying their students opportunities for choice. However, since the range of abilities widens as we work with older grades, we still need to be flexible.

In the remainder of this book I pick up threads introduced in this chapter, teaching writing as process (Chapter 6), increasing students' repertoires of forms of representation and genre (Chapter 7), and integrating assessment and evaluation with learning and writing (Chapter 8).

Reflections on the Chapter

Think about/talk about/write about:

Principles into Practice

- Use Figure 2.6, From Principles of Writing to Practice, to find specific examples in this chapter of each principle as it is put into practice.

Classroom Contexts for Writing and Learning

- Examine both classrooms described in this chapter to see how writing is integrated as part of classroom workplace literacy.
- Compare and contrast the ways in which the two teachers integrate writing within the language arts and across the curriculum.

Learning Experiences

- Analyze the learning activities in both classrooms, using the criteria for designing writing/learning activities (provided in Chapter 4).
- Examine how each teacher provides instruction: the methods used, grouping for instruction, and how assessment and evaluation are integrated.
- Discuss how the teachers provide support for students in their learning and writing.
- Explain how the two classrooms incorporate personal and social aspects of writing and learning.
- Compare and contrast how the two teachers implement writing workshop in their classrooms.

REFERENCES AND FURTHER READING

Baratta-Lorton, M. (1976). *Mathematics their way: An activity-centered mathematics program for early childhood education.* Menlo Park, CA: Addison-Wesley.

Chase, E. (1984). *The new baby calf.* Toronto: Scholastic.

Early, M. (1989). Using key visuals to aid ESL students' comprehension of content classroom texts. *Reading Canada Lecture,* 7(4) 202–12.

Harrison, T. (1982). *A northern alphabet.* Montreal: Tundra Books.

Keats, E. (1962). *A snowy day.* New York: Viking.

Miller, E. (1967). *Mousekin finds a friend.* Englewood Cliffs, NJ: Prentice-Hall.

Peers, J. (1995). *Free stuff for kids, 13th ed.* Toronto: Stoddart.

Rylant, C. (1985). *The relatives came.* New York: Bradbury Press.

CHAPTER 6

Learning the Craft of Writing: Processes, Strategies, and Skills

CHAPTER OBJECTIVES

To discuss a process approach to teaching writing

To provide strategies for fostering writing fluency and enhancing meaning-making

To discuss issues surrounding the teaching and learning of skills

To present strategies for integrating skills instruction for spelling, punctuation, syntax ("grammar"), and usage

To explore ways of celebrating writing through publishing and presenting

PERSONAL REFLECTION

As I was working on this book, I came across an interesting description of Athena, Goddess of Wisdom for the ancient Greeks. Athena, who presided over battle strategy during war and over the arts and crafts during peace, was often depicted with a spear in one hand and a spindle in the other.

As Goddess of Crafts, Athena was involved with making things that were both useful and aesthetically pleasing. She was most noted for her skills as a weaver, in which hands and mind must work together. To make a tapestry or a weaving, a woman must design and plan what she will do and then, row by row, methodically create it. This approach is an expression of the Athena archetype, which emphasizes foresight, planning, mastery of a craft, and patience (Bolen, 1984, p. 81).

While at first glance battle strategist and weaver roles seem very different, on further reflection I can see that they are similar in many ways. I also believe that their common characteristics come into play in writing.

Something to think about

Consider Athena—wise woman, strategist, craftsperson, and weaver—and how her attributes are manifested in the process of writing.

I use this discussion of Athena to segue into this chapter because I think it captures the essence of the craft of writing. During the early years of my teaching, writing in school was looked upon either as a creative process or a mechanical one. Emphasizing the creative aspect meant that teachers should encourage children to express their ideas in writing. So that I would not inhibit my students' expressiveness, I thought this meant that I should accept whatever they wrote during creative writing periods, which were scheduled on Fridays. However, during other periods in which writing took place, I made sure to correct everything the children wrote with a red pen—and as a conscientious teacher I took care to find every error.

Now I see that the way I taught writing then was not effective, either for encouraging creative expression or for mastering conventions of print.

Furthermore, writing is not a case of creativity *or* correctness: it is both. If writers' ideas are brilliant, but no one can decipher them, then their brilliance will go unrecognized. If what is written is mechanically correct but has little meaning or purpose, then it is not worth reading. A teacher's task is to address both creativity and conventions in meaningful, appropriate ways. In this chapter, I focus on teaching writing as process, an approach that enables students to enlarge their repertoires of strategies and skills for effective writing.

The Writing Cycle: Prewriting to Presenting

Although the term *writing process* is often used, in reality, there is no single process of writing, but rather, many processes that vary with individual writers, purposes, and contexts of writing. I prefer the term **process writing** because it emphasizes process without implying a single, unvarying procedure. Process writing is an approach to teaching writing based on knowledge about how children learn and strategies writers employ in various contexts and genres. Although process writing is often divided into stages—prewriting, writing, and postwriting are common—it is important to remember that writing

REFLECTION

It was not until I found out about the process approach to writing that I learned how to balance meaning-making and mechanics. At the time I "discovered" process writing, mechanics were emphasized in school and many educators were concerned that this "new" process approach implied a pendulum swing back to the era of creativity in writing and a concomitant neglect of skills. Thanks to people such as Donald Graves (1978, 1983) and Lucy Calkins (1986), among others, the focus of writing shifted to meaning-making and skills began to be seen as part of writing processes. In other words, skills would be taught as students needed them, in the context of their own writing, and as aids to making and communicating meaning rather than as ends in themselves.

Think about your own school experiences of writing. What was emphasized? What were considered to be the skills of writing? Did your experiences vary throughout your school years? How?

is recursive and integrated rather than a series of linear, discrete steps. We must also keep in mind that there are differences in composing style that vary with individual writers, functions, genres, and contexts. Nevertheless, in working with young writers, it is helpful to consider a developmentally ordered sequence beginning with the development of *fluency*, followed by *clarity* and *coherence*, and finally, *correctness*. For example, when we begin a piece of writing, we need to focus on ideas, so worrying about mechanics at this point is inappropriate—it detracts from our purpose, impedes the flow of ideas, and inhibits expression. Spelling, punctuation, and other conventions of writing do take on importance when we prepare a piece for publication, especially if the intended reader is unknown to us or if the context is formal.

Many teachers find it helpful to use a particular sequence of instructional steps or stages as a guide for addressing various aspects of writing. So that teachers and students can talk about writing processes, they need to learn and use a specific set of vocabulary, a **metalanguage.** You will find that there are many variations in how various terms are used. So that you will understand the discussion in this chapter and the ways in which I use particular words, here is a short list of definitions:

- **Prewriting**—getting started; thinking about what you want to say; generating ideas; planning.
- **Drafting**—putting ideas into words, shaping ideas, or discovering what you want to say.
- **Editing**—revising; reviewing and reworking ideas and words for meaning, clarity, coherence, and/or effect.
- **Proofreading**—checking what has been written for conventions or mechanics (e.g., spelling, punctuation, omissions, usage, syntax).
- **Publishing**—making a final copy to share with others.
- **Presenting**—sharing and celebrating the writing.

In your own classroom, you may want to use different words than the ones I use. Do keep in mind that regardless of what terms you choose, you need to be explicit with your students about how you use them and what they mean. In many instances, terminology is specified in provincial curriculum guides. Whatever the case, it is helpful if everyone on the same school staff uses the terms consistently to minimize confusion for students.

In classrooms where writing is fostered and where students have opportunities to share their writing, particular topics and genres can become con-

Something to think about

What does the following developmentally ordered sequence imply for the teaching of writing?

↓

Fluency—facility; ease in getting down ideas or a ready flow of words

Clarity—being clear or precise, making sense; and **coherence**—being consistent, logically or naturally connected

Correctness—meeting conventions of Standard Written English

tagious. For example, if one student writes and shares a story about dinosaurs, other students may be motivated to write their own dinosaur stories. In this way, presenting is a stimulus for prewriting. Similarly, teachers can capitalize on what students accomplish in one writing activity by encouraging them to develop ideas further or to write sequels. Thus, steps or stages can instead form an ongoing cycle (Figure 6.1). For this reason, many teachers use the term **writing cycle** or **authoring cycle** (Harste, Short, & Burke, 1988)—one writing activity flowing into another.

Regardless of whether we think of stages or cycles, it is important to keep in mind that our intent is not to take a lock-step approach to writing. Every piece of writing need not be edited, proofread, or published. Because fluency and positive attitudes are important goals, it is necessary to have students do lots of short, informal, first-draft writing. In the primary years, students might publish perhaps one piece in ten; in the junior grades, perhaps one in five. Thinking about the purpose of the writing will help teachers and students determine whether or not they should continue to work through a piece and carry it through to publication and presenting.

Something to think about

Which goals—fluency, clarity, coherence, and correctness—are the major focus of each of the instructional stages: prewriting, drafting, editing, proofreading, publishing, and presenting?

Figure 6.1 Writing Process or Cycle

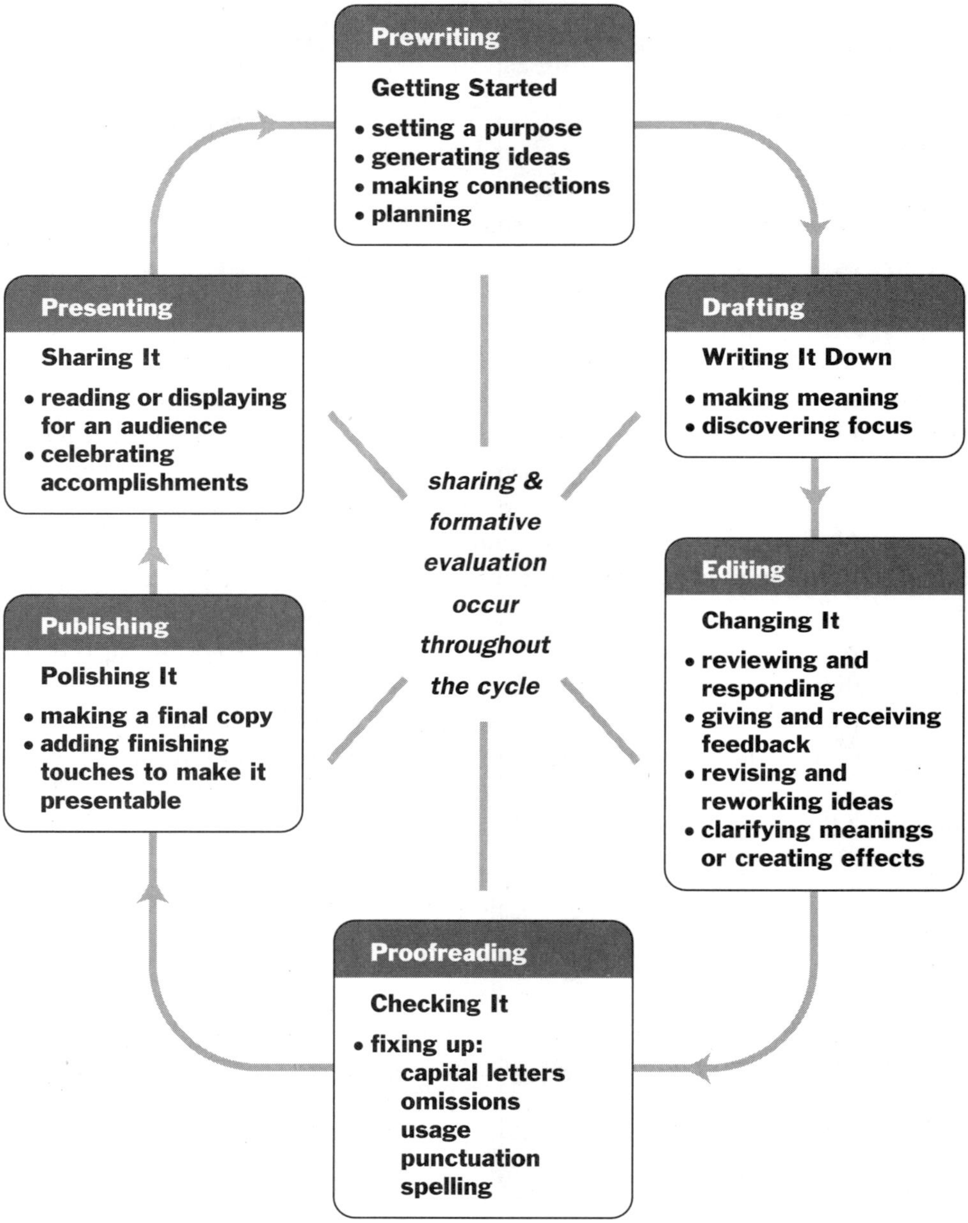

> **Something to think about**
>
> Think about the purposes or functions of writing (you may want to refer to Figure 1.2 in Chapter 1). With what writing tasks might students proceed to publish and present?

The Writing Folder

When teachers use a process approach to writing, students write a lot more than in traditional classrooms, so it is important to think about how to manage and organize students' written products. Students should have a writing folder, a large envelope, or a writing notebook in which to put their drafts. I prefer notebooks for specific purposes such as journals and learning logs. For all other drafts I prefer folders. Some primary teachers prefer large kraft envelopes. The very fact that all writing is placed in the folder is an indication that the writing is valued enough to be saved. The folder keeps all the students' writing in one place and is a valuable source for evaluation and reporting. (Remind students to make sure their name, the date, and a DRAFT stamp is on each piece.) Not all pieces of writing will be carried through to the publication stage (some work begun will not be worth completing). From time to time, students select one draft from the folder to carry through the process to publication or to practise a specific proofreading or editing skill. Sometimes drafts rejected at one time for editing may at a later date spark an idea for further writing. It is a good idea to ask students to write double-spaced to make future changes easier.

Process Writing in the Primary Years (Kindergarten–Grade 3)

The major goals in the primary years include positive attitudes toward writing as an activity and to oneself as a writer, metalinguistic concepts about the nature and purpose of writing, and fluency.

Most of the writing primary students do involves prewriting and drafting followed by sharing. Prewriting is particularly important for younger children, for students who are experiencing some sort of difficulty (such as a learning disability), or for students not yet fluent in English (or the standard dialect). The more time these young writers spend engaged in first-hand experiences and in generating and talking about ideas, the more easily their ideas will flow when they attempt to put them on paper. It is also helpful for these young writers to interact with an adult who helps them verbalize their ideas and who accepts and extends what they say. Recording key words and phrases on a chart or chalkboard can help them make connections between oral language and written language. Making connections between other forms of expression is one of the major emphases in the primary years. While it is true that speech and writing are different in many ways, in the early years of school we highlight the similarities between them.

Because young children's writing is not conventional in mechanics, many parents and teachers believe that the best way to get young children writing is to focus first on conventions such as spelling, printing, and punctuation. However, this belief is unfounded. Emphasizing mechanics, especially at the drafting stage, is one of the best ways to impede the development of fluency. And, as discussed later in this chapter, graphophonic knowledge and skills are best learned in the context of meaningful writing activity and when children are developmentally ready.

Something to think about

Revisit Figure 2.3 in Chapter 2 and review the characteristics of primary children (beginning, emergent, and developing writers). Think about the kinds of experiences that would foster their writing development.

KINDERGARTEN CORNER

Writing Processes

The major goals in kindergarten are to develop positive attitudes toward writing and toward oneself as a writer and to develop metalinguistic concepts about the nature and purpose of print. Kindergarten children need to talk and to have their ideas recorded in print so that they can learn about the connections between oral and written language. They should also have many opportunities to express their ideas through a variety of media, including writing in whatever ways they are able.

Idea Box:
Children Read Their Own Writing

Sometimes it is hard to read what a young child has written. Having children read their own writing builds their self-esteem and also helps others to know what they have written. I tell children that I really enjoy hearing authors read their own work because it is powerful, it helps me to hear the writer's voice, and sounds the way the author intended. I also say to children, "Tell me about your picture." I have learned to do these things because there have been times when a child has been upset that I did not read his or her work correctly or when I have made a faux pas such as saying, "Wow, that's a great horse" when a child has drawn some other creature!

Primary children need many opportunities to express their ideas in writing without worrying about correctness. Just as we celebrate children's early attempts at talking, we need to celebrate their writing. One of the best ways to do this is to have children publish and share orally what they have written. Teachers and parents need to have developmentally appropriate expectations for children's published work—*published does not mean perfect.*

Process Writing in the Junior Grades (Grades 4–7)

In the junior years, positive attitudes and fluency continue to be major goals of the writing program. As students move through the junior grades, there is an increasing emphasis on clarity, coherence, and correctness. A central focus is on helping students learn to adapt writing to suit particular purposes, audiences, and contexts in the language arts and across the curriculum.

In the junior grades, teachers build on the foundations established in the primary years. It is important to keep in mind that the gap between more able and less able writers widens as students grow older, and many of the experiences suggested for the primary years are appropriate for older students too. This is especially so for students who are not developmentally advanced, who have learning difficulties, or who are not yet fluent English speakers. Positive attitudes and fluency are still major goals in Grades 4–7, so much so that many teachers, myself among them, believe it is important to spend several

> **Something to think about**
>
> Revisit Figure 2.3 (Chapter 2) to review the characteristics of children in the junior grades (developing, consolidating, and expanding writers). Think about the kinds of experiences that would foster their writing development.

months at the beginning of the school year creating a positive climate and doing lots of short, first-draft writing. Once positive attitudes and fluency are established, teachers introduce editing.

Editing is important because it is the heart of writing craftsmanship. Acquiring skills in editing is a lengthy process and requires a lot of scaffolding and guidance on the part of the teacher. It is very important for the teacher of junior students to keep in mind that our focus should be on the learning process rather than on the finished product and the emphasis should be on clarity and coherence. Because students are becoming mostly conventional in spelling in the junior years, it is appropriate at this stage to focus on proofreading skills. *However, even in the junior grades, published work may not be perfect.*

In the junior grades, the writing demands placed upon students increase. For example, they are expected to write in a wider range of genres across curriculum areas and to become more skilled in the various aspects of writing. I have found teachers of junior grades to have widely varying beliefs and expectations about students' writing. Some teachers assume that their students know little or nothing and approach them as blank slates; others expect students to have mastered all or most of the conventions of Standard Written English. Neither position is true—in all elementary classrooms you will find a range of abilities. This makes the teaching of writing complex and demanding since it is the teacher's role to enable students to learn and write in developmentally and culturally appropriate ways, and to provide challenge and support in ways that meet diverse needs.

Fostering Fluency

There are two key ideas to keep in mind that relate to fluency: having (or realizing that you have) something to write about, and feeling free to express your

> **Something to think about**
>
> How do you feel about displaying students' work that is not perfectly correct? Why? How would you handle a situation where a junior student has produced an interesting piece of work that contains nonstandard spellings, even after proofreading and correcting?

ideas. In my early days of teaching, I thought that children needed to be given what I called "story starters" to get them writing. Now I realize that children have many, many ideas to write about; what they need are strategies for accessing what they know. But just as important, or maybe more so, is the freedom to write without worrying about everything having to come out perfectly—in other words, the right to be wrong. We have all heard, and probably experienced, what is known as "writer's block," for few people are able to write on demand. Young writers can be taught a variety of prewriting strategies so that when they begin writing, their ideas will flow more freely. As well, they need to be reassured that spelling, printing, and other mechanical aspects of writing are not prominent in the beginning stages. A process approach to writing fosters fluency by beginning with a focus on ideas: prewriting, generating ideas; and drafting, writing ideas down without concern for mechanics.

Prewriting

Young writers need to learn a repertoire of prewriting strategies. One reason for this is that different people find different strategies effective or personally useful, and unless they have tried out a number of techniques, they don't know what works for them. Another reason is that different writing functions and genres make varying demands on the writer. For example, if I want to write a story I might make a storyboard or storyline map; if I want to write an article for a research journal, then I prepare by collecting information and making notes. In this chapter, I introduce prewriting in a global way with a focus on teaching children strategies for developing, generating, and accessing ideas. In the following chapter I discuss prewriting as it relates to specific genres.

Topics and ideas for writing come from a writer's experience or imagination, a personal real-life event, or a shared experience designed by the teacher.

REFLECTION

Teachers and student teachers I have worked with have often asked me about how to encourage students to write more, especially in journals. When I probe to find out about when and how journals are used in their classrooms, it seems that problems occur when students are asked to write in their journals without a chance to talk first. I have found that getting kids to write is no problem when I "prime them" first. For instance, like Ms. Chan in Chapter 5, I begin the school day with a morning meeting. During this time, there is much discussion and as children talk I record ideas on the board. If I want the children to write in their journals that day, before they leave the meeting area I review the ideas on the board and invite them to write about those topics, if they wish. For example, if one student talked about her soccer team, I might suggest that some of the children might want to write about their own sports activities. I ask the children to think for a minute about what they might want to write about and then to turn to a neighbour and talk about it. Instead of having the children all leave at once, I ask who is ready to start writing and send those children off. I suggest that those who need more talk time stay behind, and we chat a few minutes more until their ideas start to percolate.

I think another problem factor with journal writing is that it's overused. Journals are an excellent way to start the year and to use from time to time afterward, but in many classes students are expected to write in their journals every day throughout the school year and they get tired of it. I think it is better to use journals as one writing activity among many and to offer them as one option in Writing Workshop time.

REFLECTION

I have learned many lessons from children. One of the most important ones was from a little boy in Grade 3 who told me that it was important to get his ideas down quickly even though his printing might be messy "because ideas are like butterflies. If you don't catch them quickly, they will just fly away!"

Think back to the discussion of classroom climate in Chapter 3 and how the ideas presented there relate to fostering fluency.

Something to think about

Think back to what you read in Chapter 4 about shared experiences and designing writing/learning activities. Consider how the ideas presented there relate to prewriting.

Because one of the best foundations for writing is a multitude of hands-on, minds-on activities, much of what teachers design for learning curriculum content serves also as meaningful prewriting experiences. As mentioned earlier, we begin with first-hand experiences whenever we can; where this is not possible, we provide secondary experiences through listening, reading, and viewing.

Input can also be furnished through patterns or models. In the primary years, many teachers use patterned writing to get children started. One way to do this is to use frame sentences, such as "I can _______. I can _______. But I can't _________." Another approach is using a patterned book such as *Brown Bear, Brown Bear, What Do You See?* by Bill Martin Jr. (1983) or *The Important Book* by Margaret Wise Brown (1949). First, the teacher reads the story aloud and then the children write their own versions using the author's pattern. Using a pattern as a stimulus for writing on occasion is interesting to children, especially when it is presented as a form of linguistic play. Many teachers like patterning because they believe it helps children feel successful.

There is, however, a downside to using patterns and models. While this approach furnishes a framework for the children, provides standard spellings for most of the words they write, and promotes a polished-looking product, it can be overused. Children may come to rely on a pattern and find it hard to write without one. The overuse of patterns can also lead to stilted, monotonous writing. A parallel occurs in the junior grades with the use of models for writing. If we want children to develop fluency, then we must provide them with many opportunities to do free-flow writing—in other words, to express their ideas in writing as they would do in their talk. Hillocks (1986) discovered in his meta-analysis of research on writing that the study of models, imitation of patterns, or reliance on rules is ineffective.

For me, learning about the importance of prior knowledge and how to help students access it has revolutionized the way I approach teaching. Here are some generic prewriting strategies I use frequently with students of all ages:

Activity:
Visualization

Visualization techniques are effective for helping young writers exercise their imaginations. Rather than showing children the illustrations when you read a story, you can stop at various points to ask them to create pictures in their minds or make "mental movies." Another way is through **guided visualization.** Here is an activity I used for Remembrance Day.

I had the children think about a peaceful place, make a picture of it in their minds, and put themselves in their pictures. I asked them to think about what they could see, smell, hear, and so on. I also had them focus on what they were doing and saying to make their world peaceful. After we had done this, I had the children draw and write about what they had imagined.

Here are some pointers when using guided visualization:

- Have children close their eyes (turn off the lights if you wish).
- Speak slowly and quietly, in a calm yet serious tone.
- Pause sufficiently so that children have time to create their images.
- Use the five senses in your prompts.

I know from personal experience that guided visualization can produce vivid images and ideas. When I was in Grade 5, my music teacher, Miss Parsons, did a guided visualization as she played Smetana's *The Moldau*, a tone poem about the river's journey from its beginnings as a spring bubbling out of the ground until it reaches the sea. More than forty years later, whenever I hear that piece of music those same images come to mind and I remember that teacher!

- **Brainstorming**—thinking together and sharing ideas; some ideas are better than others, but no idea should be rejected in this activity (the more ideas there are, the better the chance there will be some good ones).
- **Think, pair, share**—as discussed in Chapter 4, students think individually first, share with partners, and finally share with a larger group (or the whole class); more ideas are generated by a group when people think individually first.
- **Word banks/caches/lists**—word collections can be general (e.g., Halloween words) or in categories (e.g., for fairy tales: characters, places, magic things) (see Figure 6.2).

- **Webbing, clustering, or semantic mapping**—a form of brainstorming that starts with the topic in the centre; ideas are added to the centre or to each other (shown in Figure 6.3); connections can be made in various ways, but I think it is important to make the link the way the student who contributed the idea wants it. At the end of the activity, the class can suggest cross-connections and more lines can be added.
- **KWL (Know-Wonder-Learned)**—using a three-column format (see Figure 6.4) or three-coloured web, students generate what they know and what they wonder about a topic; the learned part is added later. (Students use one colour for *Know,* a second colour for *Wonder,* and a third for *Learned.*)

PERSONAL REFLECTION

I often find that good ideas pop into my head when I am doing something other than writing, especially when I am relaxed. Most of my best ideas seem to come when I am running. I used to cross my fingers (literally) and hope I could remember them until I got home. Now I use an idea I borrowed from my brother, Billy Mitchell. Because he writes all his own material for his stand-up comedy routines, he keeps a notebook and pen in a fanny pack that he wears all the time. That way when he gets the germ of an idea he can write it down immediately. Now when I run I wear a fanny pack with a notebook and pen inside for idea-keeping on the run.

Do you have particular ways of idea-keeping? When and how do you use them?

Activity:
Idea-Keeping

There are a variety of ways children can record ideas they might want to write about. They can generate a list or web of ideas at the beginning of the school year; for example: things I am interested in, things I like to do, things I wonder about. Or at the beginning of a unit, they can generate ideas related to the topic. Ideas can also be kept in a writing folder, a small notebook, or inside the cover of a journal.

Figure 6.2 Word Bank, Cache, or List

Fairy Tale Places

kingdom
palace
castle
land far away
woods
forest
cottage
village
market

Drafting

Even if one has engaged in a prewriting activity, drafting is always an exploratory process and tentative in nature. We don't formulate ideas completely in our heads and then write them down. Instead, we construct meaning through the process of writing. Drafting is a process of discovery and the emphasis is on ideas—what writers say, not how they say it. Young writers need to be encouraged to take risks, knowing that their ideas can be reworked later. They also need reassurance that ideas will flow more freely in a state of alert relaxation rather than when they are forced. As well as fluency, we want to enable students to gain enthusiasm and confidence as writers.

Figure 6.3 Web, Cluster, or Semantic Map

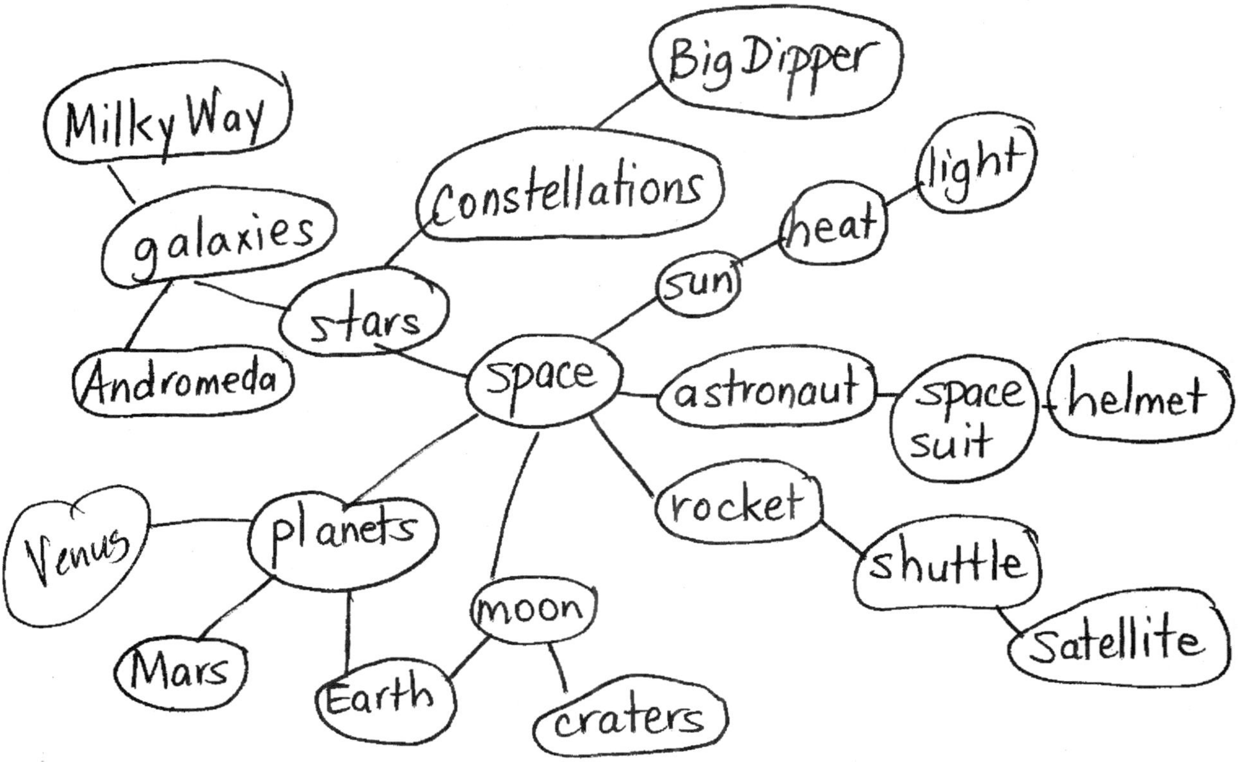

Figure 6.4 KWL Charts

What we know about space:	What we wonder about space:	What we learned about space:
– There are planets. – Earth is our planet. – The sun is very big and hot. – Rockets can go into space. – There are millions of stars.	– How many planets are in our solar system? – Is there life on other planets? – Do other planets have moons?	– There are 9 planets in our solar system. – The Earth is the third planet from the sun. – Our galaxy is the Milky Way. – Our sun is a star.

How do we develop fluent, uninhibited writing and what some people call a "spelling conscience" at the same time? One approach is to encourage students to use **placeholder spelling** (Wilde, 1992), that is, to write a word the way they think it is spelled, and to mark it, for example, by underlining or circling. In this way, the writer's ideas continue to flow, but at the same time when they reread what they have written, they will be reminded to check for the standard spellings of marked words.

Something to think about

Recall what you know about children's development in writing, referring to Figure 2.3 (Chapter 2) if needed, and consider at what stages of development teachers should encourage invented spelling without concern for correctness, and at what developmental stages they should encourage placeholder spelling and checking for standard spelling.

Activity:
Informing Parents about Drafting

While we may reassure students that it is ideas that matter, they may receive a different message when they take drafts home. I have found parents to be most supportive when they understand why we don't mark all errors or correct every piece of work. It is part of a teacher's job to inform parents about teaching practices. Here are the ways I help parents understand the nature and purpose of drafting:

- I teach students to use a DRAFT stamp on their drafts. Self-inking DRAFT, EDITED, and PROOFREAD stamps (X-stamper brand) are available in many office supply stores.
- I send home a newsletter that explains drafting and introduces the use of the DRAFT stamp at the beginning of the school year.
- I stamp DRAFT on the covers of books such as journals and learning logs and paste an explanatory letter (see Chapter 3, Figure 3.3) inside the front cover.

Voice

An important goal of the writing program is developing a writing **voice** or personal style of expression. Voice develops when students have opportunities to write daily, although much of this writing is informal and never gets beyond the first draft stage. The voice of a writer comes through more effectively when the topic selected is one with which the writer is personally involved—from personal experience, things the writer cares about, or things the writer knows about. Choosing one's own topic for writing leads to greater quantity and quality of writing, especially for boys in the primary grades (Graves, 1975). Writing begins to feel "natural" when we engage in it regularly and frequently, when hands and minds are continually exercised.

Free-Writing

Free-writing activities are effective for developing fluency and voice. In free-writing, the writer should write quickly but without rushing, not stopping to revise or check spelling. This technique is intended to help writers turn off their "inner critics" or "internal editors" and become less inhibited. Compulsive, premature editing not only makes writing hard, it often makes it stilted. There are several variations of free-writing:

- **Free-writing** is a nonstop free flow of words. The writer turns off his or her internal editor and reflective self and writes nonstop. The product is not important here; sometimes the result will be good, but sometimes it will be garbage!
- **Focused free writing** fixes the writer's attention on a particular topic or idea (i.e., everyone is asked to write about the same topic), but like free-writing, encourages the writer's unique perception and voice.
- **Sustained writing** is free-writing or focused free-writing that is sustained for a specified time limit. Sometime referred to as SWAT (Sustained Writing All Together [teacher too]), it is a parallel to Sustained Silent Reading (SSR).

KINDERGARTEN CORNER

Using Unlined Paper

Kindergarten children should be encouraged to write without worrying about neat printing and staying on the lines. In kindergarten and the first half of Grade 1 (and longer, if needed), children should be provided with unlined paper. This gives them one less thing to wrestle with and allows them to more easily weave writing and drawing as they compose.

Developing Clarity and Coherence through Editing

Editing is **re-vision**—taking a step back from what has been written in order to see it more clearly. It is not a simple matter of making the writing better for an audience, but of developing ideas further and clarifying meaning. Published authors usually meet with an editor or group of editors who go over their work and make suggestions for improvement, and this is the approach I advocate in the classroom. Research indicates that improved student writing can result when students share their writing with their peers and with the teacher (Hillocks, 1986). However, students do not become successful at giving or receiving editorial feedback automatically or quickly. They must be carefully taught, and the learning process takes time.

In order to accept the idea of changing their writing, students need a climate of trust and acceptance and a background of sharing and talking about ideas and language, and their fluency and confidence must be established. *It is unwise to rush into editing too soon,* whether it be with children who are not yet developmentally ready (most primary children, for example) or too early in the school year. In process writing, there are two aspects of editing: reviewing or responding to what has been written, and making changes to the content or ideas. I advocate separating these two phases for instructional purposes.

Research shows that in the junior grades (Grades 4–7), editing is the most important instructional phase of the writing process. For these students, more learning and growth in writing ability can occur through editing than through any other stage in the writing process. Primary children, for the most part, are not able to separate themselves from their writing sufficiently to make any major editorial changes. However, even very young writers can begin to focus on writing to look for the parts they like best. This critiquing lays the foundation for revising in the later grades. Some primary children are able to make changes in their writing by adding more (to begin with, they usually add it at the end of a piece), by substituting a more interesting word, or by adding a describing word. Primary teachers should keep in mind that editing is *not* a major emphasis, but it is appropriate to gently encourage children who are interested in and capable of making minor editorial changes to do so.

Responding to Children's Writing

When we respond to children's writing, we need to keep first and foremost in our minds the focus on the learning process rather than on the written product. When writers are taking risks in their learning, they will be working in their zones of proximal development, and this means they may make errors.

REFLECTION

When I first began to use a process approach to writing, I found it very hard not to correct children's spelling or punctuation. Because writing is visual, it is hard to look past errors to see children's ideas. I have found several things that help me get beyond this:

- I leave the pencil in the child's hands.
- I leave my pen on my desk.
- I sit on my hands or put my hands in my pockets so I can't take over the child's work.
- I ask the child to read her or his writing to me.

How do you feel when someone responds to your writing? How do you like people to respond? Why?

No errors means staying with what is known and safe, what one can already do, so errors are often signs of growth. Children learn to respond to one another's writing to a great extent from the modelling of adults. Here are some guidelines for responding to children's writing:

- Respond to content and ideas, not mechanics—this will come later.
- Be specific.

- Begin with positive feedback only in the early stages (in the primary grades, or with students in the junior years who have not yet developed fluency and confidence).
- When you introduce the idea of making changes, begin with a positive comment and then make only one suggestion for a change.
- As writers become experienced, you can make a few more suggestions, but keep these focused and related to the same concept.

Peer Response

Start simply and slowly. It takes patience and repeated modelling to help students understand the editing process. I recommend that techniques and strategies be introduced initially to the whole class. Later on, students can practise and apply their skills in small groups. It is wise to establish a few basic rules before you begin. These should include the following:

- Comments should be constructive and positive. Negative or unkind comments about someone's work are unacceptable because they may destroy a writer's confidence.
- Comments should be directed to content, to the ideas the writer is trying to express.
- Strengths of the writing should always be identified first. Only then should suggestions for improvement be made.

I have found Authors' Circle (see the Activity box on page 178 to be a powerful vehicle for creating a community of writers and modelling appropriate responses. I introduce Authors' Circle early in the school year along with Writing Clubs (described in Chapter 4 and illustrated in Chapter 5). Once students are familiar with writer response, I have them form authors' mini-circles. These are groups of four to five students (the teacher is not included) who take turns sharing and responding to the writing. Here's a management tip: group members should put the pieces they are sharing face down on the desk or the floor; the only one to have a paper in his or her hands is the author who is reading aloud at the time. This makes for more effective listening.

KINDERGARTEN CORNER

Sharing Circles

Authors' Circles can begin in kindergarten. I prefer to call them Sharing Circles and expand them to include all creations made by the children, including drawings, paintings, writing, three-dimensional constructions, and so on. In responding, be specific and stick to positive comments only. Help children learn to respond to one another by asking focusing questions such as, "Why do you like the elf in the picture best?"

Writers of all ages need opportunities to share what they have written with others.

Editing Conferences

Once students have learned to respond to one another and are accustomed to the idea of suggestions for making changes, they need to learn how to examine

Activity:
Authors' Circle

Authors' Circle provides sharing time after drafts have been written and an opportunity for children to give and receive feedback.

- Begin with short pieces of writing. Ask for one or two volunteers.
- Have an author read her or his draft aloud.
- Ask the audience to identify what they consider the best parts or strengths of the piece. Discuss what was good, going into great detail about what makes it so. You may want to write responses on the board. (The first few times, you may have to supply most of the comments yourself.)
- Sometimes include a draft of your own. Students cannot learn too early that *everyone* has to edit to make writing better.

It is helpful to have a chart with a list of suggestions for starting responses. A sample chart is shown in Figure 6.5.

Figure 6.5 Authors' Circle Chart

In our Authors' Circle time, we:

- read our drafts aloud
- listen to each other
- respond and share our feelings
- ask for and give our comments

Here are some ways to start:

- I like what you said about ...
- I like the way you described ...
- I like the part when ...
- I like the words ... because ...
- Your writing makes me feel ...
- Your writing makes me think ...

Figure 6.6 Editing Charts

IDEAS

Are the ideas
- understandable and clear?
- focused on the topic?
- interesting and appropriate for the audience?

OPENING

Does the beginning
- "hook" the audience?
- set the "stage"?
- state the main idea?

SEQUENCE

Do all the sentences
- follow a logical order?
- flow smoothly from one to another?
- focus on the topic?

WORD CHOICE

Are the words
- precise and clear?
- fresh and interesting?
- varied and original?

SENTENCE STRUCTURE

Has the writer used
- varied sentence lengths?
- varied sentence types?
- varied word and phrase orders?

ENDING

Does the ending
- tie the ideas together?
- sum up the thoughts?
- give a feeling of closure or conclusion?

their own writing critically and to give and receive feedback. Writers need to ask themselves questions about their own writing, such as:

- What am I trying to say?
- What have I said so far?
- Where is this leading?
- How do I feel about this piece?

They also benefit from opportunities to ask others (a teacher or peers):

- How does this sound?
- Do you understand what I'm saying?
- How else could I have approached this?
- Do I need to add or explain anything?

In the junior grades, students can learn to examine various components of their writing such as the opening, ending, content, word choice, sentence

Peer editing is an important part of process writing in the junior years.

structure, and sequence. I use charts such as the ones shown in Figure 6.6 to do this. I introduce each chart with the whole class as I use it, and then post it on the wall for further reference when students work in peer editing groups. Students can also learn to address specific genre-related aspects of writing (discussed in the following chapter).

Editing conferences can take a variety of forms: an individual student with a teacher (initiated by either), groups of students with a teacher (Writing Clubs and Spotlight on Writing Groups, described in Chapter 4 and illustrated in Chapter 5, are examples of these), and peer editing groups. Peer editing groups without the teacher should only be used once students are familiar with editing and have had experience in working in teacher-guided situations. Sometimes editing conferences are relatively open-ended; at other times, for example, Spotlight on Writing Groups, they are structured to achieve particular purposes.

I like to have a table designated as the Conference Centre for conferences that I participate in and for a group of students having a peer editing conference. If the entire class is organized into peer editing groups, the groups will need to be placed around the classroom so that group members are close to one another but sufficiently far apart from other groups so that they do not disturb one another. Management can become an issue when groups get too large. Depending on your purpose, groups can vary from two to five students. I find partners the best way to start.

Editing Strategies

There are five basic processes through which all editorial changes are made. *Adding* and *substituting* are the easiest and thus the best ones to start with, followed (in increasing difficulty) by *rearranging*, *combining*, and *deleting*. Younger or inexperienced writers can learn to

- add one detail
- substitute more interesting words
- change endings
- cut apart a paragraph to rearrange sentences for a different meaning or effect
- expand sentences
- make up effective titles
- rearrange words within a sentence

Older or more experienced writers can learn to

- add supporting details
- remove unneeded words/ phrases
- substitute more specific words
- coordinate ideas
- arrange details in a logical order
- vary sentence length and structure
- adapt form and style for particular purposes and audiences
- incorporate dialogue
- eliminate overused words and expressions
- improve introductions and endings
- combine sentences
- make effective transitions
- create particular effects

Editing Lessons and Mini-Lessons

Over time, students can learn to edit through focused lessons and mini-lessons. These guided experiences provide demonstrations of editing strategies, and opportunities to learn about the thinking processes of writers when they edit and to apply them in a supported setting. I find it effective to use the chalkboard, charts, or overhead projector, to "think out loud as I write," and to encourage students to verbalize their own thinking. A good beginning, in the later primary grades, is learning to write interesting sentences by substituting words, extending sentences by adding words and phrases, and rearranging words and phrases within sentences. I do this by engaging the children in a sentence play activity that focuses on a particular skill. I begin with a lesson on substituting interesting words; in a subsequent lesson I do sentence extension. With Grade 3 students, I follow this with lessons in sentence rearranging (see the Activity box for details).

The approach shown in the Activity box on page 183 can be extended in the junior grades. Here is a suggested sequence:

1. Teach the strategy at the sentence level; you may want to begin with a review of substituting, extending, and rearranging if you need to and, later on, introduce sentence combining (see Activity box).
2. Have students select a draft from their folders and apply the idea to one sentence in a paragraph (two or three sentences may be appropriate with students in the upper grades).
3. Model the strategy within the context of a paragraph using an overhead projector.

Activity:
Sentence Substitution, Extension, and Rearranging

Create a simple sentence and choose a focus for the lesson, for example:

The	car	went.
	↓	↓
	truck	raced
	limo	sped
	Ford	skidded
	Lamborghini	crawled

The ________	car	went ________	________.
silver	↓ ↓	quickly	down the road
sleek		slowly	up the hill
expensive		dangerously	on the ice

The first example shows substituting. The second example shows extension; this sentence could subsequently be used for a lesson in rearranging.

1. Brainstorm words or phrases (one word or slot at a time) and record them in lists below the word or blank (on the board or on chart paper; use the latter if you want to build on the activity over a series of lessons).
2. With the children, make sentences orally, mixing and matching from the word lists.
3. While the enthusiasm is still high (don't spend too long on the oral sentence-making), ask the children to write as many different sentences of their own as they can within a five-minute period (sustained, focused writing) using words on the board or any others they can think of.
4. Children pair up and read their sentences.

You can take this a little further if you wish:

5. Each child chooses his or her favourite sentence; checks for capital letters, periods, and spelling (proofreading).
6. Each child prints this sentence on a clean piece of paper, illustrates it, and puts it together with the others as a class book (publishing).

4. Have students select a draft from their folders and apply the idea to a whole paragraph; this could be done with partners to begin with, then independently.

Modelling and collaboratively applying editing strategies using an overhead projector, followed by children applying the strategy to their own work, is probably the single best way to help junior students learn many editing skills; for example, those shown in Figure 6.6. Regardless of the focus of the lesson, always keep in mind that learning to edit one's work is likely the single most difficult task of a writer and continues to be so throughout one's lifetime. It cannot be rushed, and it will not be mastered by the end of the elementary school years.

Cultivating Correctness

While traditional approaches to writing have focused on correctness, especially spelling, punctuation, syntax, and usage, a constructivist view puts purpose and meaning foremost and considers correctness in terms of appropriateness to context rather than as a goal in itself. Process writing is flexible, not lock-step, and not every piece of writing need be corrected. On the other hand, to deny the significance of correctness would be to ignore our sociocultural context. Simply put, being able to write correctly can open doors in academia and in society in general. Not to empower students to achieve this would be irresponsible.

REFLECTION

For many years in my teaching career I dutifully taught spelling and punctuation and gave practice exercises and spelling tests. Yet many students who had completed a worksheet successfully or spelled words correctly on a test made errors in their writing, errors that showed they could not apply the same skills they supposedly had mastered or passed on a test.

What does it mean to have learned to spell a word or to have learned to use commas?

Activity:
Sentence Combining

Research indicates that sentence combining can help improve students' writing. It is an excellent way to integrate the teaching of an editing strategy, punctuation, usage, and syntax meaningfully. For example, subordination, use of linking words, and commas in apposition can be taught in this context. Here is a possible sequence:

1\. Put some sentences on the chalkboard (the first time, you may want to use only two).

2\. Brainstorm with the class to discover how many different ways you can combine the short sentences into one longer sentence. There are three guidelines: the new sentence must make sense, it must be syntactically acceptable in Standard English, and it must retain the meaning. The last point can lead to important discussions. For instance, suppose these are the sentences the class is working with:

> John was alone. John was sitting by the tree.

A student might come up with something like "Lonely John was sitting by the tree," which would lead to a discussion about whether the words "alone" and "lonely" mean the same.

4\. The important thing in this activity is the metalinguistic play and discussion, not the "right" answer.

5\. This can be followed by identifying in a paragraph (on a transparency) where short sentences might be combined and then brainstorming several possible alternatives. Then ask students to apply the strategy to one of their own drafts.

There are two aspects to cultivating correctness in students' writing. One is learning knowledge and skills in spelling, punctuation, usage, and syntax; the other is learning how to proofread to identify changes that need to be made to conform to the conventions of Standard Written English. I advocate an integrated approach to skills instruction because a wide body of research clearly indicates that children do not apply to their own writing what they learn in isolated lessons. I also favour teaching children proofreading strategies and skills to enable them to take responsibility for their learning and writing.

Remember that *conventions of print are a part of writing, not ends unto themselves*, the third principle established in Chapter 1. When students are taught mechanics in isolation, they do not learn such skills effectively. Neither do they learn this important principle. From my point of view, which is supported by research, continuing to teach mechanics in a decontextualized way is indefensible. It is beyond the scope of this book to go into every detail about teaching spelling, punctuation, syntax, and usage appropriately. However, I discuss here some key ideas because of their relevance to writing in the elementary school.

Spelling in the Writing Program

We know that learning to spell is, to a great extent, a developmental process that moves toward conventional spelling (see for example Chapter 2, Figure 2.3). A large-scale assessment in the United States (National Association for Educational Progress, cited in Wilde, 1992, pp. 23–24) that examined samples of students' writing found that average 9-year-olds spelled 92 percent of words correctly and average 13-year-olds were 97 percent accurate. Even the poorest 9-year-old spellers were 80 percent correct. The study concluded that most poor spellers do not have a spelling disability; they have a developmental progression similar to "normal" students, but three to four years younger, and a less sophisticated repertoire of spelling strategies than students of their own age.

Many teachers overestimate the role of formal spelling programs and underestimate the contributions of reading and writing to the acquisition of spelling. Reading and writing are the best ways to learn to spell. Children

Something to think about

Consider the following quotation from Marion Crowhurst (1994, p. 220) and its implications for teaching writing:

> Spelling often assumes a significance out of all proportion to its importance. Spelling is neither as important nor as difficult as many other aspects of writing.... Yet many people, both members of the general public and teachers, talk as if spelling were the most important aspect of writing.

learn many words, especially high-frequency ones, by seeing them over and over, and whenever they try to put thoughts to paper, they draw on their knowledge of letter–sound relationships, spelling patterns, and so on.

Nevertheless, spelling instruction is often a contentious issue. I find that teachers, student teachers, and parents usually have more concerns about spelling than any other aspect of writing. For this reason, I explore spelling in some depth in this chapter. For a more comprehensive treatment of spelling (and punctuation), I recommend Sandra Wilde's (1992), *You Kan Red This!: Spelling and Punctuation for Whole Language Classrooms, K–6*. She provides an in-depth exploration of both research and instructional strategies. Here is a brief summary of her research findings:

Informal learning (learned easily, in context; needing little or no instruction):

- predictable spelling patterns (including most consonants and digraphs, e.g., *th*, *sh*)
- morphemic patterns (e.g., prefixes and suffixes)
- historical and arbitrary spellings (e.g., *knight*)

Benefiting from instruction:

- some developmental patterns (e.g., lax or "short" vowels)
- variant spellings (e.g., tense or "long" vowel spellings)
- orthographic patterns (e.g., doubling consonants, dropping *e* to add *ing*)
- high-frequency words with irregular spellings (optional)
- personally interesting words (optional)

Instead of spending unnecessary hours on formal instruction, teachers can address spelling through informal spelling activities and mini-lessons with groups of children:

- *Informal spelling activities* can be integrated into language experience activities, making class word books and alphabet books, word play activities, writing alliterative poetry, Mystery Messages (see Chapter 5), and so on.
- *Informal mini-lessons* can focus on "word families" (words that are derived from a common root or that have a similar spelling pattern), rhyming words, root words, prefixes, and suffixes. These types of mini-lessons often occur incidentally within other language activities with a group of students.

REFLECTION

I find that some students are overly anxious about spelling and want me to help them with it (or to tell them how to spell words) while they are drafting. I refrain from giving too much assistance during drafting because I want children to become independent writers. I have been in many classrooms where children are constantly asking the teacher how to spell words. When teachers provide spellings for students as they are drafting, it interferes with the children's development of fluency and independence. It also reinforces the idea that spelling is important in the draft-

Spelling can also be a focus of informal, one-on-one mini-lessons with students in the context of their own writing as the teacher circulates through the classroom during Writing Workshop. In this case, it is important to consider what is appropriate in terms of a student's development and also whether spelling is an important focus of the activity.

Formal lessons and mini-lessons are sometimes appropriate for the class as a whole or as specific, small-group instruction for those students who need it. Here are some aspects of spelling that may require a more explicit instructional focus:

Orthographic patterns, such as doubling consonants, dropping *e* before *ing* and changing *y* to *i*, are often overgeneralized by young writers to cases where they do not apply (for example, *jumpping*) and confuse words that are similar (for example, *hoping* and *hopping*). Children sort out spelling patterns such as these much more quickly when the teacher provides some explicit instruction. Once an orthographic pattern such as dropping *e* before adding *ing* has been taught, it is appropriate to remind children of the spelling pattern when proofreading their writing.

Vowel spellings tend to cause more problems for young writers than any other aspect of spelling. Most primary children confuse the various **short vowel** sounds (as in bat, bet, bit, bob, but), particularly short *e* (as in bet) and short *i* (as in bit), especially in the early stages, but much of this is developmental. Charles Read (1975) did some experiments with young children to try to find out the source of common misspellings. He discovered that young children *feel* where sounds are made in their mouths and make associations with

Something to think about

Young writers have to sort out *word boundaries*. Sometimes they will overgeneralize the making of *compound words* and write phrases that are "semantic chunks" as a compound word (for example, "a lot" as "alot" and "have to" as "hafto"). Sometimes they will write one longer word in two parts (for example, "yesterday" as "yester day") or in "syllabic chunks" (for example "Frankenstein" as "Frak n stin" or "Frank in stine"). Refining the concept of word boundaries, particularly in relation to compound words, can continue into the adult years. Sometimes I am not sure if a lexical item is one word or two, or whether it is written with a hyphen. For example, do I write "play school," "playschool," or "play-school"? Are there some particular lexical items you have difficulty with or find confusing?

how sounds feel and the closest letter name. Short *i* feels similar in the mouth to the letter name *e*, and quite different from the letter name *i*. Read concluded that children's misspellings are very logical and that they reveal children's working hypotheses about letter–sound relationships. As children gain more experience with reading and writing, and with a little help from the teacher, most of the confusions with short vowel sounds sort themselves out. Primary children do benefit from *some* instruction in short vowels, but they do not need massive amounts of skill-and-drill practice. (This is a common area of overkill.)

Another challenge in vowel spellings is variants for the **long vowel** sounds (as in cake, see, like, nose, and use). For example, the long *a* sound (which is actually a diphthong, or two phonemes, rather than a single sound) is spelled in different ways in each of the following words (some without an A): day, make, rain, break, reindeer, eh, weigh, Santa Fe. Vowel variations can cause confusion for children in spelling and distinguishing homonyms, such as been and bean. Most children benefit from some instruction with these words that sound the same but are spelled differently. Sometimes children will overgeneralize the idea that words with different meanings are spelled differently (homonyms) to multiple meanings of a word that has one spelling (for example, that "bat" would be spelled differently when it means a hitting stick and when it means a flying mammal). Students need to learn the various spelling patterns so that they can come up with placeholder spellings as they are drafting, which can be checked later.

Something to think about

Here is something to try for yourself so that you can re-create how children solve a short-vowel spelling puzzle: (1) Say "bit" (out loud), then say the vowel sound by itself; now hold onto that shape in your mouth and say the letter name *i*; (2) say "bit," say the vowel sound by itself, hold that shape in your mouth, and then say the letter name *e*. What did you notice about the way the sounds felt in your mouth and the ways your mouth changed shape? Which letter name *(i* or *e)* is closer to the vowel sound in the word *bit?*

Spelling strategy instruction is another important part of an effective spelling program. Students can be taught how to generate approximate, alternate spellings through "sounding out," using known spelling patterns (e.g., from rhyming words), morphemic analysis (i.e., root word and affixes), and analogies to known words (e.g., nation and station). They can learn to monitor their own spelling ("Does this word look right? Can I find its root word and affixes?") and to use spelling resources to confirm or revise their predictions.

Spelling resources should be made available and children should be taught how to use them. Spelling resources may include class-made charts, a "word wall" (see the Activity box), posters, class word books, atlases, and thesauri. Dictionaries may be useful in the junior grades, but even at this level, students need to learn appropriate strategies for using them. The problem with using dictionaries for spelling is that you have to have a reasonable idea, or several possibilities, of how a word may be spelled. So students need to learn how to generate several possible spellings for a word before they look in a dictionary. For primary children, dictionaries (even "junior" versions) are of little help. At one time, I made each child a personal spelling dictionary, but now I prefer not to use them because I find some children overrely on them in the drafting stage. Instead, I encourage children to use placeholder spellings and check them *after* they have written their drafts with a Pocket Dictionary (described in the Activity box and shown in Figure 6.7).

Word lists have long been a part of traditional spelling programs. Many teachers and parents believe that they are essential elements of any language arts program. Some teachers feel pressured into using weekly spelling lists and spelling tests. Unfortunately, many of the practices commonly used with word

Activity:
Word Wall

I found a word wall particularly useful in my primary and Grade 4 classrooms. At the beginning of the school year, I put up a picture of a skunk and a sign that said "Little Stinkers" (you could also put up a picture of an imp and a sign that says "Spelling Demons"). I chose high-frequency words I noticed children were misspelling in their writing and, with the children participating, wrote them on manila tag strips and put them on the wall. Some of the words were functional words, such as "because" and "their," others were more personal to the children, such as "soccer" and "Vancouver." Sometimes the children would suggest words for the word wall. Keep in mind that the word wall is created anew with each class and is cumulative throughout the school year.

lists are ineffective. Some of these include: everyone studying the same set of words, studying too many words, spending too much time (more than 15 minutes a day) on spelling and spelling-related activities, using a post-test method (rather than pretest and post-test), copying and writing words three times or more, completing workbooks or worksheets of spelling exercises, and treating spelling as a separate subject rather than as part of writing.

Now this does not mean that we have to toss word lists out all together. If we feel the need to have a spelling word list program, we can adapt it to make it more meaningful and relevant for the children by

- individualizing the word lists (otherwise students waste time studying words they can already spell or they get frustrated because the word list is too difficult)
- limiting the number of words studied (five words is plenty for primary students, a maximum of ten words for the junior grades)
- spending no more than fifteen minutes a day on spelling activities
- incorporating a list of high-frequency words (optional); if so, use a Canadian list (e.g., Thomas, 1979; Thomas & Scott, 1987)
- using a pretest, post-test method if you incorporate a high-frequency word list; students should check their own pretests because this accounts for the major portion of their learning to spell the words on the list

Activity:
Pocket Dictionary

Attach a library pocket for each letter of the alphabet to a piece of bristol board (as shown in Figure 6.7). In each pocket, place a matching card. To check the spelling of a word, children figure out the initial letter, take the card from the right pocket and read the card to see if the word is already there. If it isn't, they bring the card to the teacher, who prints the word on the card. I prefer to start with blank cards each year, and when I spell the word for a child, I ask her or him to help me spell it, using this as a teaching opportunity.

Figure 6.7 Pocket Dictionary

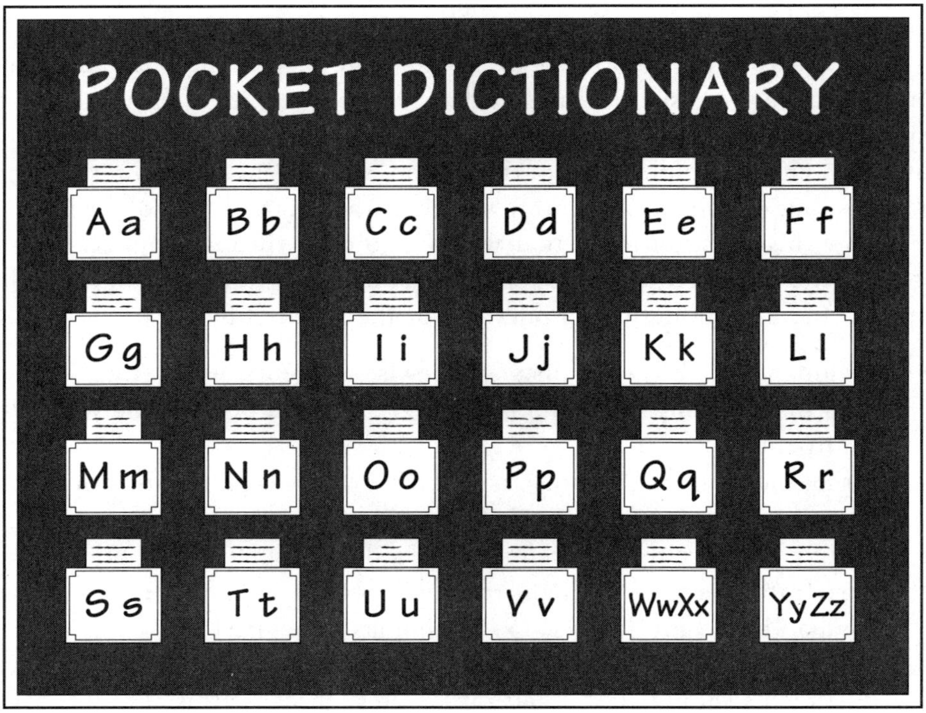

Activity:
Spelling Study Steps

Copying words or writing them out several times is really a wasted effort. Instead, teach children a variety of strategies that include word analysis, visualization, writing, checking, and comparing. Here is one example of how you might sequence these:

1. Look at the word and say it in a quiet voice.
2. Look at the parts.
3. Say each letter.
4. Close your eyes, visualize the word, and spell it orally.
5. Check the word letter by letter.
6. Write the word on scrap paper or a little chalkboard.
7. Check and compare letter by letter. If it is not correct, repeat from the beginning.
8. Cover the word, rewrite it, and check again.

- teaching children to use an appropriate method for studying words (see the Activity box) instead of repetitious writing and copying
- integrating spelling with writing by (1) using students' own writing as a source of personal spelling words, (2) teaching children spelling strategies that they can apply while drafting and proofreading, and (3) teaching children to proofread their own writing for the spelling patterns and words they have learned

Individualized spelling programs are not as complicated as you might think. Here is one way I have organized an individualized spelling program; I have used this method myself with Grades 2 to 7. (I would not use this approach with kindergarten or Grade 1 children. The focus in these years should be on ideas rather than spelling; any attention to spelling should be done through informal activities rather than learning lists of words. Even traditional spelling programs usually start at Grade 2.) The individualized spelling program I describe here incorporates a pretest from a Canadian word list (Thomas, 1979), students' personal words, and "spelling buddies."

Personal word banks. Each student needs to generate a personal word bank for spelling. These are derived primarily from their own writing. I have a file box with an index card for each student, and when I read students' work or we have writing conferences, I add words that I think they should work on. (Teachers need to use their judgment here and take into account the child's spelling ability and the usefulness of the words.) Students who are good spellers also like to add words they find interesting and challenging. In addition, when I read students' journals and learning logs, I record on the inside back cover the misspelled words that I think they should learn (and write the correct spellings, of course).

Pretesting from an appropriate word list. At the beginning of the week, the teacher does a pretest (five to ten words, depending on age of students) from a grade-appropriate Canadian list (for example, Thomas, 1979). As students proceed through the elementary years, the gap in spelling ability widens and students become conscious of their abilities. Teachers in the junior grades might want to pretest with two different spelling lists, one more challenging than the other. Immediately after the pretest, the teacher takes one word at a time and writes the correct spellings on the chalkboard, saying the letters aloud. *Each student checks his or her own pretest*, because this accounts for the major portion of the learning of the correct spelling (Thomas, 1979). Students write correct spellings next to any errors, making note of the parts of the words that were correct and the parts that were incorrect.

Creating individualized weekly spelling lists. Every student will have five to ten weekly spelling words. I suggest using five words per week in Grades 2 and 3, six to eight words in Grades 4 and 5, and ten words in Grades 6 and 7. Each student creates his or her own list, beginning with those words spelled incorrectly on the pretest. Students then add more words from their personal word banks, which include words from their individual cards in the card file and from inside the back covers of their journals and learning logs. When students take a word from these sources, they put a line through it to keep track of words selected and words available for future spelling lists. The teacher can also write on the chalkboard a few words related to topics in social studies, science, current events, and so on for those students who want an extra challenge.

Establishing weekly spelling routines. To avoid spending too much time on spelling activities, it is important to establish routines and teach them to the children. The Activity box describes a weekly routine I have used for Grades 2 to 7. Make a chart of daily spelling activities, post the chart in the classroom, and refer to it when teaching the routines. Children learn these routines quite quickly, and then the individualized spelling program pretty well runs itself. Except for the Monday pretest, I incorporate the daily spelling activities as one of the must-do activities in Reading and Writing Workshop.

Activity:
Weekly Spelling Schedule

Here is a sequence of spelling activities that takes a maximum of fifteen minutes per day (except for Monday, which may take a little longer because of the pretest).

Monday — Pretest; students check their own words; students make up their own individualized spelling lists for the week (I use a spelling notebook); teacher checks the list (so students don't study incorrect spellings by mistake).

Tuesday — Children do spelling study steps (see the Activity box on page 193).

Wednesday — Buddies trade weekly spelling lists (their notebooks); test and check each other (using scraps of paper or little chalkboards); use words orally in sentences.

Thursday — Optional activities; for example: play spelling games, use words in sentences, find root words and affixes, generate word families or rhyming words, proofread drafts to find and check weekly spellings.

Friday — Buddies trade weekly spelling lists (their notebooks) and test each other (writing words on strips of paper); students place the spelling test papers as a bookmark in their spelling notebooks and hand them in for the teacher to check; the teacher checks the post-tests and circles misspelled words so that students know which words need to be included on the next week's list.

Learning to Punctuate

Like spelling, learning to punctuate is a developmental process, and much of what students learn comes from reading and writing. As children realize that punctuation helps convey meaning, they begin to use it and gradually bring those uses into conformity with accepted usage (Hillocks, 1986). When children learn to punctuate, they create "invented punctuation," which is akin to invented spelling. Some aspects of punctuation are easily learned and are best dealt with informally; others benefit from instruction. The most effective methods for teaching punctuation include modelling in the context of writing; for example, language experience activities and collaborative writing. Punctuation can also be discussed in the context of sentence combining and related activities. For example, placing a comma in different places in a sentence may change its meaning.

Many punctuation skills can be learned easily and quickly when students perceive the need. To teach punctuation in context effectively, keep in mind the following points:

- Familiarize yourself with the curriculum for your grade level. Take note of weaknesses that appear in your students' writing.
- Use student samples of written work and a "let's fix this up" attitude to teach punctuation. You can make transparencies from students' writing for this purpose.
- Teach appropriate skills after first drafts have been written and before proofreading. For example, if the writing involves dialogue, teach or review quotation marks and then have students focus on quotation marks when they proofread.
- Reinforce punctuation as an aid to understanding rather than as a discrete skill (see the Activity box on teaching quotation marks).
- Teach skills incidentally; for example, the use of commas in a sentence-combining activity.

For an in-depth review of the research and specific teaching strategies and mini-lessons, I again recommend Sandra Wilde's book (1992), *You Kan Red This!: Spelling and Punctuation for Whole Language Classrooms, K–6.*

What about "Grammar"?

To begin, let's clarify what is meant by "grammar," since this term is used in a variety of ways. Crowhurst (1980) suggests that "grammar" is commonly used in the following ways. First, it is sometimes used to refer to syntax

Activity:
Teaching Quotation Marks Conceptually

While there are many rules associated with quotation marks, such as whether to start a quotation with a capital letter or not, where to place commas, and so on, even primary children can learn how quotation marks signal in a text that someone is speaking. Here's how I introduce quotation marks to primary children:

- I draw a smile shape (like this: ).
- Next I draw an "open mouth" shape by adding a "bottom lip" (like this: .
- Then I rotate this shape, left and right (like this: ).
- Then I draw quotation marks below the two rotated shapes (like this: ).

I explain to the children that these are like little "mouth marks" that show when a person opens his or her mouth to talk. So they can be called talking marks because they are placed around the parts of the text where someone is talking. We then do a shared reading activity where children take the role of a speaker (or speakers) and I act as narrator. I also include hand actions for opening and closing mouths when we see the talking marks.

When I teach or review quotation marks with junior students, I have students identify spoken parts of a text by highlighting or circling them and then putting in the quotation marks. I introduce the term "quotation marks" but still use "talking marks" in the same context.

(which is the preferred term), the system of rules that governs a language (for example, word order) and enables its speakers to produce and understand sentences. Second, it is used to refer to models that systematically describe this knowledge of language (for example, analysis of sentences and parts of speech). The two most common models used in education are traditional and transformational grammar. Third, "grammar" is sometimes used to refer to conventional notions of what is socially acceptable in particular contexts, in other words, **usage** (which is the preferred term). "Improving bad grammar" usually means trying to eliminate nonstandard usages.

Syntax concerns the principles by which words are ordered and relate to one another. Without any conscious knowledge of syntactic structures, by the time they enter school children have learned most of the syntactic patterns of

Something to think about

I remember exercises in identifying parts of speech and parsing sentences (underlining the bare subject with one line, the bare predicate with two). Do you remember grammar lessons at school? At what age? Were you good at grammar"? Did you like it? Do you think it helped you improve your writing abilities?

their spoken language (Loban, 1976). Syntactic errors are an inevitable part of first- and second-language development, but most of them disappear as children gain experience. A massive amount of research confirms that formal grammar instruction (of all kinds, including traditional and transformational grammar) has no beneficial effect on either elementary or secondary students' writing (Hillocks, 1986). Some studies show it to be detrimental because it takes time away from writing—which is the best way to improve writing—and promotes negative attitudes toward writing. Furthermore, the study of grammar is far too abstract for children under the age of about 16.

This does not mean, however, that teachers have to avoid the use of terms such as "noun" or "adjective." These are part of the **metalinguistic** vocabulary that can be helpful in talking about writing. With primary children I prefer terms such as "describing words" and "action words," and only use them in context; for example, in the sentence extension activities described earlier and in discussions about editing. In the junior grades, I introduce the terms "noun," "verb," "adjective," "pronoun," and so on. Even so, I emphasize the concept, not the term, and continue to use phrases such as "describing words" in the same context. I don't expect students to use this **metalanguage** independently, nor would I have them do exercises in identifying parts of speech.

Research shows that sentence combining may have a, though minor, positive effect on students' writing. Sentence combining focuses on manipulating and generating syntactic elements, but in the context of discussion in this type of activity we often refer to parts of speech. Some students in Grades 6 and 7 are ready to learn about subject–verb agreement, consistency of verb tense, and pronoun reference (for example, "they" in reference to children and "his" or "her" in reference to a child). This should only be done, however, in the context of their writing, with a focus on meaning and "sounding right."

As such, this skill may be considered part of editing because it is meaning-related. I prefer to treat it as part of the proofreading process because it is primarily an issue of conventions or the surface features of writing. This issue is an example of staying flexible in the writing process instead of being arbitrary. It doesn't really matter much how you label or classify this kind of revision. It also illustrates that the primary function of writing conventions is to clarify meaning.

Proofreading

Over the years teachers have spent countless hours proofreading students' work to identify errors. Research indicates this is largely wasted effort—students do not learn from teachers' corrections of their work. Here is what to do instead:

- Spare the red pen! Use a pencil to mark errors, or make suggestions on a separate piece of paper. Keep an individualized card file for spelling words students need to learn, or write these words on the inside back cover of the students' notebooks. These words can become part of students' individualized spelling lists.
- Don't mark every error you spot. Sometimes, focus your proofreading on a particular skill you have already taught, for example, commas in lists or "dropping the *e* before adding *ing*" spelling rule. On some occasions, check the first half of the piece and then get the student to find the rest of the same type of error.
- Indicate in the margin where there is an error in a line (e.g., SP for spelling).
- Make note of the major skills a student needs to work on (for example, run-on sentences), and use this information for determining small-group instruction for students with a common need.
- Best of all, teach students how to proofread their own and others' work.

Something to think about

Have you ever received a paper back from a teacher covered with red ink? How did this affect you?

Something to think about

Review the functions of writing (Chapter 1, Figure 1.2). For which functions and tasks would proofreading be appropriate?

If students believe that every piece of work must be checked and corrected, they soon begin to use only those words they can spell, avoid unusual punctuation situations, and keep sentences simple to avoid making mistakes. This means no risk, little growth, and less excitement and discovery. On the other hand, if students are free to write knowing that their ideas are more important than mechanics, that they can go back later to change and fix up what they have written, that they may have help with correcting, that they will not be labelled failures if they have to make such changes, this results in taking risks, growth in writing, and more positive attitudes toward writing.

The purpose of proofreading is to prepare a piece of writing for publication. There is no reason to proofread and correct writing that is for personal use or for which the writer is his or her own intended audience. With students I make an analogy between proofreading and cleaning up for company: if the writing is informal and the audience familiar there is no need to proofread, just as there is no need to clean the house when a good friend stops by for a chat (although in my house we may have to clear the newspapers off the couch so there is a place for her to sit). On the other hand, if the writing is formal and addressed to someone we don't know or want to impress, we do the best job we can, just as we would make our home spotless (maybe repaint too) if a dignitary, such as the queen, were coming to visit. If we plan on presenting what we have written orally rather than in print, then instead of checking spelling and so on we rehearse to polish our phrasing and expression. In short, purpose, audience, and degree of formality determine whether to proofread or not.

Proofreading can be taught effectively through modelling. This can begin in the primary grades as part of regular morning activities just as Ms. Chan, the primary teacher, does with the Mystery Message activity in Chapter 5. With primary children I use the acronym COPS as a reminder of what to look for; with older students I add the U:

C – capital letters
O – omissions (words or endings)
U – usage
P – punctuation
S – spelling

A chart such as the one below (from Deanna Nichols, Sooke, B.C.) can be used.

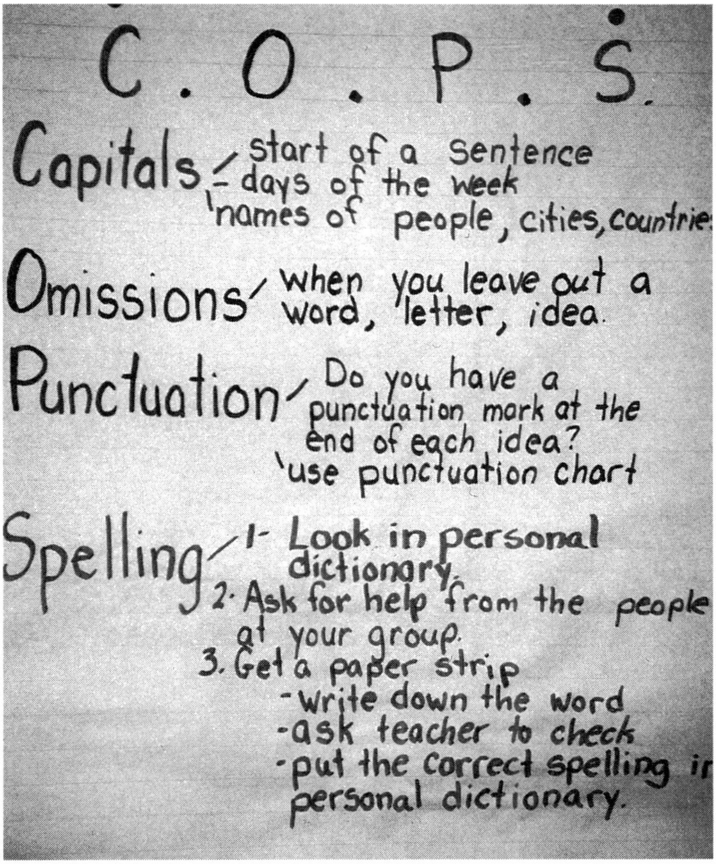

Students use proofreading aids more effectively when they help develop them and use them in the context of literacy lessons and mini-lessons on a regular basis.

When we write and read, we focus on meaning (or should) and may not pick up errors. When we proofread, however, we need to focus on the mechanics. Here are some ways that can help:

- If you are proofreading your own work, put it aside for a while to get distance from it; then when you proofread you will see the errors more clearly (by the way, this is also beneficial for editing).
- Trade papers with someone else and proofread each other's work; it is always easier to see someone else's mistakes (older students or "big buddies" can help younger ones).
- Read the writing aloud (a "writer's mumble") so you can hear the mistakes you don't see.
- Use charts or checklists as references.
- Proofread backward—yes, backward. Some people find this the best way to pick up spelling errors (except homonyms) because you cannot read for understanding. Start with the last word and "read" right to left, bottom to top.

Aids for proofreading include spell-checks on the computer (although these are not fail-safe and can, I think, lead to a false sense of security), checklists, and charts (see Figure 6.8 for examples). As with editing, introduce charts or checklists one at a time in a lesson or mini-lesson. Then post the charts or put checklists in the writing centre and encourage students to use them. Students in the junior grades can learn to proofread with a partner or in small groups. They can form cooperative groups in which each member checks one particular item, for example, the ones shown in Figure 6.8. Students in Grades 4 to 7 can also develop personal proofreading lists for specific items they need to work on. These are cumulative and emerge through writing conferences with the teacher and peers.

Celebrating Writing

Publishing and presenting provide the motivation and purpose for all the hard work of writing. They emphasize the value and importance of writing, provide an audience, build self-esteem, and bestow a feeling of accomplishment. Writing should be published or presented whenever the opportunity arises,

Figure 6.8 Proofreading Charts

CAPITAL LETTERS

Check for capital letters:
- at the beginning of each sentence
- the word I
- names of people
- names of streets and places
- names of days and months
- titles

SPELLING

Check to see if all words are spelled correctly.

Make a list of the words you had trouble with and add them to your personal spelling list.

SENTENCE AND PUNCTUATION

Check to see that sentences end with a

. Jack went for a ride.
! We won!
? Where shall we go?

OMISSIONS

Read your piece aloud. Insert missing words or word endings with a caret:

                    ing   the
John was walk home from store.
                    ^   ^

SENTENCE SENSE

Read your piece aloud.
Snap your fingers or clap when you hear the end of the sentence.
Cross out any extra **ands** and **thens**.

COMMAS

Check to see if commas are used in lists:

The rabbit ate lettuce, celery, carrots, radishes, and spinach.

when the writer wants to, and as soon as possible while enthusiasm is greatest. One caveat: *Published does not necessarily mean perfect!*

Publishing Possibilities

It is often amazing to see the effort students will put into publishing their work. As well as doing their best printing or handwriting or using the computer, they add illustrations, covers, and so on. They may also include other finishing touches such as dedications, acknowledgments, or an About the Author section. Students' writing may be published in or on

- Books—individual books, class books, cloth-bound books, coil-bound books, shape books, zigzag books, big books, mini books, flip books
- Scrolls, murals, banners, posters
- Reproduced class booklets, newspapers, newsletters, magazines
- Bulletin boards, carrels, room dividers, easels, chart stands
- Wall hangings, window blinds, clotheslines, mobiles
- Audiotape or videotape, computer

Some ideas for publishing and displaying students' work are shown in Figures 6.9 and 6.10. The following chapter provides additional ideas.

Presenting

Time should be set aside on a regular basis for students to share their work with the class. Sharing happens informally throughout the writing process for various purposes. Presenting provides a chance for students to be acknowledged for their efforts and accomplishments—it is a time of celebration. Children should not be forced to share what they have written, however. Hesitant students can be encouraged to share by privately rereading for practice first, having the teacher read their work aloud (with their permission), through a tape recording, or sharing with a nonthreatening audience such as a small group (Writing Club, for example, or a few trusted classmates) or a younger child.

Children benefit from other presenting opportunities and audiences as well as their classmates; for example, older and younger buddies, other classes, school administrators, the librarian and learning assistant, parents and relatives. They can also reach wider audiences in many ways. See page 207.

Figure 6.9 Publishing Ideas

Shape Books

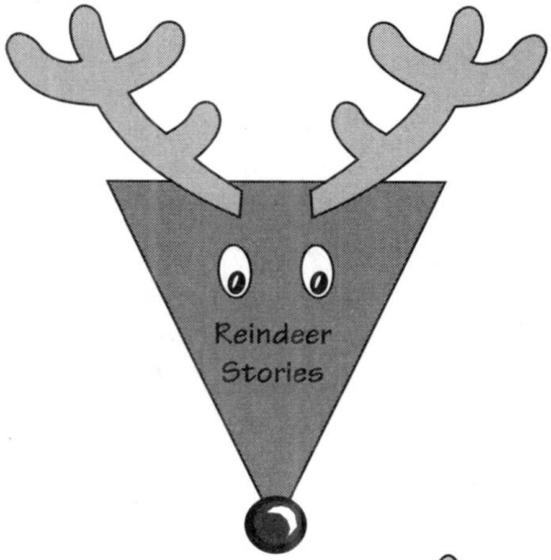

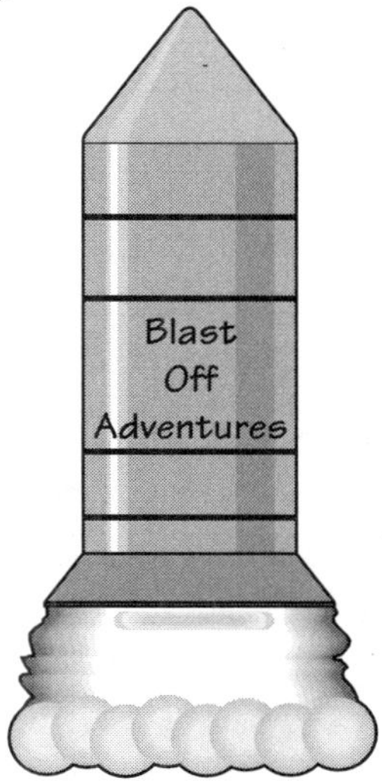

Zig-Zag Books

Figure 6.10 Display Ideas

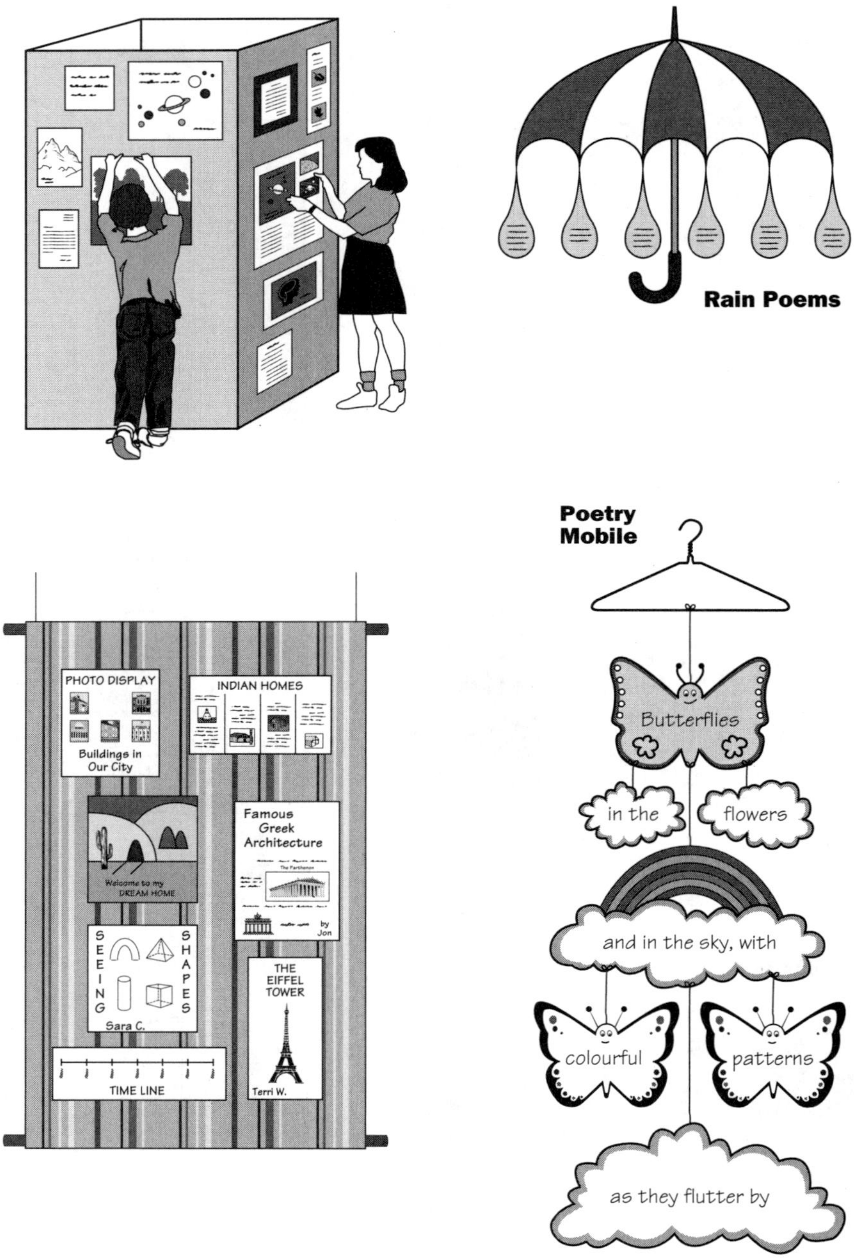

- Submit their work to a newspaper or magazine.
- Display their work in a store, shopping mall, or community centre.
- Hold a writing fair and inviting residents from a seniors' home or the general public.

Reflections on the Chapter

Think about/talk about/write about:

Principles into Practice

- Use Figure 2.6, From Principles of Writing to Practice, to find specific examples in this chapter of each principle as it is put into practice.

Process Writing

- How does a process approach to writing compare to the way you were taught in elementary school?
- What are the benefits of a process approach to writing?
- What aspects of process writing do you think parents and the public need to be informed about? How might teachers do this?

Fluency

- How do you feel about your own fluency of expression as a writer? How do you think you developed in this way?
- How do you feel about your own voice as a writer? Were you ever taught about voice in elementary school?

Editing and Proofreading

- What are the benefits of separating editing and proofreading?
- What did you learn about teaching editing that can help you as a writer?
- What are your beliefs and values about creativity and correctness in writing? How did you construct these ideas and attitudes?

Publishing and Presenting

- Have you ever published or presented your own writing? In what contexts? How did you feel?
- What are some other ways that students can publish or present their writing?

REFERENCES AND FURTHER READING

Bolen, J. (1984). *Goddesses in everywoman: A new psychology of women.* New York: Harper & Row.

Brown, M.W. (1949). *The important book.* New York: Harper.

Calkins, L. (1986). *The art of teaching writing.* Portsmouth, NH: Heinemann. (2nd edition, 1994).

Crowhurst, M. (1980). Grammar in the elementary school. *Highway One, 3*(2), pp. 44–54.

———. (1994). *Language and learning across the curriculum.* Scarborough, ON: Allyn & Bacon.

Graves, D. (1975). An examination of the writing processes of seven year old children. *Research in the Teaching of English, 9*(3), 227–41.

———. (1978). *Balance the basics: Let them write.* New York: Ford Foundation.

———. (1983). *Writing: Teachers and children at work.* Exeter, NH: Heinemann.

Harste, J., Short, K., and Burke, C. (1988). *Creating classrooms for authors: The reading–writing connection.* Portsmouth, NH: Heinemann.

Hillocks, G. (1986). *Research on written composition: New directions for teaching.* Urbana, IL: National Council of Teachers of English. ED 128 818.

Langer, J. (1991). Literacy and schooling: A sociocognitive perspective. In E.H. Hiebert (Ed.), *Literacy for a diverse society: Perspectives, practices, and policies* (pp. 9–27). New York: Teachers College Press.

Loban, W. (1976). *Language development: Kindergarten through grade twelve.* NCTE Research Report No. 18. Urbana, IL: National Council of Teachers of English.

Martin, Jr., B. (1983). *Brown bear, brown bear, what do you see?* New York: Henry Holt & Co.

Read, C. (1975). *Children's categorizations of speech sounds in English.* New York: Harcourt Brace Jovanovich.

Thomas, V. (1979). *Teaching spelling: Canadian word lists and instructional techniques.* Toronto: Gage.

Thomas, V., and Scott, R. (1987). *The Canadian spelling program II.* Toronto: Gage.

Wilde, S. (1992). *You kan red this!: Spelling and punctuation for whole language classrooms, K–6.* Portsmouth, NH: Heinemann.

CHAPTER 7

Expanding Young Writers' Repertoires of Genres and Forms of Representation

CHAPTER OBJECTIVES

To discuss issues related to the teaching of forms of representation and written genres

To provide a variety of forms of representations and suggestions for teaching them

To explore ways of interweaving process and genre approaches for teaching written genres in the language arts and across the curriculum

PERSONAL REFLECTION

As I began work on this chapter, I tried to think of events in my own schooling when I was taught particular forms of writing. I do remember being taught how to make graphs, maps, charts, and diagrams. These forms were taught in social studies, science, and math. I cannot recall any experiences of learning to write stories, reports, or poems as specific genres. Yet I have a repertoire of written genres. Is it the case that I was taught them directly but do not remember how or when? Or did I learn them through reading?

Do you remember learning about particular types of writing—stories, poems, reports, and so on? Were you taught directly or left to discover them on your own?

In this chapter I focus on ways of enabling students to expand their repertoires of forms of representation and written genres. Like other aspects of language arts instruction, writing is not immune to controversies about skills versus creativity, process versus product, and so on. Of particular relevance to this chapter is the current dispute between those who advocate process writing and those who argue for explicit instruction in the formal features of particular types of writing (in other words, the format). It seems to me that what teachers and researchers need to do is to look at all the evidence, weigh the merits of different methods, and construct a perspective that makes sense, is supported by research, and is compatible with one's own belief system and values. The ideas in this chapter represent my own meaning-making about how best to expand young writers' repertoires by incorporating what I believe to be the advantages of and best techniques from both process and formal approaches. I begin with a discussion of the concept of **representing** and ways of expanding students' knowledge of various forms of representation in the language arts and across the curriculum. Next, I discuss process and genre perspectives and how to integrate them in the teaching of description, narrative, poetry, argument, and exposition.

Forms of Representation

A traditional view has divided the language arts into listening, speaking, reading, and writing. Since language, in its broadest sense, encompasses oral, written, and visual forms of communication, many newer programs and curricula promote visual literacy and include the processes of *viewing* and *visual representation.* Viewing is seen as parallel to listening and reading; representing is analogous to speaking and writing. Viewing may occur on its own (e.g., viewing slides without a commentary) or be accompanied by listening (e.g., watching and listening to a film) or reading (e.g., interpreting a chart). Likewise, visual representation may be nonverbal (e.g., communicating through sign language) or it may accompany speaking (e.g., in puppetry) or writing (e.g., making a graph).

In this book, I use the terms *representing* and *forms of representation* in a very broad sense to include all the ways we can express meaning through any or all of the processes of speaking, writing, and visual representation and that may be interpreted through listening, reading, and viewing. The term "representing" reflects the integrated nature of language. It is an important concept for teachers of writing because it is flexible and enabling; it opens up opportunities for students to construct and express their ideas. Writing is interwoven with representing: it is incorporated in many forms of representation directly (such as diagrams, word webs, charts, and so on) and is used in the process of creating and developing forms that are presented visually or orally (for example, in planning a play or preparing a speech).

Something to think about

Sometimes learning to use a particular word or phrase can make a big difference in the classroom. Instead of saying to students, "Write down your ideas," you can ask them to "represent your ideas" or "show me your thinking." How might the different expressions influence what students do?

Form Follows Function

It is important to remember the adage that "form follows function." In other words, how something is structured or organized is not decided arbitrarily, but in response to particular purposes in particular contexts. For example, when someone writes a letter, she or he includes the date so that the reader knows when the letter was written, a salutation to signify to whom the letter

Figure 7.1 Representing from A to Z

A
about the author
acrostic
acrostic poem
advertisement
agenda
- real or imaginative
alliteration
announcement
anthology of
- stories
- poems
autobiography
autobiopoem

B
bibliography
- annotated
- of references
Big Book for primary grades
biography
book
- by a class
- by a small group
- by an individual
- wordless book
- patterned book
book cover
book jacket flyleaf notes
booklet
brochure
bulletin board display

C
captions
cartoon
chapter
- single chapter
- opening chapter
- additional chapter
- chapter story
character sketch
chart
coded message
commentary
- current event
- fashion show
- historical event
- sports event
concept map
conversation
- retelling
- imaginative
court case
critique
crossword puzzle

D
data chart
debate
- "Ping-Pong"
- argument
descriptions
dialogue
- real or imaginative
diagram with labels
diary
- personal
- imaginative
diary written in role
dictionary
- thematic or topical
- illustrated
- multicultural
directions
display

E
editorial
encyclopedia
- article
- Big Book
- thematic
essay
- of opinion
- formal essay
- research
- outline
exhibit
experiment
explanation

F
fable
fairy tale
- retelling
- original
- parody
- alternate point of view
family
- history
- tree
field trip
- preparation
- student-led
- summary
- reflection
filmstrip
flannel board story
flow chart
Freyer chart

G
game
game board
glossary
graffiti board
graph

H
hink-pinks (1-syllable riddles)
hinky-pinkies (2-syllable riddles)
hinkety-pinketies (3-syllable riddles)
hypotheses

I

index
interview
- family members
- class visitor
- simulated

instructions
introduction

J

jokes and riddles
journal
- personal
- fictional

K

key to a map, chart, or graph
KWL chart (know, wonder, learned)

L

labels
learning log
learning centre
legend
lesson
letters
- personal
- to the editor
- to an advice column
- to one's hero
- to politicians

list
- of ideas
- of observations
- of procedures
- of questions

M

map
- current event
- fictional place
- geographical
- historical event
- storyline map
- treasure site
- 3-dimensional

mathematical problems
matrix data chart
memorandum
menu
- nutritional
- imaginative

message
mural
music
- score and/or lyrics
- songs and/or parodies
- additional verses
- original verses

myth

N

newspaper
- announcement
- article
- classified ads
- column
- feature story
- advice column
- editorial
- want ads
- fictional

New Year's resolutions
notes
- note cards
- note slips
- note boxes
- reminder note
- thank-you note

novel

O

opinion statement

P

patterned writing
- repetitive
- alliterative
- cumulative
- alphabetic
- days of the week

"Ping Pong" debate
poem
- cinquain
- concrete
- diamante
- found poem
- free verse
- haiku
- lantern
- patterned
- rhyme
- string

pop-up book
poster
procedures
proverb

Q

questionnaire
questions
- for a game
- for a quiz
- for interviews
- for research
- for study
- for review
- for a visitor

quiz show
quotations

R

rap
"Reach for the Top"
rebus
recipe
- real or imagined

report
- oral
- written
- poster report
- research

résumé
- real or fictional

retelling
review

– of book
– of film or event
riddles
role-play

S
satire
script
self-evaluation
self-report
sequel
short story
speech
speech balloons
storyboard
story map
story web
summary

T
table
tall tale
telegram
television program
thinking boxes
thinking bubbles
timeline
– historical
– personal
– biographical
travel poster
trial
Trivial Pursuit questions

U
unbelievable story or scenario
unusual character

V
valentine
Venn diagram

W
web
– cluster
– mind map
– semantic map
word play

X
X-ray diagram
exit slip

Y
year-end review or reflection

Z
zigzag book or display

is addressed, a return address so that a reply may be written, and a signature at the end so that the reader knows who wrote the letter. A reader expects these elements to be there (and in a specific order) so that he or she can make sense of the letter. In the same way, mathematicians express ideas through particular forms so that all members of the mathematics community can understand them.

Forms of representation are best learned in context, not only in the context of the discipline or subject, but also in the context of meaningful activity. Children need to learn forms of representation not as discrete entities, but to shape their ideas for particular purposes and to suit the specific situation. In school, we cannot replicate exactly what goes on in the wider world. For example, we cannot all *be* scientists, but we can engage children in doing science and cultivate scientific ways of thinking and of using language. We can, for example, use scientific language to talk about scientific concepts, and we can help children learn scientific forms of representation to communicate scientific ideas.

In some cases, ideas can be expressed in a variety of ways. For example, if I want to tell someone I love him, I can say "I love you," sing a love song, write a poem, give him a hug, make a valentine, write a love letter, and so on. In other cases, information must be communicated through a particular form (for instance, writing a prescription for medicine). Students need to learn specific ways to suit particular contexts and also to learn an array of forms so they can have options from which to choose when the situation allows more flexibility.

Teaching Forms of Representation

While children may discover some new forms on their own through reading and independent exploration, in many cases, particularly in science, social studies, and mathematics, they benefit from explicit instruction. In Chapter 4, I discussed designing appropriate writing/learning experiences. Some of the ideas introduced there are included in this list of suggestions for teaching new forms of representation:

- Create learning contexts or situations in which students will have a purposeful opportunity to learn and use the new form.
- Engage students in doing an activity, and introduce the new form as a way of communicating ideas.
- Model and demonstrate how the form is created and used, and engage children actively in the process.
- Be descriptive rather than prescriptive; help students see the purposes behind the form.
- Talk about what is happening; include conceptual and metalinguistic vocabulary.
- Provide guided practice and other kinds of support before you expect students to use the new form independently.

Once students have learned a new form of representation in this way, use it from time to time as part of the classroom teaching/learning repertoire, and encourage students to use it as one choice of representation in open-ended activities.

Introducing students to a variety of forms of representation is important not only for academic reasons, but for affective ones as well. Learning new forms of representation is exciting and challenging; it also allows more choices in open-ended activities and promotes success for more learners. Figure 7.1 provides an array of representations that elementary school students are able to learn and use.

Process and Genre: Competing or Complementary Approaches?

> **Something to think about**
>
> What forms of writing do you think most children might be familiar with before they come to school? How do you think they learn them?

Expanding students' repertoires of forms of representation and genres is an important instructional goal.

In Chapter 2, I discussed various perspectives on the teaching of writing. Of particular relevance in this chapter are the opposing views of those who see writing as primarily a personal endeavour and those who see it as a sociocultural one. Many advocates of process writing emphasize the personal, expressive aspects of writing and use of discovery methods such as free-writing as opposed to explicit teaching. These individuals often value narrative as the primary mode of expression and equate the process of learning to write to becoming an author. Critics point out that this philosophy ignores many demands of academic and workplace writing and of society at large. Some (e.g., Delpit, 1988; de la Reyes, 1992) argue that process writing disadvantages children from nonmainstream groups and that these children need explicit instruction to empower them to be successful at school and in society. On the other hand, research has shown that process writing is effective for many aspects of writing instruction and in developing positive attitudes toward writing, while the study of models and following of rules was found to be ineffective (Hillocks, 1986).

Learning and Teaching Genres

Until recently, genres were viewed basically as stable, fixed text types and the focus of instruction was on teaching format, or formal features. Larger groupings—description, narrative, poetry, exposition, and argument—were conceptualized as discrete categories, each encompassing subtypes, or specific genres, such as folk tales and reports. Now, genres are thought of as *social actions* that occur in particular types of situations within a discourse community. Formal features are seen not as ends in themselves but derived from and related "to the writer's social motive in responding to a recurrent social situation of a certain type" (Freedman & Medway, 1994, p. 3).

Something to think about

Recall the results of Hillocks (1986) meta-analysis of writing instruction. Which mode of instruction is the most effective?

Genres are flexible and fluid, and categories overlap; for example, you will find descriptions embedded in stories and reports. As human life changes, new genres evolve and develop. A good example of this is the new genres created through the use of e-mail. Another social dimension of genre is in its dialogic nature: writers use their knowledge of how to shape language from their experiences in similar situations, and they learn how to take into account how their audience may respond. Because genres are context-dependent, the notion that they can be taught out of context is problematic. As Aviva Freedman and Peter Medway argue, "Craft knowledge [of genres is] a matter of enculturation rather than instruction" (1994, p. 13), or as Lev Vygotsky (1978) would put it, genres should be *cultivated rather than imposed.* To me, this implies a process approach to genre.

How Can Process and Genre Be Integrated?

Instead of seeing process writing and teaching genres as conflicting positions, I propose that we consider integrating process and genre in a complementary fashion. Rick Coe (1994) suggests we think of genre as process; how we approach genre depends

> on our situations and contexts of situation, and most especially on our students, on what they already know, on how they are experienced. Students need to learn discourse in genres, but that does not necessarily mean teachers must teach genre knowledge explicitly, nor that students' knowledge cannot be tacit. (p. 163)

Like Coe, I believe that sometimes it is best to teach a new genre directly and at other times it is more appropriate to use an inductive or discovery approach, or as Coe says, "To create situations in which students can reinvent the wheel of a genre" (p. 164). The guidelines suggested for introducing new forms of representation—creating learning contexts, engaging students in activities, modelling, metacognitive talk, and support for independence—apply equally to learning written genres. Since formal features are now understood to derive from and relate to a writer's purpose and the social context of writing, any consideration of form should be descriptive rather than prescriptive (Freedman & Medway, 1994). Here are some things to consider in blending process and genre:

- Emphasize ideas rather than form in the early stages (i.e., with younger children and in the first part of the school year at all grade levels).
- Begin by immersing children in a genre you want them to learn; for example, before you engage them in writing legends, read aloud legends to them, stock the classroom library with books of legends for them to read, show films of legends, and so on. Focus their attention on the form of the legend to help them identify its features; later, collaboratively create a list of criteria or attributes.

- Use the attributes or criteria generated by the class at the prewriting and/or editing stages; while the use of models has been shown to have limited value when teachers provide them and students copy them, a benefit has been indicated when students generate criteria and apply them to their own work (Hillocks, 1986).
- Help students understand the function of particular features of a genre; for example, why letters include the date, address, salutation, and greeting.
- Help students understand the importance of audience and context of situation.
- Use a process approach—prewriting, drafting, editing—but incorporate genre-specific techniques and strategies where they are meaningful.

When Is a Focus on Genre Appropriate?

Sometimes focusing on a genre is appropriate; at other times it would conflict with another objective (for example, the development of fluency or editing to clarify meaning). Here are some questions that can help teachers decide whether or not to focus on formal or structural features:

- *Is form an appropriate focus for these learners?*
  A focus on fluency is more important than form for younger and inexperienced students and in the first part of the school year with all elementary school students.
- *Is a specific form essential for the particular function or purpose of the writing?*
  Form is usually not important in personal/expressive and epistemic writing and may not be with some other functions of writing, depending on other factors.
- *Who is the intended audience of the writing?*
  If the audience of the writing is oneself, form is not prominent, nor is it when the audience is someone very close to you (a dear friend, for example). On the other hand, form may be important for audiences unknown to the writer or when the addressee has the power to make judgments or decisions about the writer (as in a job application).
- *How formal is the context of situation?*
  The more informal the context, the less importance is attached to form. For example, in interpersonal communication between good friends we do not

worry much about form (beyond essential requirements that enable communication), but we certainly do when we are writing a formal business letter.

- *Is the form in question familiar to students by way of speaking, reading, and other experiences?*
  When students have a strong background of experience with a genre (personal stories, for example), they may not need much instruction in its formal features. On the other hand, when they have relatively little experience with a genre (written argument, for example), they may benefit from some attention to its formal features.
- *Is the form in question particularly important for academic or workplace success?*
  Some types of writing, particularly exposition, are important for future success in school or work. In these instances, most students benefit from some explicit attention to form.

Interweaving Process and Genre

In the remaining part of this chapter, I examine five major categories of writing—description, narrative, poetry, argument, and exposition—and pro-

REFLECTION

Part of learning the craft of weaving is developing a conscious awareness of form and technique. Apprentice weavers are taught to discern basic elements of design and traditional patterns, not to limit them to what has already been done, but to enable them to create their own textiles and develop their individual styles of weaving. Similarly, apprentice writers need to learn about written genres. Paradoxically, focusing too intently on form, particularly in the early stages, inhibits both weavers and writers. A more effective approach is learning through exploration and hands-on experience with guidance, support, and metacognitive talk within the context of the activity from more accomplished members of the weaving or writing community.

Have you learned any artistic endeavour (e.g., painting, dancing) or athletic pursuit (skating, swimming)? Think about how you learned about aspects of form. Did you learn them independently, or were you taught? When and how did you master particular techniques?

vide suggestions for ways of weaving together techniques from process and genre approaches. In traditional programs, the first three categories were usually addressed within the context of language arts, while argument and exposition were commonly associated with science and social studies. In an integrated approach to writing, these curricular boundaries dissolve; narratives, for example, can be used in social studies. My intent here is to illustrate how to weave the teaching of genre with a process approach rather than to provide an exhaustive supply of suggestions. I hope that the ideas presented will help you create your own strategies.

Description

Traditionally, it was thought that narratives were the most basic genres. Some people still argue for the primacy of narrative; I am not among them. I chose to start with description because my own research (Chapman, 1994, 1995, 1996) found that young children's written genres in Grade 1 began this way, with single-clause labels that evolved into descriptions of their pictures. Descriptions can occur as specific genres (for example, character sketches) and embedded in other genres such as stories (descriptions of characters and places) and reports (a description of an animal, for example).

Bernie Mohan (1986) developed a schema for classifying discourse that places descriptions in the most basic category. I have used Mohan's framework for organizing some forms of representation and written genres (Figure 7.2). You will notice that description, narrative, argument, and exposition are included in this chart, but poetry is not. Rather than tackling descriptive writing directly (i.e., "I want my students to do descriptive writing; how can I devise an activity to do that?"), I propose that teachers think of situations in which descriptive writing is meaningfully embedded or is a logical outcome of the activity. Countless opportunities abound in science, social studies, art, and literature response. Because descriptions are based on observations of specific cases, prewriting activities that enable young writers to write effective descriptions are those that emphasize experiencing and observing; talk provides the medium for linking the two. Experiences can be real or imagined, personal or shared, and observations can incorporate all five senses, not just sight. First-hand experiences such as field trips and science experiments are the most concrete; asking children questions can help them focus and hone their observation skills. This also forms a link to the fine arts: becoming effective

Figure 7.2 Genres and Forms of Representation According to Mohan's Categories of Discourse

	Specific (1 case)	Comparative (2 cases)	General (more than 2 cases)
OBERVING	label, caption list of attributes diagram map specific description (e.g., my house) specific web character sketch about the author acrostic brochure story map or web	comparison and contrast Venn diagram 2-column matrix	classification definition glossary tree chart general description (e.g., houses) general web concept map matrix (more than 2 columns)
SEQUENCING	timeline action strip chronology chronicle narrative (e.g., folk tale) retelling storyboard agenda biography autobiography directions instructions procedures recipe description of process cycle flow chart dialogue script	cause and effect prediction hypothesis	theory set of principles rules guidelines explanation conclusions
DECISION-MAKING	personal opinion decision problem identification problem posing or generation decision tree flow chart editorial	alternative solutions debate argument trial	evaluation recommendation rating scale rubric critique

Note: Each category includes tables and charts of various kinds.

REFLECTION

One year when I was teaching Grade 3, an incident occurred that made me realize how well children can learn about a genre through active engagement. Earlier that school year we had explored fables within the context of a theme on animals. I had read many fables to the children, and then we created a chart of characteristics of fables that included:

- animal characters that act and talk like humans
- very short stories
- there is a problem in the story
- a character in the story learns a lesson (a moral)
- many fables were written long ago by a man named Aesop

Below, we added a list of about ten stories that met these criteria and could be classified as fables. I encouraged the children to add more titles from their own reading. Over the next month or so, the list grew and grew, and I remember the enthusiasm of the children as they wrote title after title on the chart.

Later that year, I was reading to the class James Marshall's (1972) *George and Martha* when one student, Michelle, put up her hand and said, "Mrs. Chapman, George and Martha stories are modern fables." When I asked her how she knew, Michelle said, "Well, they are short stories with animal characters who act and talk like humans. There is a problem in the story, usually because of George, and George always learns a lesson. But this is a modern fable because it wasn't written a long time ago in Greece by Aesop." Well, I hadn't even thought about the George and Martha stories as modern fables, but I learned from Michelle that they are!

How does this incident demonstrate Michelle's knowledge of genre?

observers is important for artistic and aesthetic development as well. Prewriting can also include drawing, visualizing (see the visualization Activity box on page 168), and drama. Words and ideas can be recorded in attribute lists or webs or through combinations of writing and sketching such as pictures with captions, or diagrams with labels.

Improving students' descriptive writing abilities in the primary years occurs mainly through providing rich prewriting experiences and making connections through oral language. In Grades 4 to 7, editing also has a role to play. After students have written a draft that is descriptive in nature, teachers

Activity:
Story Board

Story boards are planning devices for stories. They are used in the production of movies and television shows (professional writers use a series of blank frames like cartoon boxes to represent different scenes in the production). The best way to introduce story boards is through reading aloud to the class and completing the story board collaboratively to show the elements of the story just read. Once students are familiar with the format, they can use it as a planning device for writing their own stories. The simplest story boards have just three parts—beginning, middle, and end—and they can be introduced in kindergarten (the children make illustrations for the parts of a story read to them). With Grades 1 and 2 children I introduce the element of *story problem* by putting a small sad face in the first box (to show the character is sad because he has a problem) and a happy face in the last box (to show the problem has been solved). I explain that the middle of the story is like the filling in the sandwich—it's the interesting part (and in a story it is how the character goes about solving his or her problem). A more detailed story board can be introduced in Grade 3 with the addition of focal questions. Figure 7.4 shows some story board examples. Teachers of junior grades may prefer to use blank frames as story boards, as professionals do. They can also use story boards to plan and organize plays and other performances.

can focus editing around collaboratively established criteria for effective descriptions. This can be done in several ways:

- Choose a good descriptive piece from a selection of literature; read it aloud to students (perhaps asking them to close their eyes and visualize the character or scene); and talk about why the description is effective (for example, lots of details, use of adjectives and specific verbs).
- Have students create a picture (a mythical monster, for example) and write paragraph to describe it; play a matching game in which you display some of the pictures, students read their descriptions aloud, and the class tries to identify which monster is being described; then discuss the qualities of the writing that made the matching easier.

- Read aloud to the class two or three selections of varying effectiveness in description and have students follow directions to draw pictures or act out what was described; discuss what made descriptions effective or not.

Criteria charts, collaboratively created through teacher-guided experiences and discussions, can then be used by students to revise their drafts. Begin with a single strategy, for example, adding describing words or substituting more precise words. When students construct criteria for effective writing, when they engage in activities that enable them to see criteria purposefully, and when they have opportunities to apply these criteria to their own writing, the resulting learning is meaningful and enduring.

Narrative

In my studies of first-grade genres (Chapman 1994, 1995, 1996), narratives emerged when the children began to write about their personal lives and recorded events in sequences. Time is perhaps the core element of narratives that distinguishes them from other genres. (Narrative is a large-genre category that includes many specific genres, such as folk tales, fairy tales, biographies, and so on.) In Mohan's (1986) schema, narratives are classified as one-case-specific sequencing (Figure 7.2). Although the term *story* is often used loosely to refer to any sequenced piece of writing, many of the "stories" written by young children (and many of the "stories" in basal reading programs) are simply sequences. Central features of narratives that elementary school students can learn about include

- introduction: character and setting (time and place)
- complicating action or problem
- attempts at resolving the problem
- closure or resolution

Story grammar (Gordon, 1983) is one approach (or rather, a set of approaches) to teaching narrative. It makes explicit the central features of narrative. Sometimes it is used prescriptively; I prefer an inductive, descriptive approach similar to the one discussed in the previous section on description:

- Immerse students in quality narratives by reading aloud, stocking the classroom library, and choosing stories for shared literature experiences.

- In the context of these experiences, over time, discuss elements of narrative such as character and problem; talk about what makes a good story (for example, interesting characters, problems people can relate to, vivid use of language).
- Engage students in drama so that they experience narrative "from the inside out."
- Encourage students to write in narrative when it is appropriate, for example, when relating their own experiences or chronicles of events, retelling favourite stories in their own words, or creating original stories.

When you see that students are writing fluently and confidently in narrative (it is best not to rush), for example, in the middle or latter part of the school year, introduce the notion of story grammar explicitly in the context of a story you read aloud to them, and develop a chart of story grammar elements. The story grammar chart can be presented as a list or as a *story web*.

Activity:
Storyline Map

This idea was developed by Joy Pequin of Saanich, British Columbia. In her multi-age primary class, Joy had a child who was extremely visually impaired and had difficulty understanding the idea of story sequence. Joy got two long skipping ropes, tied them together, and ran them along the floor of the classroom. The class had talked about story sequences or plots as linear journeys and circular journeys. She engaged the children in retelling a story she had just read to them, and in the process the class decided it had eight main parts. She had eight children space themselves along the rope, and the rest of the children walked along it. As they met a child on the rope, that child told his or her part of the story, so the children were walking the journey in the story. The first time they did this activity, the story had a linear plot; the next story had a circular plot. This idea was a wonderful way for all the children to learn about plot development, but it was particularly meaningful for the student who was blind. All of the children were able to successfully draw a storyline map for the stories they had heard and read. Once children have learned the concept of a storyline map through listening and reading, they can use it to map out a plot for an original story as a prewriting activity.

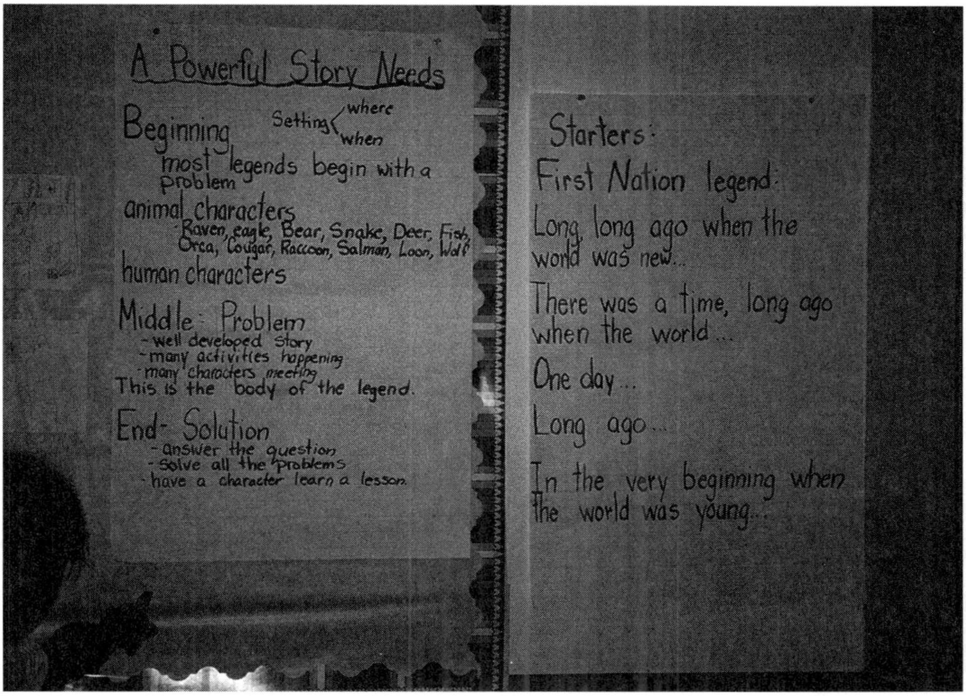

Developing charts of story grammar elements with students can help them develop conscious knowledge of narrative genres.

I prefer a story web because it can be used as a general template and filled in with specifics from a story. I also like the flexibility of the story web because it can be adapted to suit different types of narratives, such as folk tales and fairy tales. (Figure 7.3 shows a general story web and a fairy tale web.) The story grammar chart developed through reading can then be used in a variety of ways for writing, such as

- collaboratively creating a story using the chart
- editing a narrative previously written—students select a narrative from their writing folder (see Chapter 6) to critique using the story grammar chart; then they use the chart to revise their drafts
- using a planning device for writing an original story; planning devices include story webs, story boards (see the Activity box and Figure 7.4), and storyline maps (see the Activity box and Figure 7.5)

Figure 7.3 General Story and Fairy Tale Webs

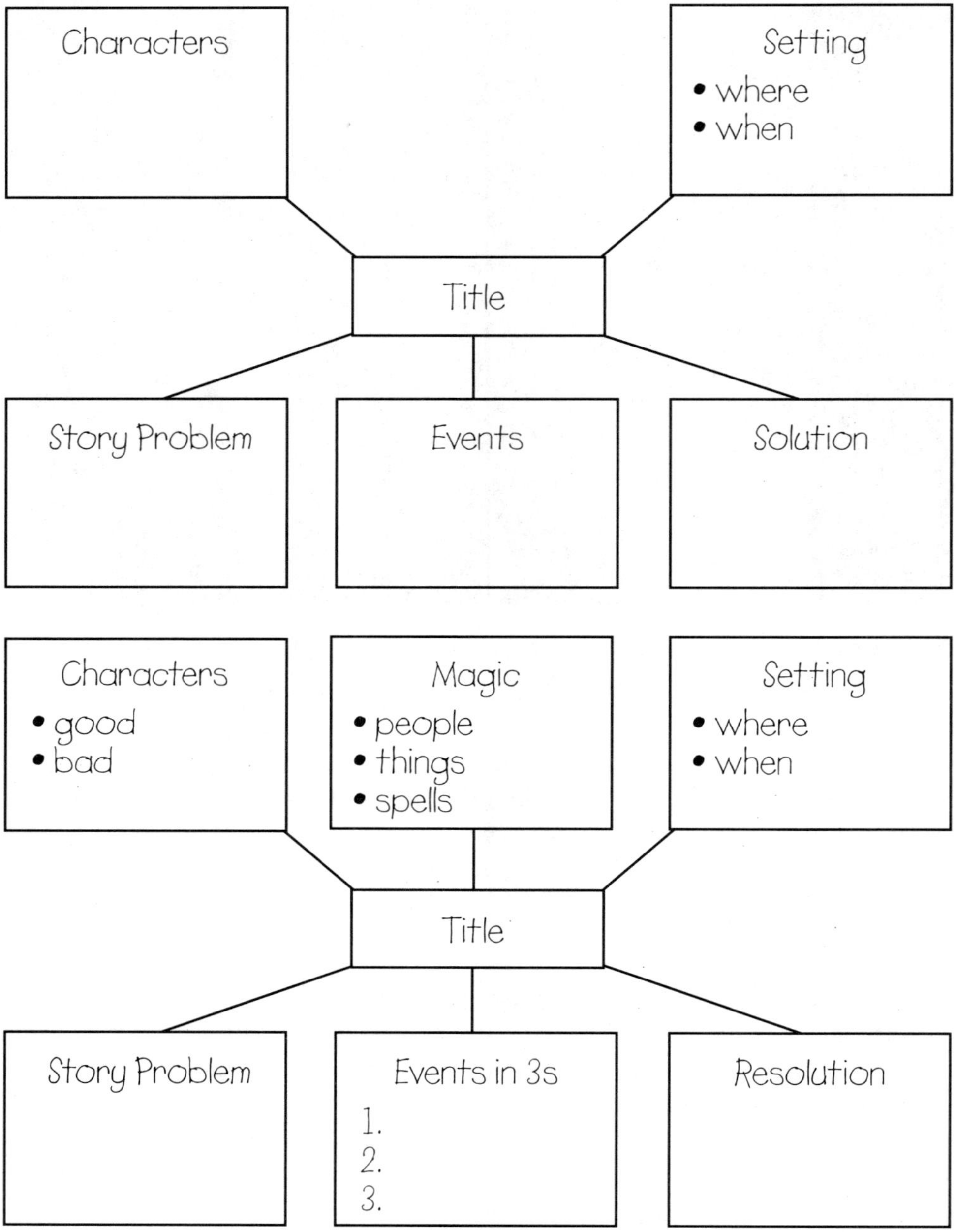

Figure 7.4 Story Boards

Beginning	Middle	End

Beginning 	Middle	End 

Beginning	Middle	End
characters setting • where • when story problem	events	resolution

Figure 7.5 Storyline Map

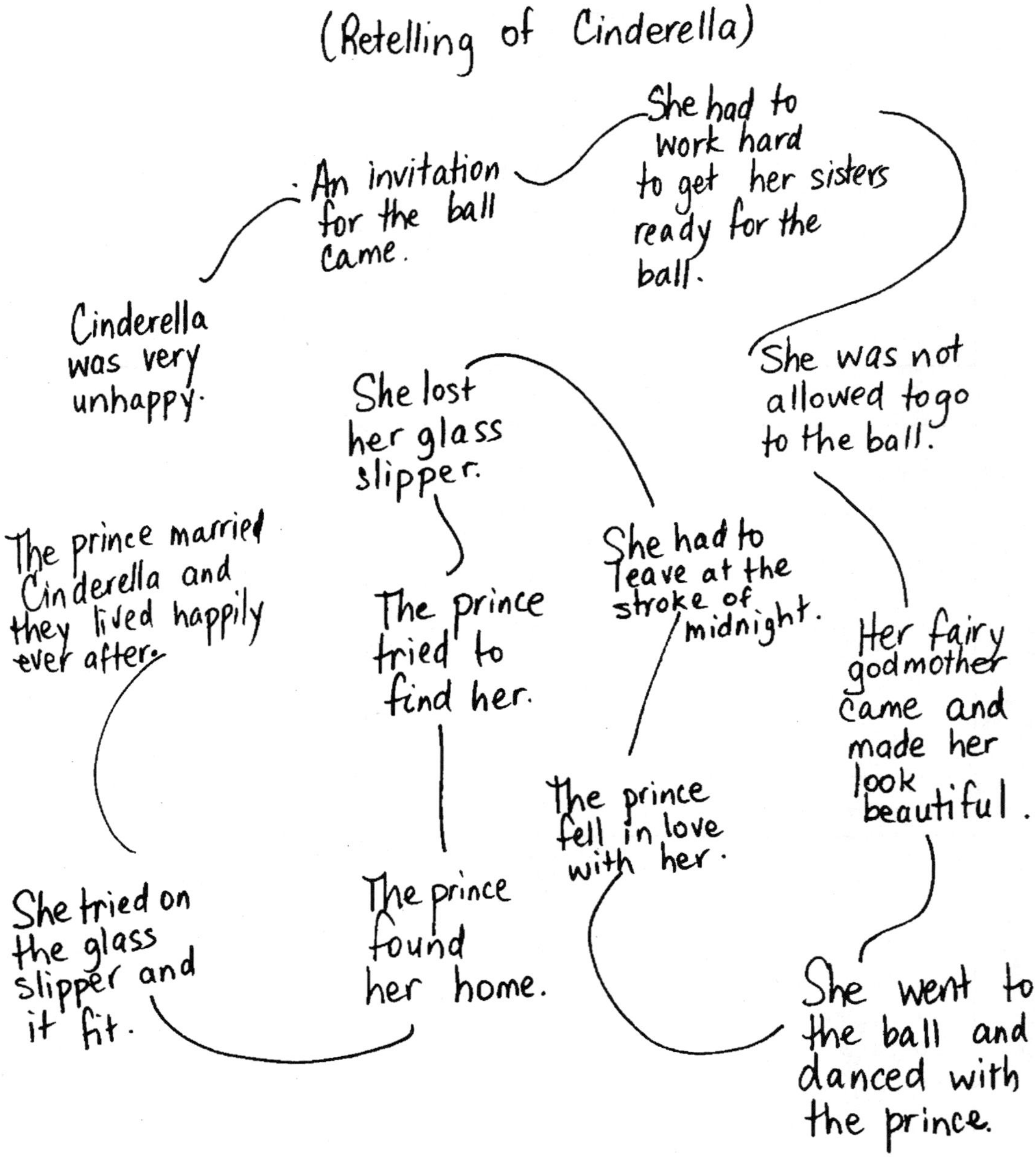

- engaging students in a series of activities that will culminate in the writing of a narrative, for example: creating a character and a setting (descriptive writing); deciding on a critical incident or problem as a focal point for the story; developing a plot line; this method may be used for whole-class, small-group, or individual writing

Elementary school students can enjoy a wide variety of fictional narrative genres, including folk tales, fairy tales, tall tales, fables, legends, and myths. Remember, however, that narrative does not always mean fiction. Autobiographies and biographies are also narratives. As well, there are other genres and forms of representation that are similar to narratives because they involve sequencing. Figure 7.2 lists some of these genres.

Poetry

The best way to introduce students to poetry writing is having it read aloud by a teacher who is enthusiastic about poetry. Children can be introduced to many different kinds of poetry and encouraged to play with words and ideas to create pleasing effects. In the elementary school, the emphasis is on enjoyment and metalinguistic play rather than on form. Poetic genres should be offered as invitations rather than assignments—having to write a poem is probably the best way to kill motivation to do so.

Poetry writing can begin informally in the primary grades through reading and sharing poems and patterned writing. These readings should be accompanied by lots of talk about language. Young children particularly enjoy word play activities involving repetitions of sound, for example, alliteration. In the junior grades, the emphasis should be on unrhymed poetry, otherwise children become overly concerned with making things rhyme, which results in stilted, nonsensical writing.

The prewriting stage invariably includes oral reading of poetry with discussions of ideas and sounds and meanings of words. This is followed by generating ideas for children's own poems through techniques such as clustering, brainstorming, or word caching (see Chapter 6). A playful, relaxed attitude toward shaping ideas and words into poems (drafting) results in more pleasing and interesting poetry than if the writer worries about pattern or form. Before asking students to write poems individually, it is often appropriate to write collaboratively, either as a class or in a small group. It is also a good

REFLECTION

Probably the best poetry my students (Grade 3s) ever produced was about the wind. It was a particularly windy day outside and I began the day by reading aloud a poem about the wind. Next, I engaged the children in dramatic movement. We turned off all the lights and became wind—starting with small gusts; building to roaring gales, hurricanes, and tornadoes; then dying down and becoming calm. As the children moved, I asked them to call out words and ideas, which I recorded on the chalkboard. After the wind had died down, we talked some more and added more ideas. Throughout the year we had done different kinds of patterned writing, and for each I had made a chart. I posted these charts so the children could use any of them if they wished, but also encouraged them to make up their own patterns and forms. The children and I were so pleased with the results that they each selected their favourite wind poem (they had all written several) and we put them together as a class collection. Every student received a photocopy of the entire set, which they then put together in clothbound books. These were then given to their mothers as Mothers' Day presents.

What was it about this activity that enabled the children to write such wonderful poems?

idea for children to produce several drafts rather than just one. This way, they can select the one they like best for sharing orally and, perhaps, revising.

Editing should begin with oral sharing and positive responses. Only once this has been done should form be attended to more carefully. For example, if students are trying their hand at haiku, have them count the number of syllables and reword to fit the 5-7-5 syllabic form. Because poems are often quite short, children can take great care in publishing them artistically, for example, in calligraphy or on the computer, mounting them on shaped paper, adding illustrations, and so on. Figure 7.6 illustrates some nonrhyming poetic or patterned forms that elementary school children enjoy writing.

Argument

While children often feel at ease in expressing their opinions, they often have difficulty writing effective arguments, mainly because they lack the knowledge and skills to support their case. I know that writing assessments in

Figure 7.6 A Potpourri of Poetic Forms

Poem Type or Form	Description	Examples
List poems	• Brainstorm lists of ideas related to a topic • List poems can be strings of single words, pairs of words, or phrases • Start and/or end with the topic	Bats Cats Goblins Ghosts Haunting Halloween Burning candle glowing brightly flickering gently wispy smoke softly curling dying down.
Pattern poems	• Use a variety of patterns, e.g., – repetition of first word(s) – days of the week – the alphabet	Spring is trees awakening, Spring is flowers blooming, Spring is grass turning green, Spring is new life appearing, Spring is a beginning. On Monday, I munched on melon, On Tuesday, I tasted toast ...
Alliteration	• Create an image using words that start with the same sound	Six silvery snakes slithered slowly And stared at the spotted spider ... hiss.
Acrostic poems	• Write vertically the word that is the subject of the poem • Start each phrase with that letter; describe the topic	Laughing together Ordinary people Very happy to be Evermore in love.
Sensory poems	• Brainstorm ideas on the topic, categorize them by senses • Whenever possible, use real objects to brainstorm about • The poem can focus on one sense (e.g., sound) or all	My apple looks shiny and red It smells tangy Feels crunchy in my mouth Mmm ... tastes delicious! Sounds in the classroom: the screech of chalk on the board the grinding of pencils in the sharpener the tapping of feet on the floor the hush of students thinking.
Found poems	• Cut out words you find in magazines, cereal boxes, etc. • Arrange them in an order you like	Food New and improved Organically grown Delicious Apple and Cinnamon The best you've ever tasted!

Figure 7.6 A Potpourri of Poetic Forms (cont.)

Poem Type or Form	Description	Examples
Instant poems	• Build by adding and removing words: – write 3 words – repeat first line, add one word – take off first word, add a new word; repeat as often as you wish	Creepy crawly creature Creepy crawly creature slithering Crawly creature slithering slowly Creature slithering slowly by Slithering slowly by, unnoticed.
Cinquain	• A simple, 5-line verse • Form: line 1—1 word (noun) line 2—2 describing words line 3—3 action words line 4—4 words express a feeling line 5—1 word, a synonym for line 1	Mountain Majestic, rising Touching the clouds Snow against blue sky Peak
Diamante	• The purpose is to show contrast or a change, from one subject at the top of the diamond to another at the bottom (often the opposite of subject) (word #1) • line 1—1 noun (subject #1) line 2—2 adjectives line 3—3 *ing* words line 4—2 nouns related to first word plus 2 nouns related to last word line 5—3 *ing* words line 6—2 adjectives line 7—1 noun (subject #2)	child rambunctious, happy playing, laughing, learning youth, growth, maturity, age striving, working, parenting older, wiser adult
Haiku	• The central image is usually about nature and the tense is present • Format: line 1—5 syllables line 2—7 syllables line 3—5 syllables	Loud, crashing thunder And then the rain pouring down A rainbow appears.
Terse verse	• A short poem with a long introduction • The form is a riddle with a definition plus an answer that rhymes • Variations: hink-pinks—1-syllable rhymes hinky-pinkies—2-syllable rhymes hinkety-pinketie—3-syllable rhymes	A small aggressive vegetable is A mean bean An easily accessible lollipop is A handy candy An unsolved event from the past: A history mystery

Figure 7.6 A Potpourri of Poetic Forms (cont.)

Poem Type or Form	Description	Examples
Concrete poems	• The central idea of the poem is depicted both verbally and visually	

~ The sleek, silvery snake slithered secretly and silently through the grass ~

Activity:
Ping-Pong Debate

Here is one way to introduce argument:

Preparation:

- Choose a topic that has opposing sides, for example: Should whales be kept in captivity (in aquariums)?
- Divide students into two teams and assign positions (for and against).
- Ask students to think individually first (ideas can be written down), then brainstorm in a team huddle to find reasons to support their argument.

Playing the Game:

- The game is played like Ping-Pong—a member of one team makes a statement, then a member of the opposing team makes a statement (it may be a rebuttal or another idea).
- The game goes back and forth; when the ball comes back into their court, team members who have already had a turn must count to five before they speak again to allow everyone a chance to participate.
- The teacher stops the game before all ideas are exhausted, watching to ensure that everyone has spoken, if possible.
- There does not have to be a winner.

British Columbia reveal argument or persuasive writing to be the least well written genre. It may well be that there is a developmental factor involved here, but it is also likely that students have less experience in this type of writing than narrative, description, and exposition.

Before we can expect students to write effective arguments, they need opportunities to engage in oral ones. An excellent way to introduce argument is through a simplified form of debate such as the Ping-Pong debate described in the Activity box. Although the debate is conducted orally, students use writing in their preparation. After the game, engage the students in a discussion of each team's support for its case. It is not sufficient just to generate ideas; students need to know why some ideas are better than others.

What counts as effective persuasion depends on the context and audience. Complicating matters still further is that there is no unifying persuasive form. For example, in Canadian law courts, arguments are conducted in ways that

Activity:
Writing in Role

Writing in role is a powerful medium for learning. Young children engage in dramatic play naturally, so the primary grades are the best time to introduce children to writing in role. I have found this approach highly effective with students in the junior grades as well. When students have a choice, learning through drama is a strong favourite.

Here is one example of writing in role integrated with story drama:

- Read a story to the class that includes a problem related to a topic or theme you are working on: for example, if the class is learning about water (the water cycle, uses of water, etc.) a suitable story would be *The King's Fountain* by Lloyd Alexander (1971).
- Stop at a place where a problem has been identified; in this story it would be when the king threatens to cut off the water supply to the village so that he can build a fountain.
- Engage the students in story drama. Students take on a role; they can all take the same role (one of the villagers, perhaps) or choose who they will be (such as advisers to the king, or adults or children who live in the village).

(continued)

Activity:
Writing in Role (cont.)

- In role, students write a letter or speech to the king to persuade him not to take the water from the village.
- Take the role of the king yourself or ask a student to volunteer.
- Volunteers read their letters or speeches (in role) to the king.
- The king responds; there is discussion about why he is or is not persuaded to change his plans (if you are the king, you can do this directly; if a student is king, the teacher acts as an interviewer and asks questions to probe the king's thinking).
- This is followed by a class debriefing and discussion of effective persuasion. Do villagers think the king can be persuaded?
- At this juncture, students could have an opportunity either to resume their roles or take on a new one and revise their letters or speeches.

Activity:
Writers' RAFT (Role, Audience, Form, and Topic)

This strategy is useful for planning writing activities. It can be used by students in planning shared experiences, or as a prewriting activity to generate ideas and make decisions about the form a piece of writing might take. Here is an example: the class is learning about pioneers; the class brainstorms *roles*, or people who were pioneers (for example, a farmer, a rancher, a young wife), and *audiences*, people the first individuals might communicate with (which could include names on the first list). Next, the class brainstorms possible *topics*, stated in sentence form (for example, "Pioneer life is very hard," or "Travelling west is very exciting." Finally, they brainstorm various *forms*, such as songs, letters, and so on. Students play with the ideas on the various lists to come up with ideas for writing, such as:

- A young pioneer wife writes a letter to her mother back home to tell her about the hardships of pioneer life.
- A farmer composes a song to sing with his friends about the excitement of travelling west.

are a mystery to most people who are not lawyers. (Most of us probably construct our ideas about legal arguments from television.) Canadian Aboriginals use a very different form of legal argument, one that is narrative in form. I have found drama, for example, writing-in-role and role-playing, to be particularly effective in teaching persuasive writing to elementary school children. (Integrating writing and drama, including writing in role and role-playing, is not limited to argumentation, of course.) There are several ways to engage students in writing in role and role-playing. The Activity box provides one example.

It is beyond the scope of this book to explore drama more deeply and to show how it can be integrated with writing. For further reading, I recommend *Role Drama* by Carole Tarlington and Patrick Verriour (1991) and Verriour's (1994) *In Role: Teaching and Learning Dramatically.* Another idea, Writers' RAFT, developed by Carol Santa (1988), is an effective strategy for planning writing-in-role activities (see the Activity box). I find it particularly useful for persuasive writing (as illustrated in the junior classroom in Chapter 5), but it can be used with other genres as well.

Exposition

In the elementary school, the major focus of expository writing is on information reports, usually in conjunction with science and social studies. Information reports may be introduced in the primary grades; they are an important part of the language arts program in the junior grades. The process of inquiry is more important than form in the elementary school. In other words, when a student engages in writing a report about whales, learning how to access, collect, and organize information (process) is more important than learning about whales (content), which is, in turn, more important than the report on whales (product). However, because report writing is a prominent component of secondary and postsecondary schooling, students need to learn about this genre in order to be more successful academically. Most students have minimal experience with report writing, and if left to their own devices they either have little idea of how best to proceed or they copy from books. For these reasons, I believe report writing is most effectively learned through a process approach that integrates explicit, direct instruction on strategies for acquiring and organizing information and on structural features of the genre.

Traditionally, teachers have spent a lot of time preparing questions and detailed outlines that tend to be specific to an assignment. If we want students to learn the process of report writing, it is more productive to teach them strategies for developing their own focal questions and outlines. Learning to collect and organize information is a major objective. The ideas presented here provide a context for a lesson portrayed in Chapter 5, and that lesson illustrates the concepts presented here. I approach the issue of report writing developmentally, beginning with a description of how I would begin report writing with primary children and explaining how I would proceed to build sequentially through the elementary grades.

A Developmental Approach to Report Writing

The report-writing process I describe has been used in many primary and junior classrooms and has evolved over time. It represents a sociocognitive constructivist or transactional approach to language and learning, and is an example of a model of an inquiry-centred curriculum developed by Gordon Wells and Gen Ling Chang-Wells (1992), described in *Constructing Knowledge Together: Classrooms as Centers of Inquiry and Literacy*, which I recommend for further reading. It also builds on ideas formulated by Dorothy Grant Hennings (1982). Students can be introduced to report writing through shared experiences within a unit of study or theme. Starting with a common topic that is explored by the whole class provides maximum support through modelling and collaboration. This can begin informally in kindergarten and Grade 1 through hands-on explorations of social studies and science topics and by encouraging children to access prior knowledge and generate questions. (See Kindergarten Corner: Factual Writing.) Although teachers' plans should always be adapted to the learning abilities and needs of the children in the class, I have found the following general sequence to be a useful guide:

- *Kindergarten and Grade 1*—Introduce children to factual writing in an informal way, with a focus on accessing prior knowledge and generating questions, for example, through the Know-Wonder-Learned strategy (described in Chapter 6) and language experience activities related to science and social studies topics; create class books (or big books) on factual topics (see Kindergarten Corner: Factual Writing); encourage children to write their own factual books in Writing Workshop time.

- *Grades 2–3*—Continue to focus on accessing prior knowledge and generating questions; introduce note-taking, classification (cut-and-paste method) and writing sentences from notes (described later in this chapter); do class research projects on a theme with sections written by children individually or in pairs and assembled as a class big book report (described in the following section); children write in sentences rather than paragraphs; continue to encourage children to write factual books in Writing Workshop time.
- *Grades 3–4*—Continue with accessing prior knowledge, generating questions, note-taking, and classifying with the cut-and-paste method; students work on separate reports on topics related to an overall theme; in Grade 3, children work in small groups and write in sentences; in Grade 4, children may work individually and also be introduced to paragraph writing (modelled through collaborative writing).
- *Grades 5 and up*—Students work on individual reports on specific topics related to an overall theme and also self-chosen topics of interest; introduce new strategies for note-taking (described further in the chapter).

This approach to report writing is a gradual one, but one that has been successful in many settings. Earlier experiences provide a solid foundation upon which subsequent learning can be built. As students progress through the elementary school their expository writing skills develop incrementally, but with this gradual immersion, by the end of the junior years, most students will be successful writers of exposition. It is a good idea to discuss report

KINDERGARTEN CORNER

Factual Writing

Factual writing can begin even before children are writing independently with invented spellings. Debbie Wheatley, a kindergarten teacher in Delta, British Columbia, introduced her students to research about reindeer. They did a KWL, looked at pictures of reindeer to find information, and made a reindeer web. Debbie asked the children to tell her an idea in a sentence. Some children wrote in invented spellings; she recorded the ideas for others. The children illustrated their ideas and made a class book.

writing with the teacher-librarian in your school. Most of them are eager to be involved and provide assistance. Many teacher-librarians have developed a process and sequence for teaching students research skills, and they can be valuable partners in teaching report writing. They know the resources available in the school and are familiar with problems children encounter in the library when they come to work on projects and reports.

First Steps in Report Writing

Discussion throughout the process of writing reports focuses primarily on ideas and strategies rather than on form, although it is appropriate to point out aspects of form informally within the context of the activities. In the following examples, children are introduced to note-taking and classification. I have found it best to introduce each skill separately, beginning with note-taking in Grade 2.

Introducing Note-taking. Here is one way to begin note-taking:

1. Choose a focal topic, for example, "bears."
2. Organize two charts in the following way: to make the charts suitable for note-taking (and for categorizing later on), fold unlined newsprint (60 cm x 90 cm) into three lengthwise columns, and then fold in half crossways three times so you end up with eighteen boxes. In the first box on one chart, write KNOW, in the first box on the second chart write LEARNED, using a different colour for each chart.
3. Label a third piece of newsprint WONDER. Do not fold this one.
4. Using a KWL strategy (see Chapter 6), brainstorm "what we know about bears," record ideas *in note form, not sentences, each idea in a separate box* on the KNOW chart (the chart that is not folded). Then, brainstorm *questions*: "what we wonder about bears," recording them in a different-coloured marker on the WONDER chart (the chart that is not folded). Post the charts.
5. Over the next few days, read aloud stories to the class and show videos, films, or filmstrips. Record new ideas on the LEARNED chart *in note form* (like the KNOW chart) with a third colour.
6. Discuss connections with the KNOW, WONDER, and LEARNED charts: Were all of our questions asked? Were the things we knew confirmed? (Sometimes children will discover that what they "knew" was incorrect; for example, that pandas are not bears.) What new facts did we learn?

7. Cut out the ideas from the KNOW and LEARNED charts, discarding any disproven ideas (such as "pandas are bears").
8. With the children, sort the ideas into a logical order (you may need to use the floor).
9. With the children, model the process of writing from notes by taking a few of the ideas and writing sentences for each of them. You may write these sentences on the board, on sentence strips, at the top of separate pages that will be part of the class book, or using a computer connected to an overhead projector.
10. Children each choose a fact they are interested in and write their own sentences. Writing at the top of the page ensures there is sufficient room; the illustrations go below.
11. Have children make illustrations, assemble the report, and add a title page.

After students have engaged in a class research project on the same topic, they are ready for a class project with sections written by children individually or with partners. The larger topic should be shared, for example, "space," within which students identify specific topics for collaborative and individual research (e.g., the sun, the moon, stars, galaxies, our solar system, Venus, Mars, etc.). The individual parts could be assembled in a Big Book Report about Space.

Introducing Classification. Once students are familiar with the note-taking process, I introduce classification. The writing process extends over a week or more, but the time is well spent. Here is one way to proceed:

1. Follow the initial steps described for note-taking (choosing a topic; using the KWL strategy to access prior knowledge, generate questions, and collect information; cutting out ideas and discarding disproven ideas). Now you are ready to classify or categorize the facts.
2. With the children, sort the note boxes into categories (you may need to use the floor); discuss why the ideas go together (the main idea or subtopic).
3. Paste each category of ideas on new charts, leaving a space at the top. Discuss titles for each category and write them at the top of each chart.
4. With the class, write a draft for each section using chart paper or a computer connected to an overhead projector. Begin with the title and then write lists of sentences with Grade 3 students or paragraphs with Grade 4s.

> **Something to think about:**
>
> Many nonfiction books for primary children are written in a narrative style rather than a traditional expository form. This is intended to make nonfiction more interesting and appealing to young children and to make reading for information easier. Do you think information is more accessible in a story format than in an expository one? Why or why not?

5. Make a title page (and a table of contents, if you wish).
6. Have children make illustrations and then assemble the report. The charts result in a big book format.

Report Writing: From Prewriting to Presenting

Eventually, we want students to be able to do research and to write reports on topics of their own choosing (or assigned by a teacher) independently. Report writing is most effectively learned when students research specific topics collaboratively or individually within a unit of study or theme that is being explored by the class as a whole. Through an inquiry-based project and report writing, students construct understanding as they compose; in other words, they learn through writing and learn to write in the report genre at the same time. In this section, I describe a process approach that integrates explicit teaching of the report genre.

Prewriting experiences are extensive in report writing. In fact, they take the majority of the time for the overall project. They are designed to enable students to construct knowledge and to access information through

- doing and observing
- interviewing
- reading
- viewing pictures, videos, filmstrips
- field trips and excursions
- talking
- listening
- technology (CD-ROM, Internet)

Many of these experiences are provided for the class as a whole. In addition, students will need opportunities to acquire information individually or in small groups, for example through reading, viewing filmstrips, using CD-ROM, and so on. Within the larger, shared context of the unit of study or theme, students individually or in small groups can

- *Select a topic or focus*—A good topic is one that the student is interested in and has some knowledge about, but is not an expert in.
- *Gather materials*—In some cases, a student selects a good topic but there is a dearth of information, so the topic needs to be revised or adapted (I remember Harley couldn't find out much about the diamondback rattlesnake when he was in Grade 3, so he had to change his topic to rattlesnakes in general).
- *Access prior knowledge and generate questions*—Use strategies introduced in whole-class projects (described earlier in the chapter).

REFLECTION

I recall hearing that when Arthur Hailey worked on his novel *Airport,* he spent two years researching by hanging around airports observing people, talking to people in the industry, and so on, and about six months actually writing the book. I would not be surprised if this is true, because I know in my own work that prewriting takes a large portion of my time. I have found, however, that the time is well spent: the more prepared I am, the easier the drafting and editing are.

Think about report writing and all the skills students need to learn.

Collecting and organizing information is another important aspect of prewriting. Earlier I described how I would introduce these skills to primary children. In the junior grades, teachers may use the same approach, for example, having students use blank newsprint folded into note boxes. Another approach is to give students strips of lined paper (about 7 cm wide) for note-taking (this might be introduced in Grade 5). It is interesting how the shape and size of paper affect how we write. When we have long lines, we tend to write sentences; when we have short lines, we make lists. Using strips of paper or note boxes discourages copying. With primary children, I use a cut-and-paste approach to categorizing; older children can do this or they can use colours to highlight or circle ideas that go together, using a different colour for each category. Once categories are established, headings are generated.

Drafting based on related facts comes next. Using a new page for each category, children write the heading and then write drafts from their notes.

Primary children are usually able to write lists of sentences. I teach students how to write paragraphs from notes by modelling and doing a class book (as in the class big book report, but with paragraphs for the sections).

Editing sections of related facts for clarity and coherence is the next step in the process. Working in groups or individually, students address the following questions:

- Do the ideas go together?
- Are the ideas interesting?
- Is the information clearly presented?

Sequencing sections into a logical order follows the editing of related facts. Next comes *drafting and editing introductory and concluding sections* and organizing the parts into a cohesive whole. At this stage of the process, teachers can discuss explicitly how genres are organized to enable readers to gain information readily. *Proofreading* focuses on mechanics such as punctuation and spelling (see Chapter 6) and includes format of titles.

As preparation for *publishing* their reports, the class can examine information books to look at their format and discuss the purposes of various features such as title pages (with author's name, publication date, etc.), tables of contents, acknowledgments, diagrams and illustrations, book covers, bibliographies, and so on. When I make a class book with children in Grade 3 and above, I include these features so that I can discuss their functions and model how to do them. I also use the correct terminology (primary students love big words and seem to learn them easily in this kind of context). I teach primary students a simplified format for references, for example: Burton, R. *The Mouse in the Barn*, 1988.

Students can *present* their reports to a variety of audiences. Students who have worked on projects individually and in small groups enjoy sharing their efforts with classmates, students in other classes (big and little buddies, for example), their parents, the principal, the teacher-librarian, and so on. Class projects can also be shared with other classes. When students share their work, they should receive positive feedback. They should also have opportunities to talk about what they learned, both in terms of content and the process of report writing.

Reflections on the Chapter

Think about/talk about/write about:

Principles into Practice

- Use Figure 2.6, From Principles of Writing to Practice, to find specific examples in this chapter of each principle as it is put into practice.

Forms of Representation

- What forms of representation might you use in a typical day or week? In which contexts do you use them?
- Choose a specific curriculum area, such as mathematics. Think of all the forms of representation used in that discipline.

Process and Genre Approaches

- What are the benefits of a genre approach, a process approach, and a combined approach?

Genres

- Which genre types are you most comfortable with and feel most skilled in writing? With which genre types do you feel uncomfortable or less skilled in writing? Why do you think you feel this way?
- Choose a genre category, for example, narrative or poetry. How many different forms or subtypes can you think of (for example, narrative: fairy tale, legend; poetry: haiku, blank verse)?

Exposition/Report Writing

- Look at a variety of nonfiction trade books for young children. Try to find one example of a narrative style and one of an expository style. Try taking notes from these two books. What did you encounter in the process? Compare and contrast the process of note-taking from narrative and expository texts.
- What skills do children need in order to learn and take notes from expository texts? What strategies might teachers use to teach them?
- What skills do children need in order to learn and take notes from factual narrative texts? What strategies might teachers use to teach them?

REFERENCES AND FURTHER READING

Alexander, L. (1971). *The king's fountain.* New York: Dutton.

Chapman, M. (1994). The emergence of genres: Some findings from an investigation of first-grade writing. *Written Communication, 11*(3), 348–80.

———. (1995). The sociocognitive construction of written genres in first grade. *Research in the Teaching of English, 29*(2), 164–92.

———. (1996). More than spelling: Widening the lens on emergent writing. *Reading Horizons, 36*(4), pp. 317–39.

Coe, R. (1994). Teaching genre as process. In A. Freedman and P. Medway (Eds.), *Learning and teaching genre* (pp. 157–72). Portsmouth, NH: Heinemann.

de la Reyes, M. (1992). Challenging venerable assumptions: Literacy instruction for linguistically different students. *Harvard Educational Review, 62*(4), 427–46.

Delpit, L. (1988). The silenced dialogue: Power and pedagogy in educating other people's children. *Harvard Educational Review, 58*(2), 280–98.

Freedman, A., and Medway, P. (1994). Introduction: New views of genre and their implications for education. In A. Freedman and P. Medway (Eds.), *Learning and teaching genre* (pp. 1–22). Portsmouth, NH: Heinemann.

Gordon, C. (1983). *Improving reading comprehension and writing: The story grammar approach.* Calgary: Braun & Braun Education Enterprises.

Hennings, D. (1982). *Teaching communication and reading skills in the content areas.* Bloomington, IN: Phi Delta Kappa.

Hillocks, G. (1986). *Research on written composition.* Urbana, IL: National Conference on Research in English.

Marshall, J. (1972). *George and Martha.* Boston: Houghton-Mifflin.

Mohan, B. (1986). *Language and content.* Reading, MA: Addison-Wesley.

Santa, C. (1988). *Content reading including study systems: Reading, writing and studying across the curriculum.* Dubuque, IA: Kendall/Hunt.

Tarlington, C., and Verriour, P. (1991). *Role drama.* Portsmouth, NH: Heinemann.

Verriour, P. (1994). *In role: Teaching and learning dramatically.* Markham, ON: Pippin.

Vygotsky, L. (1978). *Mind in society: The development of higher psychological processes.* (M. Cole, V. John-Steiner, S. Scribner, and E. Souberman, Eds.). Cambridge, MA: Harvard University Press.

Wells, G., and Chang-Wells, G. (1992). *Constructing knowledge together: Classrooms as centers of inquiry and literacy.* Portsmouth, NH: Heinemann.

CHAPTER 8

Integrating Assessment and Evaluation in the Writing Program

CHAPTER OBJECTIVES

To weave together the principles of writing and learning/teaching strands to establish a framework for assessing and evaluating writing

To provide strategies for authentic assessment of writing and learning

To suggest ways of enhancing the effectiveness of writing evaluation

PERSONAL REFLECTION

I have been wrestling with the issues of assessment and evaluation for a long time. As a classroom teacher, I anguished over giving tests and writing report cards, because I felt these activities detracted from my major purpose: to help children learn and develop to the best of their abilities. The conceptual framework for assessment and evaluation I present in this chapter began to emerge when I was teaching a Grade 2–3 class part time and studying for my PhD at the University of Victoria. I had begun my doctoral program with the idea of writing my dissertation on some aspect of evaluation in the language arts. I was participating in a graduate seminar in the language arts, for which I had decided to write a paper on evaluation of writing, and was taking a course on action research. One day when I was on my daily run, I had an epiphany: Evaluation *is*—or should be—action research; assessment should occur in the context of ongoing learning activities; and teachers should use naturalistic, ethnographic methods of collecting and analyzing information. I wrote a paper entitled *Evaluation as Action Research* (Chapman, 1988), and then expanded and elaborated the ideas for an article that was first published in one journal (Chapman, 1989a) and then reprinted in others (Chapman, 1989b, 1995). When I went to work on British Columbia's ungraded primary program, the framework for assessment and evaluation I had developed was adopted provincially (British Columbia Ministry of Education, 1990). Over the years I have continued to develop and refine my ideas to include not only assessment and evaluation in the elementary school (1993a) but also teacher education (1993b). I have heard it said that the best ideas start with small discoveries, and that most people usually have only one great idea in their lifetimes. I often wonder if perhaps my framework for assessment and evaluation will turn out to be my most important contribution to education.

Think about your own experiences of assessment and evaluation. How did they affect you as a learner? Did they promote your learning? Why or why not?

In this chapter I weave together the various idea strands of the writing/learning tapestry so it can be examined through the lens of assessment and evaluation. I begin with an interweaving of the principles of writing and characteristics of ethnography, the methodological basis of action research, to establish a conceptual framework for the assessment and evaluation of writing and learning.

I then connect theory and practice by providing strategies for authentic assessment and suggestions for enhancing the effectiveness of evaluation. Although the terms "assessment" and "evaluation" are sometimes used interchangeably in everyday speech, in the context of this book

- **Assessment** refers to the process of collecting information, or data.
- **Evaluation** refers to the process of interpreting or making judgments and decisions based on the information collected.

While the two terms are interrelated—indeed, often occurring almost simultaneously—they are not synonymous.

Writing, Learning, and Ethnography

In traditional programs, educators adopt a clinical, medical model of assessment and evaluation: diagnose what is needed (through pretesting), write a prescription (devise a plan of instruction), deliver the treatment (provide instruction), and then re-examine the "patients" (through post-testing) to determine whether the treatment worked or not. If the treatment doesn't work, try other remedies (through remedial instruction). This kind of approach reflects the assumptions of a transmission approach to education (Chapter 2). While there may be some merits to such a process (for example, the notion that evaluation should precede planning for instruction), there is a move toward methods that are more consistent with a transactional model of teaching and learning. Medicine itself is moving away from the clinical model. Rather than focusing on the physical body as a discrete entity, medicine is becoming more holistic, acknowledging the relationships between psychology and physiology, and more wellness-oriented. Likewise, education is becoming more integrated, reflecting an increased understanding of the connectedness of learning and the interplay between the individual and social and contextual factors, and becoming more learner-oriented.

As discussed in Chapter 3, one of the roles of the classroom teacher is to be an action researcher in his or her own classroom. Action researchers most frequently adopt a qualitative approach to their inquiries and use naturalistic methods like those used by cultural anthropologists. Cultural anthropologists study "what people do, what people know, and things people make and use"

(Spradley, 1980, p. 5). An anthropologist's descriptions of a culture, or particular aspects of it, are called ethnographies; for this reason, the terms cultural anthropologist and **ethnographer** are used interchangeably. Ethnographers try to understand human beings in all their complexity, in context, using natural settings as the direct source of data. This is essentially what teachers try to do both in action research and in assessment and evaluation. Their focus is on learners, multidimensional human beings, within the various contexts of the classroom community. Ultimately, however, the knowledge teachers seek is not for its own sake, but to enable their students' learning.

There is a strong resemblance between the principles of writing, on one hand, and the characteristics of ethnographic research, on the other. Rather than repeat the principles stated in Chapter 1, I have selected key ideas from each and clustered them. To each of these clusters, I connect relevant concepts from ethnography (Bogdan & Biklen, 1982) so that you may see the connections between ethnography and a transactional approach to writing and learning.

- *Principle 1, Written language is complex and multidimensional.*
  Ethnographers strive for *comprehensiveness* so that they can understand people in all their complexity. To achieve this, they collect a broad base of data from a variety of contexts.
- *Principles 2, 3, and 7: Meaning-making, rather than mechanics, is the primary focus of writing. Meaning is personally and socially constructed.*
  Ethnographers seek *meaning* and understanding. They strive for *accuracy*, trying to be as objective as possible, but realizing that all inquiries are to some degree subjective. They try to eliminate bias from various sources, including their own assumptions, beliefs, and values. To increase accuracy, ethnographers also **triangulate** the data by considering multiple sources of information in the analysis and by seeking other people's perspectives and interpretations as to what the data might mean; this includes checking perceptions with the subjects of the study.
- *Principles 4 and 5: Writing is a multifaceted, integrated process.*
  Ethnographers are concerned with *process* rather than outcomes or products. Their data-collection and analysis procedures are *interrelated*: their interpretations are grounded in, or based on, the data. They form tentative interpretations during the process of data collection, which often leads to new questions or lines of inquiry; they also reflect on a body of informa-

tion as a whole after it has been collected.

- *Principles 6, 8, and 9: Writing is a purposeful activity that occurs in and is influenced by different contexts; contexts are multidimensional and include the immediate context, discourse community, sociocultural, and personal dimensions.*
  Ethnographers believe the best way to learn about people is by becoming a *participant-observer* in the focal community. The researcher is the research instrument. Ethnographers strive for **authenticity** by collecting information that represents as accurately as possible what people do under natural settings. They collect information systematically from *naturalistic sources*, through observations of what people do (processes) and the things they make (products), and through talking to them.
- *Principle 10: Writing is a product: a text, a document, and an artifact.*
  Ethnographers use the data they collect to *describe* what they have observed and as *evidence* to *document* their findings and support their conclusions.

A Framework for Writing Assessment and Evaluation

The connections between the principles of writing and the characteristics of ethnography can be used to establish a framework for assessing and evaluating writing and learning. As I elaborate each of the key concepts, I refer back to the descriptions in Chapter 5 of classrooms taught by Ms. Chan and Mr. Mitchell. Later in this chapter I will provide details and specific techniques for some of the ideas introduced here.

Assessment and evaluation are integrated with teaching and learning. As a participant in and an observer of classroom life, a teacher is in a better position than anyone else to collect and interpret information about students' learning. Assessment and evaluation are inextricably linked with instruction (Valencia & Pearson, 1987). Margaret Donaldson (1978) describes the relationship in this way:

> A very important job of a teacher—or of a parent in a teaching role—is to guide the child towards tasks where he [*sic*] will be able objectively to do well, but not

> too easily, not without putting forth some effort, not without difficulties to be mastered, errors to be overcome, creative solutions to be found. This means assessing his skills with sensitivity and accuracy, understanding the levels of his confidence and energy, and responding to his errors in helpful ways. (pp. 114–15)

Learning activities and evaluation activities are one and the same. Teachers do not have to contrive activities solely for the purposes of assessment and evaluation; what they need to do is to consider the ways that children show us what they know as they engage in an activity.

While teachers take the leading role in assessment and evaluation, they can also involve students and other professionals in the process. Ultimately, we want students to be thoughtful individuals who reflect on and evaluate their own learning. Students can be participant-observers and share the responsibility for assessment and evaluation when they engage in collaborative criteria setting, and peer and self-evaluation. Sometimes a teacher feels the need to involve other school personnel, such as learning assistance teachers, counsellors, and psychologists. These people can provide helpful information, but this never overrides what is learned through a teacher's classroom-based assessment and evaluation.

Assessment and evaluation are interrelated, reciprocal processes. Assessment and evaluation are not connected in a linear fashion. Instead, they occur in a reciprocal, dynamic relationship to each other (see Figure 8.1). Teachers ground, or base, their evaluations on information collected through assessment. It is quite often the case, however, that a teacher collects information and tries to interpret and make sense of it, only to realize that she or he needs to collect more information. This is especially the case in formative assessment and evaluation.

Ethnography reveals the importance of forming tentative, rather than fixed, interpretations during the process of data collection. We also need to be aware of the differences between observation and interpretation and the

Something to think about

Reflect back to Chapter 5. In what ways did Ms. Chan and Mr. Mitchell integrate assessment and evaluation with their classroom learning activities?

Figure 8.1 Assessment and Evaluation Process

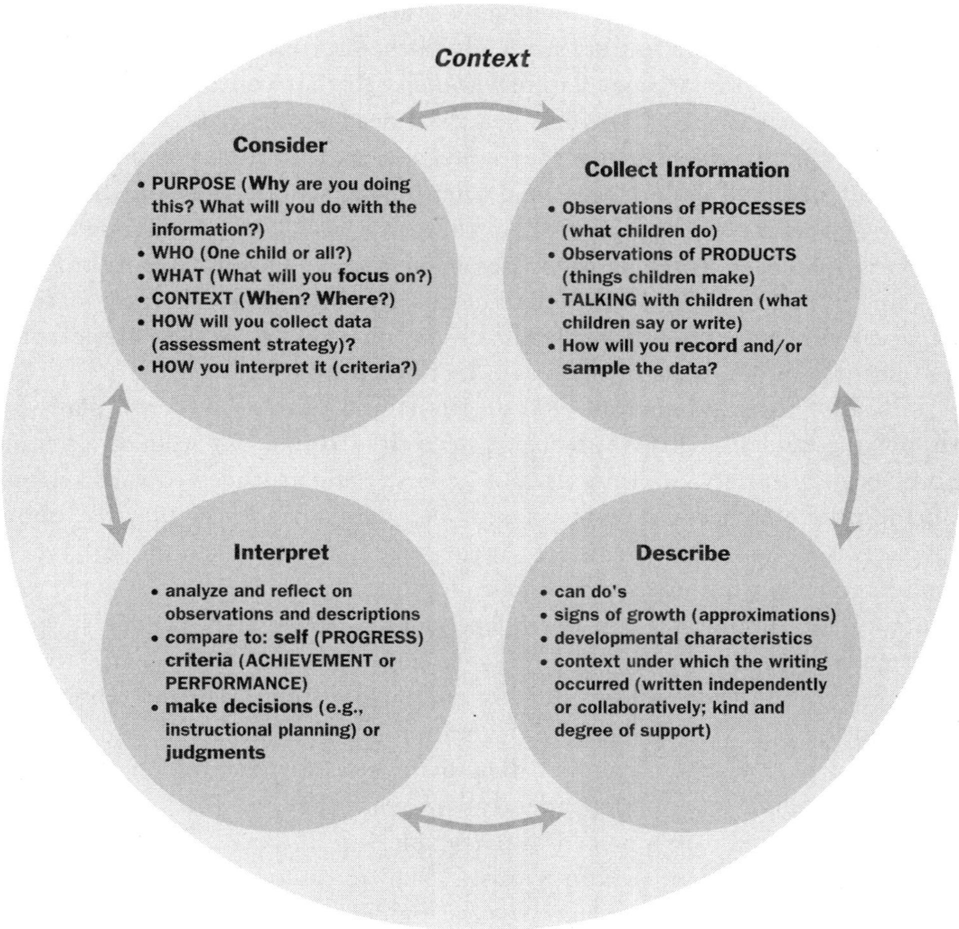

difficulty of trying to be objective. It is often the case that we jump quickly into making judgments or interpretations. When I was learning to do ethnographic research, I learned first-hand how readily this happens. Like most teachers, I found it hard to record what I saw and heard rather than what I thought. It is particularly important to hold off making judgments and decisions until a sufficient body of information has been collected during initial assessments in the early part of the school year. Students take time to adjust to being back at school and to a new classroom situation, just as teachers do.

The major purpose of assessment and evaluation is to promote learning. Assessment and evaluation are not ends in themselves. Rather, they are purposeful—aimed primarily at gaining knowledge that can be used to enable children as learners and writers. Teachers need to discover what children know and can do and also what they need to learn. Unfortunately, many people have had negative experiences in evaluation at school and sometimes felt diminished as a result of procedures that were used. Instead, students and teachers alike need to realize that assessment and evaluation are part of learning, and are constructive rather than destructive processes. They are learning experiences when students get feedback on what and how they are learning and become more aware of their own learning processes.

In order to make instructional decisions and develop in-depth plans for supporting students' growth, teachers need first to find out students' writing abilities in a variety of contexts and genres, their attitudes toward writing (including preferences for certain topics and genres), and how they feel about themselves as writers and learners. At the beginning of the school year, teachers undertake **initial assessments** to collect baseline information—what students already know and can do independently. Marie Clay (1985) suggests that teachers spend a couple of weeks "roaming around the known," avoiding intervening (teaching) too quickly and suspending judgments about students until a fairly broad base of information has been collected. Throughout the school year teachers conduct **diagnostic assessments** to determine what students are able to do independently and what they need help with. These types of assessment often precede a particular unit of work. Teachers can also use **dynamic assessment** (Dixon-Krauss, 1996) to discover (1) what a student knows and can do independently (static mode), and (2) students' zones of proximal development (dynamic mode). In the dynamic mode, teachers provide assistance and instructional scaffolding (Chapter 2).

Most of the time, a teacher performs assessment and evaluation almost simultaneously and responds to learners' immediate needs in learning situations. Mr. Mitchell did this, for example, when his students wrote and talked about mathematical principles. **Formative assessment and evaluation** occurs throughout the process of teaching and learning; it is ongoing and focuses on the learning process rather than the finished product. From time to time throughout the school year, particularly in reporting periods, a teacher reflects on a body of information to make a **summative evaluation**, usually in preparation for writing a report. Although teachers usually do not like writing report cards, they often find that there is value in looking at each child as an individual learner in an array of learning contexts. Summative evaluations enable teachers to get "the big picture" of what a student knows and can do and to see the progress he or she has made.

Teachers seek authentic evidence of students' writing and learning. Concerned that traditional ways of assessing and evaluating literacy do not match what we know about reading and writing processes (Valencia & Pearson, 1987), educators are increasingly calling for more *authentic* forms of assessment, those that, as *Webster's New Collegiate Dictionary* (1976) defines, "conform to an original so as to reproduce its essential features" (p. 75). In reality, complete authenticity is unattainable. However, teachers try to collect information that least distorts reality. The highest degree of authenticity occurs when teachers observe *naturally occurring* behaviours. The least authentic situations are those that impose a high degree of constraints on the learner, for example, testing situations. And when it comes to tests, those that are made by outside experts, for example, large-scale assessments and standardized group achievement tests, are the least authentic of all. Figure 8.2 shows a continuum of authenticity.

"External testing is no more necessary for learning in school than for learning out of school. It does not benefit those in the classroom, who can better assess in other ways" (Moffett, 1992, p. 1). Instead of testing, teachers should first look for opportunities to collect information informally through observing and talking to children and collecting those products that are natural outcomes of writing/learning activities. For example, in Chapter 5, Ms. Chan and Mr. Mitchell moved around their classrooms, observing and talking to children as they engaged in writing activities such as writing workshop. Sometimes, however, a teacher might not be able to acquire evidence of a particular writing skill through informal observation. For instance, suppose Mr. Mitchell wanted to appraise his students' knowledge and abilities in using quotation marks. Instead of giving a test, he could design a writing/learning activity to create a situation where students need to use quotation marks for an authentic purpose. He could, for example, involve students in writing

Figure 8.2 Authenticity Continuum

high authenticity ⟵⟶ low authenticity

- informal contexts
- naturally occurring behaviours
- child- or teacher-initiated activity
- least obtrusive form of assessment

Examples
- informal (open) observations
- informal (open) conversations, discussions, and conferences

- performance assessments
- situation designed to elicit information
- teacher-initiated activity
- somewhat obtrusive

Examples
- moderately structured observations, conferences, and discussions
- performance tasks

- formal contexts
- highly contrived
- externally initiated and/or designed
- highly obtrusive

Examples
- formal written tests
- oral examinations
- standardized tests least authentic

- represent complex behaviours
- demonstrate process (how)
- utilize range of tasks and contexts
- access how the learner integrates and applies knowledge

Source: Adapted from Teale (1982).

dialogues, or encourage them to incorporate conversation into the stories they are writing. These situations are examples of **performance assessments,** tasks or activities that are structured to elicit particular actions or behaviours. Performance assessments enable teachers to assess complex behaviours in meaningful contexts. Moreover, students view them as learning activities rather than assessment procedures or tests. Performance assessments are usually coupled with criterion-referenced evaluation procedures (discussed later in the chapter).

Teachers collect assessment information from naturalistic sources. "Thought is invisible until it is translated into deeds or words" (Moffett, 1992, p. 6). We don't know what is in people's heads—how they think or what they know—unless they represent it in some way. Children show us their thinking through what they do, make, and say. Thus, their actions, creations, and language provide three *naturalistic sources* of assessment information (Figure 8.3):

- Observations of processes—what children do and how they do it as they engage in writing
- Observations of products—the things children create, including their written products
- Talking and listening to children—conversations, conferences, and discussions with children, and communicating through writing

In Chapter 5, I showed Ms. Chan and Mr. Mitchell assessing their students' writing through observing them as they were writing. The two teachers used a variety of products to determine what and how students were learning and writing, for example, learning logs, journals, webs, stories, idea boxes, and so on. They also talked with children individually, in small group conferences (for example, Writing Club), and in whole-class discussions (for example, in Mr. Mitchell's mini-lesson on page breaks). Ms. Chan and Mr. Mitchell did not treat assessment as an afterthought; they were deliberate and *systematic* in their collection of information. Ms. Chan, for example, recorded her observations using an at-a-glance sheet while children worked independently, and used a conference record sheet for observations in Writing Club. Teachers also need to devise systems for collecting and organizing the products students create—the writing folder, for example.

Teachers assess students' writing/learning through observations of processes and products and through conversations and conferences.

Teachers strive for comprehensive assessment and evaluation. A teacher is able to obtain a more accurate and complete picture of a student's knowledge and abilities in writing by collecting information of many kinds and in many *contexts*. Any one situation or single piece of writing may not be representative of what a student knows or can do. All writers behave differently in different contexts; for example, students may seem quite skilled when they write in their learning logs, yet appear to be struggling when writing a report in science. Physical and emotional well-being play a role too: on any given day, students may be feeling ill or tired or may have had an upsetting experience.

It is also important to collect different types of information. A selection of written pieces, for example, while very informative, needs to be used as one source of data, to be complemented with observations of process and conversations. As teachers collect data they also need to record information about the context in which it occurred. Context information needs to be brief in order to be manageable, yet sufficiently complete to make the notes taken from observation, or a sample of work, meaningful later on. This may be as

Figure 8.3 Naturalistic Assessment Triangle

Observation of Process
(things children do)

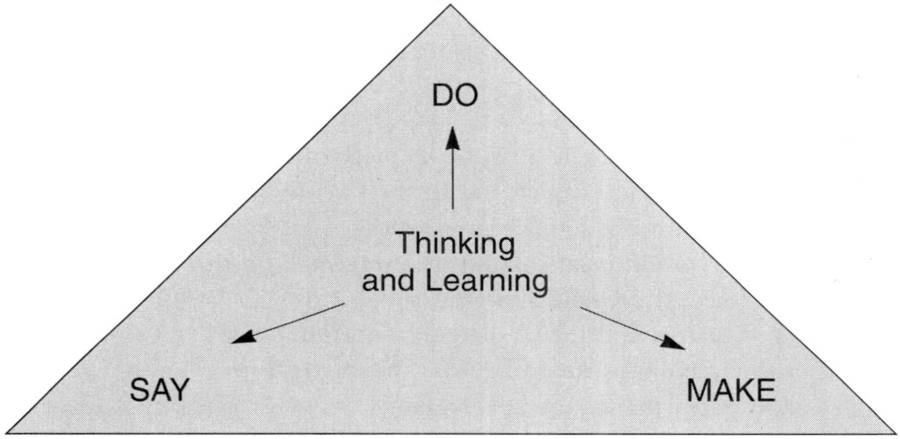

Conversations Conferences, and Discussions
(oral and written)

Observations of Product
(things children make)

Sources of Evidence

Discussions
- individual or group conferences
- informal conversations
- class or group discussions
- Writing Club
- Authors' Circle
- dialogue journals
- self-evaluations
- portfolio review conferences
- student-led and three-way conferences

Activities
- individual writing
- collaborative writing
- language experience activities
- writing in response to reading
- writing workshop
- writing across the curriculum (e.g., writer's RAFT)

Products
- journals
- learning logs
- dictated pieces
- writing folder selections
- science or social studies projects and reports
- two-dimensional forms of representation (e.g., written texts, webs, charts, labels, captions)
- writing to accompany 3D representations (e.g., signs, labels, directions)

simple as recording the date and title of a piece read aloud in Writing Club. When it comes to evaluating writing samples, a teacher needs to know whether a piece of writing was a first or revised draft, whether the student worked on it independently or collaboratively, whether the writing was assigned or self-selected, and so on.

A comprehensive assessment and evaluation of writing and learning includes a consideration of students'

- attitudes toward writing and toward themselves as writers
- writing preferences (e.g., topics and forms)
- metacognition and metalinguistic awareness
- effectiveness of communication and meaning-making through writing
- writing processes, strategies, and skills
- repertoires of genres and forms of representation
- writing in the language arts and across the curriculum
- progress and performance (achievement)

Teachers strive for accuracy in their assessments and evaluations of students. Teachers strive to be objective, while acknowledging that all inquiries are, to some degree, *subjective* because they involve decisions, judgments, and interpretations. Assessment is subjective to a degree because it involves decisions about what to focus on, what procedures to use, and what to record. Evaluation is even more subjective because it includes the teacher's speculations, ideas, hunches, impressions, and biases. It is very important for teachers to be aware of the sources of bias, including their own assumptions, beliefs, and values.

Assessment and evaluation are also *subject to error*. They are performed by human beings and are, thus, fallible. And no one external representation (what a child does, makes, or says) can reveal everything that is going on in a student's head. To increase their accuracy, teachers triangulate their interpretations by using multiple sources of information. They also increase their accuracy by triangulating their interpretations with other people's impressions of what the data might mean, including sharing the assessment evidence with students themselves to gain their perspectives on their own learning. This may be as simple as doing perception checks or asking children process questions about their thinking or how they figured something out.

Teachers use assessment data as evidence to document and describe students' writing and learning. Rather than merely assigning a grade to students, teachers need to produce "a multidimensional conceptualization of students' literacy learning in a variety of contexts and situations" (Chapman, 1989b, p. 9). Assessment information is collected on an ongoing basis, for example, in writing folders. From this broad base of data, teachers and students select samples that represent students' writing and learning in a variety of contexts over time. These are assembled in a variety of ways, such as in portfolios and progress folios (discussed later in the chapter).

The maxim "Show, don't tell" is a powerful one in writing assessment and evaluation. When teachers share their observations with children and their parents and look at samples of writing, children and parents understand better how the child is progressing. In this way, the assessment data teachers collect not only forms the basis of evaluation, it also serves as *evidence* of students' learning and can *document* their progress and levels of performance.

Authentic Writing Assessment

I begin this section with a brief discussion of the ways in which assessment changes from the kindergarten and primary years through the junior grades. Then I explain some specific assessment techniques. It is beyond the scope of this book to explore all assessment avenues, however, so I also provide references for further reading.

An ethnographic approach to assessment and evaluation has been most readily embraced by kindergarten and primary teachers, individually and through their professional associations (e.g., National Association for the Education of Young Children, 1991). This may be due, in part, to the influence of the child study movement that originated in the 1930s. Kindergarten and primary teachers usually emphasize informal observations, conversations with children about their writing and learning, and first-draft types of writing, such as journals.

In the junior grades, the scope of writing/learning assessment and evaluation broadens, incorporating a wider variety of written genres and forms of representation across the curriculum. There is also an increasing emphasis on student responsibility in the process, through developing and using evaluation criteria, self and peer evaluation, and creating and managing portfolios. Because students are more facile in written language, there is a tendency for teachers in the junior grades to use more pencil-and-paper tasks such as written quizzes and tests for assessment. However, caution must be advised here, since these forms of assessment are biased against many students, for example, ESL and ESD students and children with learning disabilities. Thus, junior teachers should still stay on the left and centre of the authenticity continuum shown in Figure 8.2, using performance tasks rather than written tests (Stiggins, 1987) whenever possible, involving students in generating and/or negotiating the evaluation criteria.

Observing Children Writing (Observations of Processes)

Observation is an important part of assessment, but to be most effective it needs to be comprehensive and systematic. Observation may be at-a-glance or in-depth, wide-net or focused. Figure 8.4 provides an overview of the different kinds of observation.

Figure 8.4 Types of Observation and Recording Devices

	At-a-Glance	In-Depth
Wide-Net	• Anecdotal comments • At-a-glance sheet (general observations) (see Figure 8.5) • Post-it notes	• Two column notes (see Figure 8.7) • Writing conference record (e.g., Figure 8.6)
Focused	• At-a-glance sheet (specific, focused) • Checklists	• Performance task checklists or guides • Observation guides (e.g., Figure 8.8)

Figure 8.5 At-a-Glance Observation Sheet

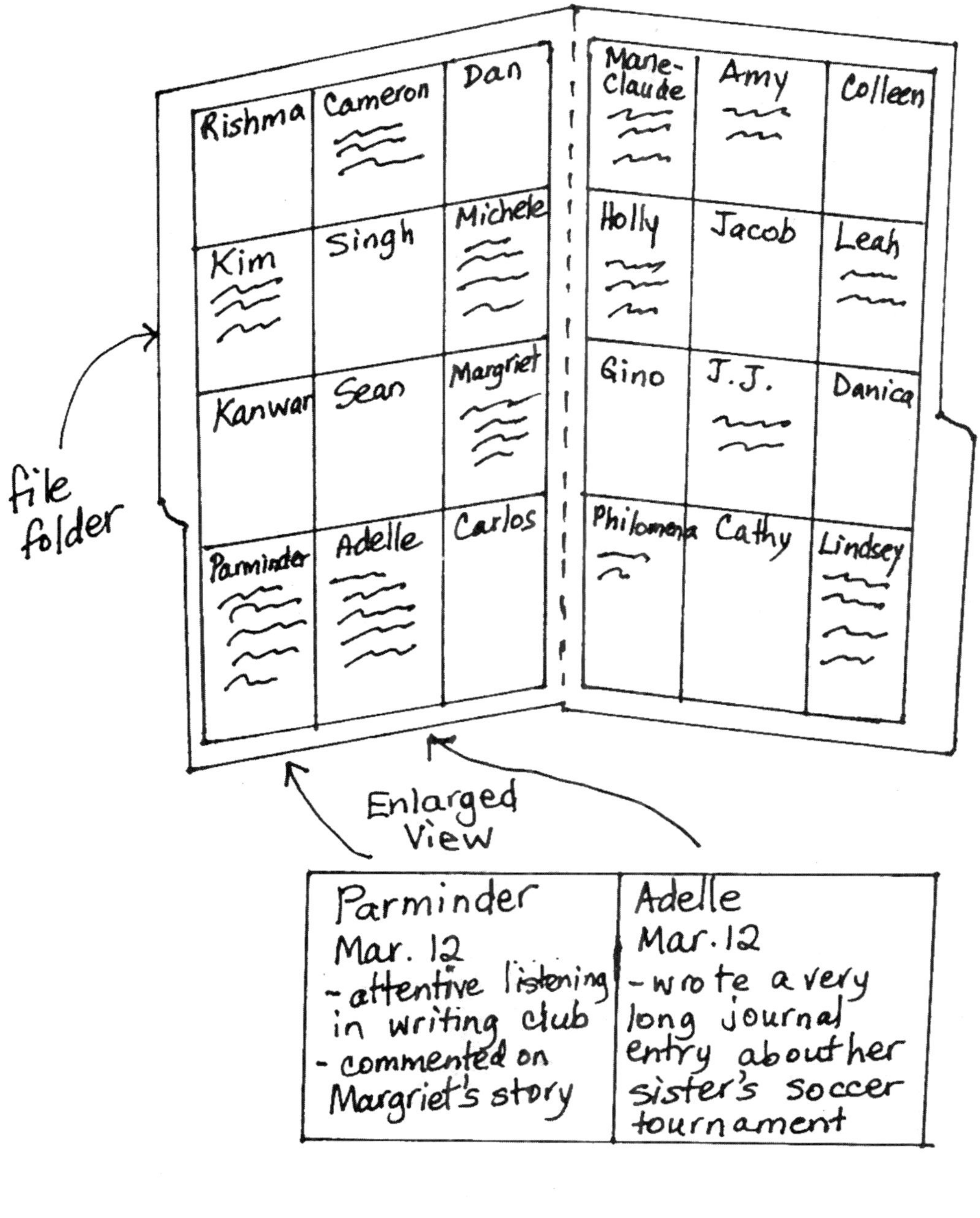

Wide-net, at-a-glance observations. Like many teachers, I have found an at-a-glance observation sheet (Figure 8.5; adapted from North York Board of Education, 1983) the most effective way to record informal observations throughout the day, for example, as I circulate in the classroom while children are at work and play. To make at-a-glance sheets for a class, you need to make grids with a box for each child's name. (Make master copies and then photocopy enough for each week.) You can use a double-page spread, half of the children's names on one page and half on another. These can be attached to the two sides of an open file folder. If you want larger boxes (or if you have a large class) you can overlap two file folders to create a three-fold spread and use three grid pages. Some teachers prefer to make a large grid for the entire class on bristol board and laminate it. They record their observations on Post-it notes that are then placed on the bristol board. (I prefer to make photocopied pages for each week and then add Post-it notes when needed.)

The advantage of at-a-glance sheets for wide-net observations is that they ensure you make notes on *all* the children, not just those who catch your attention. When I shared a classroom, my partner teacher and I found the at-a-glance sheets useful for communication; we used different-coloured pens so we would know who had written what when we referred to them later. It is important to record the date observations are made, because when report-card time arrives, you will cut apart the pages, sort them for each child (for example, by content and context), and put them in order by date.

Focused, at-a-glance observations. At-a-glance sheets can also be used for focused observations. For example, you might want to watch all of the children in Authors' Circle time during a given week to see how they respond to one another's writing. As the week progresses, the boxes will start to fill up and so the spaces show whom you still need to observe. At-a-glance sheets can also be used for recording observations of children in an audience role during writing conferences. (You might want to use different colours of paper for different contexts.) You may also want to use a writing conference record (Figure 8.6) or adapt a variety of checklists for focused at-a-glance observations. These checklists generally list students' names down the page and have columns for various categories of information. Progress charts, such as the one described in Mr. Mitchell's class, are another way of recording information.

Wide-net, in-depth observations. Many kindergarten and primary teachers set aside time for systematic observation using a one- or two-a-day method.

Figure 8.6 Writing Conference Record Sheet

Name ______________________________ WRITING CONFERENCE		
Date	Selection	Comment

Teachers choose one or two children to observe each day in a variety of contexts and record their observations. I recommend using a two-column format (shown in Figure 8.7) for taking notes. As you observe a child, try to capture what you see and hear, and record these in the column on the left side. Interpretations and judgments are bound to pop into your mind, and you record those on the right side. It is simply amazing how much information you can collect even in just a few minutes. Later on (after school, for example), review your notes and make a tentative interpretation, adding things such as comments, impressions, hunches, questions, and so on, in the right-hand column. When I do this reflection, I sometimes find I have written an interpretive comment on the left side, so I put a line through it and rewrite it on the right side.

Focused, in-depth observations. Performance tasks and project work provide opportunities for focused, in-depth observation. For example, when my students work on research reports, I observe what they do and how they are performing throughout the report-writing process (described in Chapter 7), recording my observations on the form shown in Figure 8.8. I do this as I circulate around the classroom. At other times, I schedule group writing conferences or Writing Clubs that focus on particular aspects of the report-writing process or that serve as progress checks.

Because junior-grade teachers feel the pressure of increasing curriculum demands and do not always teach the same group of students all day, observation tends to receive less emphasis than in the primary classroom. However, observation of process is a valuable mode of assessment for all age groups.

Figure 8.7 Observation Record Sheets

Two-Column Notes

Observation What I saw/heard:	**Interpretation** What I think:

T-Chart

<table>
<tr><td colspan="2">Context</td></tr>
<tr><td>Observation
What I saw/heard:</td><td>Interpretation
What I think:</td></tr>
</table>

Many teachers in the junior grades incorporate cooperative learning techniques and collaborative group work that free them from being the sole source of instruction and provide opportunities for focused, in-depth "kid-watching" (Goodman, 1985).

Observing Children's Writing (Observations of Products)

Children can represent their thinking through a variety of forms of representation (see Figure 7.1, Chapter 7), many of which include writing while generating ideas and planning or when working on the finished product. Because young children may not yet be able to express and elaborate their ideas through conventional symbolic forms, kindergarten and primary teachers use a variety of children's products, including two-dimensional (e.g., drawings, paintings, webs) and three-dimensional representations (e.g., block constructions, models, dioramas), many of which incorporate writing. Young children's writing reveals much about their metalinguistic concepts (e.g., what writing looks like, directional concepts, etc.), the strategies they use (e.g., interplay of drawing and writing, spelling strategies), knowledge of spelling and punctuation conventions, fluency, ability to elaborate and organize ideas, and so on.

A variety of written products from across the curriculum can be incorporated into writing assessment. For example, a student's research report can provide the teacher not only with information about the student's knowledge of social studies or science, but also his or her ability to select and organize information and write in an expository genre. When reports are accompanied by in-process writing, such as notes, webs, outlines, and first drafts, teachers are able to assess and evaluate a student's learning and writing processes as well as finished pieces. Writing that is used to promote or enhance learning, such as that in learning logs and journals, can provide important insights into a student's thinking and learning processes. Thus, a wide array of written products may be used to assess writing and learning within a wider curriculum framework.

Conversations, Conferences, and Discussions

Listening to children is as important as observing them and the things they have written. Adults often make assumptions or interpretations that prove to be inaccurate when children are asked about their thinking. Talking and

Figure 8.8 Report-Writing Process Record Sheet

Name ______________________________ Dates ____________________

Process	Date	Code*	Comment
Prewriting • collecting information • classifying • generating headings **Drafting** • body – sentences from notes – paragraphing • introduction • conclusion **Editing** • for relevant ideas • adds information • clarifies meaning • sequences logically **Proofreading** • spelling • punctuation • usage **Publishing** • neatness • organization – table of contents – sequencing • diagrams, illustrations • creativity OTHER			

*Codes:
I—can do *independently;* S—needs some *support;* NI—*needs* further *instruction*

listening can act as a way of triangulating perspectives. Teachers learn much about children through informal conversations as they circulate through the classroom. Writing conferences such as writing clubs (Chapter 5) or editing conferences (Chapter 6) enable teachers to focus more on individual children and to ask probing and clarifying questions about their thinking. Because of time constraints, writing conferences often are conducted with groups of students. Teachers may also want to conduct individual writing conferences with particular students from time to time or with each student at particular times of the school year.

Some teachers schedule writing conferences at regular intervals to review writing folders and select pieces for a portfolio or progress folio (often in preparation for writing report cards and conducting parent–teacher interviews). Writing conferences of this type provide an opportunity for both the student and the teacher to be learners: the teacher learning about the student, and the student learning about the assessment and evaluation process, as well as gaining a deeper understanding into her or his own literacy learning.

Managing the Assessment Data

When teachers use a naturalistic, ethnographic approach to assessment, they have much information to draw on—usually too much. This can be overwhelming without some sort of management or organizational system. Children and teachers need ongoing procedures for collecting written products, such as learning logs, journals, and writing folders (Chapter 6). When students work on ongoing projects such as research reports or picture books, they need process folders to store all the things related to a project. Teachers also need a system for collecting records of observations and conferences. I find having a file folder for each student to be the most flexible method; other teachers prefer notebooks or index cards.

Reviewing and Sampling

When we have too much information to take it all in, it is hard to see the forest for the trees. We cannot use every piece of writing or observation when we evaluate students' writing and learning, so we need to review and make selections, or sample, the assessment data. Some kindergarten and Grade 1 teachers photocopy a selection from each child's journal on a weekly or biweekly basis to reduce the information overload and make the data more manageable. Beginning in the later primary grades, children can be involved in the selection process.

From time to time, for example, at the end of every month or term, students in the later primary and junior grades can review the larger collection of written products in their writing folders, journals, and so on. This review process is an important one, since it compels students to reflect on what they have done over a period of time. Teachers can provide students with guidelines for the review process, such as the one shown in Figure 8.9.

Figure 8.9 Writing Folder Review

1. **Kinds of Writing**
   - How many different kinds of writing have you done (stories, poems, etc.)?
   - What kinds of writing do you feel success with?
   - What kinds of writing do you feel you need more practice with?
2. **Topics**
   - What topics do you write about most often?
   - What topic would you like to write more about?
   - What other topics would you like to write about?
3. **Best Piece(s)**
   - Choose one or two pieces that you think are your best. Why do you think this/these is/are your best?
   - Complete an *entry slip* for each of the pieces you have selected (one or two) and put them in your portfolio.
4. **Best Potential**
   - Which piece do you think has the most potential to become even better? Write EDIT on it.
5. **Progress**
   - Compare a recent piece with something you wrote earlier. Find three or more ways in which your writing has improved.
6. **Goals**
   - What would you like to work on next to improve your writing?

After students have revisited and reflected on their writing, they can select several pieces to include in a portfolio or progress folio. Teachers and students should both have input into what is selected. For example, students may choose one or two of their best or favourite pieces. The teacher may also ask all students to include an artifact from one or two particular writing activities so that the portfolio includes a variety of genres and forms of representation from across the curriculum. Students can share responsibility for record-keeping, for example, by filling out an entry slip (Figure 8.10) to accompany a piece of work selected for inclusion in their portfolios or progress folios. Process conferences enable the teacher to help students individually or in groups to apply criteria for selection; these conferences also provide opportunities to gain insights into students' perceptions of their literacy learning.

Portfolios and Progress Folios

Much richer and more meaningful than accumulating marks for assignments and tests, portfolios or progress folios assist teachers and students in evaluating writing and learning. They also document what students know and can do and their progress in writing. Portfolios and progress folios are purposeful collections of students' writing/learning artifacts collected over time, not merely work folders. There are many different kinds of portfolios:

- **Masterpiece portfolios** include only students' best pieces and finished products.
- **Process portfolios** include all artifacts related to a particular project; these document the students' writing and learning process in a particular genre or activity.
- **Documentary or descriptive portfolios** include samples of students' work, selected by students and teachers; they may or may not include selections from teachers' records of observations and conferences and may include teachers' comments as well as those of students.
- **Cumulative portfolios** include samples of students' writing over a period of years. Each year, students select one or two pieces to add to the cumulative portfolio; the cumulative portfolios are then passed on to the teacher the following year.

Colleen Politano and Anne Davies (1994) devised the **progress folio** because they found portfolios very cumbersome. Progress folios are similar to portfolios in that they include samples of students' writing, but they are organized according to curriculum areas. Using a large scrapbook, double-page

Figure 8.10 Entry Slip

Entry Slip

Name ______________________________ Date ________________

Context: ____

Independent/Collaborated with ________________________________

Why I chose this piece:

What I'd like you to notice:

Something to think about

In my undergraduate teacher education program, my students make a *learning folio* to document their learning processes in the course. This folio uses a double-page spread format. The left-hand page contains an artifact that has been created in the process of doing an activity, for example, a chapter map made from reading the textbook or a two-column record from an in-class observational activity. On the right-hand side, students add a page that includes context information and a reflection on the activity. In what ways is the learning folio like a learning log? In what ways is it similar to and different from a portfolio?

spreads are labelled for each area of the curriculum: science, mathematics, art, reading, writing, and so on. Each double-page spread is then divided into four sections: September, November, March, and May. At the beginning of the school year, pieces of work are selected for each curriculum area and then pasted in the appropriate September sections of the progress folio. This process is repeated for each reporting period. Like portfolios, the progress folios can include entry slips, such as the one shown in Figure 8.10.

Effective Evaluation of Writing

Evaluation is the process of making judgments or decisions based on evidence gathered through assessment. Making judgments implies some sort of comparison; different evaluative purposes use different types of comparison. Here are some brief definitions of related terms:

- **Progress** is concerned with growth; it is determined by comparing a student's present and past performances; it is self-referenced.
- **Achievement**, or **level of performance**, is determined by comparing what a learner can do to something else; it may be norm- or criterion-referenced.
- **Norm-referenced** evaluation compares learners' achievements to others of the same age or grade.
- **Criterion-referenced** evaluation compares learners' achievements to a set of criteria or standards.
- **Grading** is the process of sorting students' work into hierarchical categories that are represented by a numerical score or letter grade.

The most important types of evaluation in the elementary school are determinations of students' progress, that is, their growth as writers, and their achievement in relation to specific criteria. It is often the case that progress is emphasized in kindergarten and the primary grades, while achievement takes on increasing emphasis as students progress through the junior grades. Evaluating progress is important for writers of all ages because it is learning- and process-oriented, while achievement tends to be more product-oriented. Criterion-referenced evaluation can also promote learning and growth in writing if it is treated as part of the writing process, especially when students are actively engaged in generating and using the criteria.

Describing and Documenting Writing and Learning

In the elementary school, teachers should use their knowledge of children's literacy development and learning (see Chapter 2) as a lens through which they interpret the information they have collected. Children's errors should be viewed as *developmental approximations* that reveal what children are learning to do with written language. Rather than assigning grades or categorizing children into particular developmental stages, teachers need to describe their students' literacy learning in multidimensional ways and develop rich and representative portfolios as evidence to document the children's progress and achievement. Some teachers use the portfolios during three-way conferences (Davies, Cameron, Politano, & Gregory, 1992) or student-led conferences (Little & Allan, 1988) so that the children can reflect on their own writing/learning processes and demonstrate their progress to parents.

Criterion-Referenced Evaluation of Writing

Criterion-referenced evaluation is more learning-oriented and constructive than norm-referencing. Comparing students' writing to a set of criteria can help students improve as writers, whereas knowing how well they are doing in comparison to others is discouraging for most (except the top student, of course). Criterion-referenced evaluation is often integrated with performance assessment, described earlier in the chapter. To be effective, criteria should

- Be specific to a writing task, activity, or genre.
- Reflect the significant and important aspects of the task.
- Reflect the complexity of the task.
- Be clearly defined, explicitly stated, and known by students.
- Be observable.
- Be manageable and practical.
- Be curriculum-based.
- Be developmentally and culturally appropriate.
- Be open to negotiation and/or revision.
- Ideally, involve students in the process of generating the criteria.

Criterion-based evaluation reduces the likelihood of bias, such as the halo effect—"seeing the glass as half full" when you like a student or if the student has demonstrated excellence in previous writing activities, and "seeing the glass as half empty" in reverse situations. It also decreases cultural and gender biases; for example, expecting students with low socioeconomic status to be less able than students from more affluent homes, or expecting girls to write better narratives than boys.

The most beneficial effects of criterion-referenced evaluation result from using criteria with students as part of the writing process. An example of this is found in the description of Mr. Mitchell's class (Chapter 5) when he and his students generated the criteria for making effective page breaks. In this way, students come to understand the purpose of the criteria—they are functional and meaningful rather than arbitrary. Students internalize the criteria as they use them in their own work.

Rubrics can be used in criterion-referenced evaluation and in grading student writing. Rubrics are rating scales that describe several levels of proficiency, from high to low; I find four categories the most practical and easy to use. Figure 8.11 provides an example of a rubric for narratives that could be used in Grades 5 to 7. The best way to use rubrics is to take a general set of criteria and then create a rubric specific to the writing task, activity, or genre. The rubrics are then used holistically to categorize the pieces of writing. Rubrics can help improve students' writing when they are involved in creating them, when students use them to evaluate their own and their classmates' drafts, and when they have opportunities to use them as guidelines for editing and revising their writing.

Involving Students and Parents in Assessment and Evaluation

Students can become observers as well as participants in their own learning and share the responsibility for assessment and evaluation in varying degrees. Beginning in the primary grades, students can be encouraged to reflect on their own learning and writing in, for example, learning logs and journals and other forms of self-evaluation. They can also learn to share their perspectives on their learning and writing through student-led conferences (Little & Allan, 1988). In primary classrooms, the teacher takes on the major portion of assessment and evaluation tasks. At the same time, she or he helps the children to develop their abilities in self-assessment and -evaluation through

Figure 8.11 Rubric for Narrative (Story)

Exemplary	• hooks the reader from the beginning and sustains interest • uses language to create particular effects • provides rich descriptions of setting and characters • develops strong plot or storyline from beginning to end • uses dialogue effectively • uses figurative language effectively (metaphors, similes) • reveals a strong personal voice
Strong	• gains the reader's attention and sustains it throughout • uses interesting language and images • describes setting and characters • develops consistent and clear storyline • relates story clearly and logically • includes some dialogue and/or figurative language • gives a feeling of the personality of the writer
Competent	• gains the reader's attention at various points in the story • uses language appropriate to the purpose and context of the writing • includes all the basic elements of a story (setting, characters, problem, sequence of events, resolution) • provides some details of setting and characters • includes a specific beginning, middle, and end • relates story events in a logical order
Undeveloped	• is unable to capture or sustain the reader's attention • limits language use to basic words and sentence patterns • limits storyline to main ideas but provides few details • includes some, but not all, basic elements of a story (setting, characters, problem, sequence of events, resolution) • may not include a specific beginning, middle, and/or end • sequences ideas in a way that it is difficult for the reader to follow

involving them actively in the process, for example, by providing demonstrations of how to select pieces of work for a portfolio, using collaborative approaches to develop criteria, and encouraging young learners to perform those tasks that they are able to do. As students become older and more expe-

Something to think about

Try to recall some of the ideas discussed earlier in the chapter for involving students in the process of writing assessment and evaluation. Can you think of any other ideas?

rienced, they assume more and more of the responsibility for assessing and evaluating themselves.

As part of a move toward increasing collaboration, teachers are starting to involve parents more actively in the processes of assessment and evaluation. Parents know far more about their children than a teacher does, so early in the school year, assessment can include talking with—and listening to—parents about their children as writers and learners. At several times in the school year, schools have traditionally sent home report cards and held parent–teacher interviews. More and more frequently, teachers, children, and parents participate in three-way conferences (Davies et al., 1992). These conferences are occasions for everyone to share their insights and to appreciate one another's contributions to children's literacy learning. They also provide opportunities for teachers to help parents understand the complex nature of writing and the ways in which children grow and develop as writers.

Reflections on the Chapter

Think about/talk about/write about:

Principles into Practice

- Use Figure 2.6, From Principles of Writing to Practice, to find specific examples in this chapter of each principle as it is put into practice.

A Framework for Assessment and Evaluation

- What are some ways in which schools (or school systems) disconnect assessment and evaluation from teaching and learning? Is there ever a case when such separation is appropriate?
- Brainstorm specific purposes for assessment and evaluation.
- Consider the connections between planning lessons, including writing/learning outcomes, and assessment and evaluation.

- Consider your personal experiences in terms of the framework for assessment and evaluation discussed in this chapter.

Assessment Strategies

- With a partner or small group, select someone to observe in the context of an activity (e.g., sharing a story she or he has written). Observe the person for two or three minutes, using the two-column format to record your observations and ideas. Compare what you have written with your partner. (I do this in my classes, using a video clip of a child.)
- Have you ever created a portfolio? When, how, and why?

Evaluation

- Devise a set of criteria and/or create a rubric for a genre other than a story, for example, an argument or an expository report.

REFERENCES AND FURTHER READING

Bogdan, R.C., and Biklen, S.K. (1982). *Qualitative research for education: An introduction to theory and methods.* Toronto: Allyn & Bacon.

British Columbia Ministry of Education. (1990). *Primary program: Foundation document.* Victoria, BC.

Chapman, M.L. (1988, March). Evaluation as action research. *Teacher as Researcher, 3*(1), International Reading Association.

———. (1989a). Evaluating literacy learning: Action research for language arts teachers. *Research Forum, 4,* pp. 17–19.

———. (1989b). Evaluating literacy learning: Action research for language arts teachers. *Prime Areas, 32*(1), 8–11.

———. (1993a). Literacy assessment and evaluation: An anthropological approach. *English Quarterly, 26*(1), 30–38.

———. (1993b). An anthropological approach to assessment and evaluation in early childhood teacher education programs. Paper presented at The Impact of Culture on Early Childhood Education Curriculum Conference, Vancouver, BC, May 16–18, 1993.

———. (1995). Evaluating literacy learning: Action research for language arts teachers. *Research Forum, 13,* 17–19.

Clay, M.M. (1985). *The early detection of reading difficulties* (3rd ed.). Portsmouth, NH: Heinemann.

Davies, A., Cameron, C., Politano, C., and Gregory, K. (1992). *Together is better: Collaborative assessment, evaluation and reporting*. Winnipeg: Peguis.

Dixon-Krauss, L. (1996). *Vygotsky in the classroom: Mediated literacy instruction and assessment*. White Plains, NY: Longman.

Donaldson, M. (1978). *Children's minds*. London: Fontana Paperbacks.

Goodman, Y. (1985). Kidwatching: Observing children in the classroom. In A. Jaggar, and M.T. Smith-Burke (Eds.), *Observing the language learner* (pp. 9–18). Newark, DE: International Reading Association and Urbana, IL: National Council of Teachers of English.

Little, N., and Allan, J. (1988). *Student-led teacher parent conferences*. Toronto: Lugus.

Moffett, J. (1992). *Detecting growth in language*. Portsmouth, NH: Heinemann.

National Association for the Education of Young Children. (1991). Guidelines of appropriate curriculum content and assessment in programs serving children ages 3 through 8. *Young Children, 46*(3), 21–38.

North York Board of Education. (1983). *Look! Hear! Developing programs for primary children based on observation of learning needs*. North York, ON: City of North York.

Politano, C., and Davies, A. (1994). *Multiage and more*. Winnipeg: Peguis.

Spradley, J. (1980). *Participant observation*. New York: Holt, Rinehart and Winston.

Stiggins, R.J. (1987). NCME [National Council on Measurement in Education] instructional module on design and development of performance assessments. *Educational Measurement: Issues and Practice,* 6(3), pp. 33–42.

Teale, W. (1982). Assessing young children's literacy development: Wherefores, wheretos, whereins. Paper presented at the International Reading Association Preconvention Institute #26, Anaheim, CA, May 3–4, 1982.

Valencia, S., and Pearson, D. (1987). Reading assessment: Time for a change. *The Reading Teacher, 41*(8), 726–32.

Webster's new collegiate dictionary. (1976). Springfield, MA: G. and C. Merriam.

Epilogue: Continuing the Conversation

This book, this *texere,* represents my evolving understandings of writing and learning. Writing it has been a dynamic and complex process of weaving together what I have learned through personal experience and from other people, including authors whose work I have read, professors and teachers I have studied with, students I have taught, and many colleagues and friends I have shared ideas with. One of the most satisfying things about writing is seeing one's work completed, especially when it comes out in published form. Writing, however, is never really complete. It involves decisions about what to include—and what to omit. Once a book is printed it becomes a fixed object, a permanent record of ideas. Yet ideas are not fixed; they continue to evolve and change as new insights are gained. Even before this book comes off the press, I will have learned something new and will wish that I had done something differently.

The process of writing this book has been very much a learning process for me: I have clarified my thinking, made connections, read and researched, refined and fine-tuned ideas and words. Writing *is* learning. Like a photograph, a written text can capture only a moment in time. Yet, a text is part of a conversation; it is "in the middle" and "in process," connected to what has come before and to what will be in the future. So, this is not the end, but part of a conversation about writing and learning that will, I hope, continue as you weave your ideas with the ones in this book into the fabric of your professional life.

Glossary

achievement (level of performance) An evaluation determined by comparing what a learner can do to something else; it may be *norm-* or *criterion-referenced.*

acquisition Knowledge gained through a subconscious process on the part of the child, without formal teaching.

action researcher A practitioner who undertakes research or inquiry into his or her own classroom and instructional practices.

alphabetic principle The principle that the sounds of spoken language can be represented by letters and that combinations of sounds in spoken words are related to combinations of letters in written words; it includes an understanding of the relationships between particular letters and sounds.

assessment The process of collecting information, or data, for the purpose of making an evaluation.

authenticity That which represents as accurately as possible what people do under natural settings.

authoring cycle See *writing process.*

Authors' Circle A sharing time after drafts have been written; it provides an opportunity for children to give and receive feedback.

brainstorming Thinking together and sharing ideas.

clustering A visual form of brainstorming that starts with the topic in the centre; ideas are added to the centre or to one another. Connections can be made in various ways. Also known as *webbing* and *semantic mapping.*

composing The process of constructing meaning.

context Literally, "that which surrounds a text." There are several layers of multidimensional and fluid context; writing occurs in and is influenced by all layers: sociocultural context, community context, sphere of activity, immediate context, and personal context.

conventions of print All of the elements of the written system (e.g., layout and directionality—front-to-back in a book, top-to-bottom of a page, left-to-right on a line), segmentation into words, letter–sound relationships, spelling and punctuation. Sometimes referred to as *graphophonics*.

COUPS (or **COPS**) An activity in which students proofread for capital letters, omissions, usage (in the junior grades), punctuation, and spelling.

criterion-referenced evaluation An evaluation that compares learners' achievements to a set of criteria or standards.

cumulative portfolio A portfolio that include samples of a student's writing over a period of years. Each year, the student selects one or two pieces to add to the portfolio; it is then passed on to the teacher the following year.

development The process of evolution or maturation.

diagnostic assessments The collection of information in order to determine what students are able to do independently, and what they need help with. These types of assessment often precede a particular unit of work.

discourse The communication of thoughts in words.

discourse community A group of people who share ways of using language.

documentary or descriptive portfolio A portfolio that includes samples of a student's work, selected by the student and the teacher. It may or may not include selections from the teacher's records of observations and conferences, and may include teacher's comments as well as those of students.

drafting Putting ideas into words, shaping ideas, or discovering what you want to say.

dynamic assessment The collection of information to discover (1) what a student knows and can do independently (static mode), and (2) students' *zones of proximal development* (dynamic mode) (Dixon-Krauss, 1996; see Dixon-Krauss entry in Chapter 8 References). In the dynamic mode, teachers provide assistance and instructional scaffolding.

editing Revising. Reviewing and reworking ideas and words for meaning, clarity, coherence, and/or effect.

emergent literacy The process of reading and writing development; it begins at birth and continues throughout life.

encoding The recording or representation of ideas on the page in written symbols.

epistemic mode The use of language as a tool for thinking and learning.

ethnographer A person who seeks to understand human beings in all their complexity, in context, using natural settings as the direct source of data.

ethnography Also called cultural anthropology, the study of what people do, what people know, and things people make and use; descriptions of a culture, or particular aspects of it.

evaluation The process of interpreting or making judgments and decisions based on the information collected through assessment.

formative assessment and evaluation Collection and interpretation of information that occurs throughout the process of teaching and learning. It is ongoing and focuses on the learning process rather than on the finished product.

free-writing A nonstop free flowing of words; the writer turns off his or her internal editor and reflective self and writes nonstop. Free-writing can be *focused* (on a particular topic) and/or *sustained* for a specified time limit.

function The purpose or way in which language is used.

genre A language structure that is embedded in and develops out of a sphere of human activity. It is a flexible model, not merely a generic form that writers slot ideas into. Genre reflects an integration of *content* (what we want to express), *form* (ways of organizing our words and ideas), *function* (purposes for writing), and *context* of situation.

grading The process of sorting students' work into hierarchical categories that are represented by a numerical score or letter grade.

grammar A term commonly used in the following ways: (1) to refer to *syntax* (the preferred term), the system of rules that governs a language (for example, word order) and enables its speakers to produce and understand sentences; (2) to refer to *models* that systematically describe this knowledge of language (for example, analysis of sentences and parts of speech), for example, traditional and transformational grammar; (3) to refer to conventional notions of what is socially acceptable in particular contexts, in other words, *usage* (the preferred term).

graphophonics Relations between speech and writing, involving all of the elements of the written code (e.g., layout and directionality of print—front-to-back in a book, top-to-bottom of a page, left-to-right on a line), segmentation into words, letter–sound relationships, spelling and punctuation; sometimes referred to as *conventions of print.*

guided participation Providing support for students in the process of learning, yet encouraging them to assume responsibility for the things they can do, through *mediation* or *scaffolding*.

immediate context The particular writing situation, which is comprised of a specific set of circumstances, including the people, the environment (physical, intellectual, and emotional dimensions), and the task (e.g., purpose of the task, how the task is structured). It occurs at a particular moment in time and is bound by events immediately preceding and following.

initial assessments The collection of baseline information—what students already know and can do independently.

inner speech Internalized self-talk. (Vygotsky, 1978)

invented spellings Spellings that are constructed by young writers. These reveal children's knowledge of letter–sound relationships. They may also be called *phonetic spellings* or *placeholder spellings*.

KWL (Know-Wonder-Learned) A strategy using a three-column format or three-coloured web, with which students generate what they know and what they wonder about a topic; the learned part is added later.

language experience activities Activities in which students are engaged in first-hand experiences that are accompanied by talk (and often, written language). Activities based on the idea that "If I think it, I can say it. If I can say it, I can write it. If I can write it, others can read it."

learning Conscious knowledge gained through teaching and involving explanations and analysis.

level of performance See *achievement*.

long vowel sounds Tense vowel sounds, such as those represented by the vowels heard in *cake*, *see*, *like*, *nose*, and *use*.

masterpiece portfolio A portfolio that includes only a student's best written pieces and finished products.

mediation Guided participation in a learning task by providing directives and cues; the process of enabling a learner to make sense of personal experiences by making connections with the concrete world to develop abstract concepts, and to integrate the new with the known.

metalanguage Language that refers to language (e.g., word, sentence, adjective).

metalinguistic awareness Awareness of the nature of written language, its forms and functions.

metaliterate language Language about literacy (writing and print), for example, book, write, letter, and later, paragraph, essay.

naturalistic assessment Information collected in natural settings through observations of what people do (processes) and make (products) and through talking to them.

norm-referenced evaluation An evaluation that compares a learner's achievement to others of the same age or grade.

notational system A system of visual or graphic marks that functions according to certain rules.

orthographic patterns Common spelling patterns, such as doubling consonants, or dropping *e* before *ing*.

performance assessments Tasks or activities that are structured to elicit particular actions or behaviours. Performance assessments enable teachers to assess complex behaviours in meaningful contexts.

phoneme The smallest unit of speech sound.

placeholder spelling Writing a word the way one thinks it is spelled. These spellings can be marked (e.g., by underlining or circling) and later checked for their standard spellings.

portfolio A purposeful collection of a student's writing/learning artifacts collected over time, not merely a work folder. There are various types of portfolios: masterpiece portfolios, process portfolios, documentary or descriptive portfolios, cumulative portfolios, and progress folios.

pragmatics Relations between language and the context in which it is used; how writing functions in a particular context, the roles it plays and the purposes it serves.

presenting Sharing and celebrating writing.

prewriting Getting started writing, thinking about what you want to say, generating ideas, and planning.

process portfolio A portfolio that includes all artifacts related to a particular project, such as a report. It documents a student's writing and learning process in a particular genre or activity.

process writing See *writing process*.

progress An evaluation of students' growth; it is determined by comparing a student's present and past performances; it is self-referenced.

progress folio A portfolio that includes samples of a student's writing, but is organized according to the curriculum areas. It has four sections (September, November, March, and May) into which pieces of work are selected for each curriculum area and then pasted in the appropriate sections.

proofreading Checking a written piece for conventions or mechanics (e.g., spelling, punctuation, omissions, usage, syntax).

publishing Making a final copy of a piece of writing to share with others.

register The language that grows out of and is embedded in a particular sphere of human activity.

representing (forms of representation) The expression of meaning, including any or all of the processes of speaking, writing, and visual representation, which may be interpreted through listening, reading, and viewing.

revision The process of taking a step back from what has been written in order to see it more clearly, and to make improvements to the writing.

rubric A rating scale that describes several levels of proficiency, from high to low.

scaffolding A process by which someone (e.g., a teacher) observes what a learner does, determines the degree and type of support needed, guides the learner's participation, and gradually removes support to allow the learner to take on more of the task through the use of prompts, cues, and explanations.

semantic mapping A visual form of brainstorming that starts with the topic in the centre; ideas are added to the centre or to one another. Connections can be made in various ways. Also known as *clustering* and *webbing*.

semantics Relations between words and their meanings; sometimes referred to as *meaning vocabulary*.

sentence combining An activity in which students combine two or more short sentences into one longer sentence. There are are three guidelines: the new sentence must make sense, it must sound right (i.e., be syntactically acceptable in Standard English), and it must retain the same meaning.

short vowel sounds Lax vowel sounds, such as those represented by the vowels in *bat*, *bet*, *bit*, *bob*, *but*.

sociocultural context The global setting. It encompasses such things as socio-economic class, language, ethnicity, power relations, and gender. Sociocultural context includes a variety of communities in which people live and interact.

sphere of activity A recurring context that gives rise to particular functions and varieties of language (registers), forms of representation, and genres.

story grammar A set of approaches to teaching narrative; it makes explicit the central features of narrative.

summative evaluation Interpretation of a body of information at the end of a period of work, often in preparation for writing a report.

SWAT Sustained writing all together (teacher too). A parallel to sustained silent reading (SSR).

syllabic hypothesis A specific form of one-to-one correspondence, in which children use one letter to represent one syllable.

syntax Relations between words. The ways words are organized and sequenced and structural patterns of word order, including sentence, paragraph, and discourse-level structures. Sometimes referred to as *grammar*.

think, pair, share Students think individually first, share with partners, and finally with a larger group or the whole class.

transactional view of learning The conception of learning as a constructive process that occurs through transactions between the individual and the community. Also referred to as the *sociocognitive constructivist view*.

triangulation (1) The consideration of multiple sources of information in an analysis, and (2) seeking other people's perspectives and interpretations as to what the data might mean. This includes checking perceptions with the subjects of the study.

usage Conventional notions of what is socially acceptable in particular contexts. "Improving bad grammar" usually means trying to eliminate non-standard usages.

voice One's personal style of expression.

webbing A visual form of brainstorming that starts with the topic in the centre; ideas are added to the centre or to one another. Connections can be made in various ways. Also known as *clustering* and *semantic mapping*.

word banks/caches/lists Word collections. These can be general (e.g., Halloween words) or in categories (e.g., for fairy tales: characters, places, magic things).

writers' RAFT (Role, Audience, Form, and Topic) A strategy for planning writing activities.

writing cycle See *writing process*.

writing process An instructional approach to teaching writing. It includes strategies for generating and developing ideas, drafting, revising to clarify meaning or to make stylistic improvements, and proofreading to address the conventions of writing, such as spelling and punctuation. Also known as *process writing*, *writing cycle*, or *authoring cycle*.

written language The linguistic expression of meanings in written form.

zone of proximal development That which is just beyond one's attained level of development (Vygotsky, 1978; see Vygotsky entry in Chapter 1 References). It is determined by what a student can do with assistance or scaffolding by someone who is more advanced. The "learning zone."

Index

To the owner of this book

We hope that you have enjoyed *Weaving Webs of Meaning,* and we would like to know as much about your experiences with this text as you would care to offer. Only through your comments and those of others can we learn how to make this a better text for future readers.

School ________________ Your instructor's name ______________________

Course ___________ Was the text required? _______ Recommended? _____

1. What did you like the most about *Weaving Webs of Meaning?*

____

____

____

2. How useful was this text for your course?

____

____

____

3. Do you have any recommendations for ways to improve the next edition of this text?

____

____

____

4. In the space below or in a separate letter, please write any other comments you have about the book. (For example, please feel free to comment on reading level, writing style, terminology, design features, and learning aids.)

____

____

____

____

Optional

Your name ______________________________ Date __________________

May ITP Nelson quote you, either in promotion for *Weaving Webs of Meaning* or in future publishing ventures?

Yes _______ No _______

Thanks!

You can also send your comments to us via e-mail at
college_arts_hum@nelson.com

PLEASE TAPE SHUT. DO NOT STAPLE.

TAPE SHUT

TAPE SHUT

FOLD HERE

MAIL POSTE

Canada Post Corporation
Société canadienne des postes

Postage paid
if mailed in Canada
Business Reply

Port payé
si posté au Canada
Réponse d'affaires

0066102399 01

Nelson

0066102399-M1K5G4-BR01

TAPE SHUT

TAPE SHUT

ITP NELSON
MARKET AND PRODUCT DEVELOPMENT
PO BOX 60225 STN BRM B
TORONTO ON M7Y 2H1